PENGUIN COOKERY LIBRARY

THE CUISINE OF THE SUN

Mireille Johnston was born in Nice and educated in France, England and America. She is the presenter of twelve BBC2 television programmes on French regional cookery. She is the author of *The French Family Feast*, *The Cuisine of the Rose: Classical French Cooking from Burgundy and Lyonnais*, *Central Park Country: A Tune Within Us* and various articles published in France and in America. She is the translator and editor of the film script for *The Sorrow and the Pity* by Marcel Ophuls and of Henri Lefèvre's book *Criticism of Everyday Life*. She has taught comparative literature at Yale University, Columbia University and Sarah Lawrence College. She lives in Paris with her husband and their two daughters, Margaret-Brooke and Elizabeth.

MIREILLE JOHNSTON

The Cuisine of the Sun

Classical French Cooking from Nice and Provence

ILLUSTRATIONS BY MILTON GLASER

PENGUIN BOOKS

PENGUIN BOOKS

Published by the Penguin Group
Penguin Books Ltd, 27 Wrights Lane, London w8 5tz, England
Penguin Books USA Inc., 375 Hudson Street, New York, New York 10014, USA
Penguin Books Australia Ltd, Ringwood, Victoria, Australia
Penguin Books Canada Ltd, 10 Alcorn Avenue, Toronto, Ontario, Canada m4v 3b2
Penguin Books (NZ) Ltd, 182–190 Wairau Road, Auckland 10, New Zealand

Penguin Books Ltd, Registered Offices: Harmondsworth, Middlesex, England

First published in the USA by Random House, Inc., New York, 1976
This revised edition first published in Penguin Books 1992
1 3 5 7 9 10 8 6 4 2

Typeset by DatIX International Limited, Bungay, Suffolk
Set in 10½/13 pt Monophoto Garamond
Printed in England by Clays Ltd, St Ives plc

Acknowledgements

I wish to thank Jason Epstein, gourmand par excellence, for his
inspired curiosity and his encouragement; Milton Glaser, who can
see more and better than all of us; Sono Rosenberg, for her
precision, patience, and taste; Susan Child, who so generously gave
time, imagination and good cheer to the project; and Roberta
Schneiderman, for her skilful help in testing the recipes.

Contents

Introduction

I was born in a tall apricot-coloured house with green shutters overlooking the sea. When I think of my childhood, I remember the bright colours, the sounds, the smells and tastes of Nice. We were constantly sent to the seashore, the garden or the hills to find ingredients for the kitchen. Along the coast we searched for sea urchins and mussels; in our garden we picked courgette flowers, tiny aubergines, the tenderest broad beans. In the fields we gathered thyme and oregano; in the woods we searched for blackberries, chestnuts, mushrooms, and pine cones full of pine nuts. And after a rainfall we would collect snails, wild pink cloves and genista, whose stems we could suck like candy.

Later there were lazy afternoons when we would sip orange wine under the fig tree, where all round us would be the scent of lavender, jasmine and honeysuckle – mingling with the fragrance of fruits that would later be made into preserves – and the endless buzzing of cicadas and bees.

On festive days – a carnival, a visit from a relative, a saint's day – our house was filled with special excitement. Feathers of hens and ducks would fly in all directions; large fish filled with stalks of dried fennel would rest under a layer of lettuce leaves; large platters of seaweed and crushed ice would be piled high with mussels, clams, sea urchins; fruits would be left to marinate in large bowls of rum and sugar; and fresh pasta would be drying on sheets of linen spread on brooms, beds, chairs and tables.

All year long there were special reasons for these banquets. For example, from spring to late summer each village around Nice and each district of the city would celebrate a local saint. These *festins* lasted three days and took place on village squares shaded by large plane, palm or eucalyptus trees. They were both family and communal affairs. Two days before the *festin*, the kitchens would begin to hum like hives. Walking through the narrow streets, you could actually hear the 'chop chop' of Swiss chard being minced for *tourte de blettes*, the pounding of garlic for *aïoli*, and the grating of dry bread to sprinkle on the *farcis*. Traditionally, each housewife had to prepare six big *tourtes*, each filled with greens, onions, squash, apricots, walnuts or honey. The women also made ravioli stuffed with beef stew and spinach; *civets* of rabbit simmered in red wine and blood; roast baby goat; and huge platters of *farcis* made with vegetables cooked the same morning they were picked. An invigorating *mesclun* salad was gathered and brought by guests from the neighbouring villages.

During the three days parades, traditional masses and folk dances alternated with banquets until the last day, when a huge *aïoli* – *l'aïoli monstre* – was served on the village square and shared by the whole community. And lingering in the houses was the delicious smell of orange rind, garlic, white grapes drying on the beams above, ripe figs on screen trays, and quince preserve simmering on the back of the stove.

Modern life has swept over the Comté de Nice, but things have not changed very much. The dance music is mostly rock now and the basic costume mostly jeans and espadrilles, but the colours, the flavours, the textures of, and pleasure given by, the food have well resisted the levelling of time.

All this, which is the spirit and heart of this book, evokes not only Nice but all of the South of France. Although Niçois cooking is distinctive in many respects – an almost Oriental way of cooking vegetables in oil, a peculiar mixture of sweet and salty (spinach with raisins, sweet onions with anchovies, carrots with garlic, chicken baked with figs, and so on) – it is inextricably tied to the techniques, ingredient requirements and aesthetics of Provençal cooking. Since I remember and grew to love several Provençal dishes commonly served in Nice, I have included recipes for them as well as for strictly Niçois dishes.

A quick sketch of the character and history of the South of France may help to highlight the eclectic origins of the region's cuisine.

Much has been written about the varied beauty of Provence, and rightly so. There is true kinship between the land and its people, and nothing illustrates this better than its cuisine. It is a resourceful peasant cuisine (though refined by centuries of practice), with powerful basic ingredients – saffron, fennel seeds, olive oil, garlic, anchovies, and aromatic herbs – to enhance the flavour of fresh vegetables and simple cuts of meat.

The northern Provence of Giono, Cézanne and Pagnol is ascetic, dry and secretive. Its olive trees, cypresses, fields of lavender and rocky hilltops are swept by the mistral. Nevertheless, it is full of unexpected treasures: truffles under the dwarf oak trees, juniper berries, hills of rosemary and thyme. It has deep gorges, woods of chestnut trees and little villages perched on top of steep hills: Gattières, Châteauneuf, Cabris, Gourdon. Most of the rather dry and highly flavoured dishes, such as *aïgo bouido, crespeou, capoun, caillettes, tourte aux noix et au miel* and *nougats*, come from this region.

To the south is the lush, fertile Provence of Renoir, Matisse and Picasso. It is well irrigated and offers an abundance of fruits and vegetables. This is where *tian de légumes, artichauts à la barigoule, troucha* and *salade niçoise* were born.

Finally, along the *côte* there is an explosion of luxuriant vegetation and colours: eucalyptus, mimosa, palm and orange trees, and roses and jasmine. From Marseilles to Nice to Monte Carlo there are lovely pastel houses, flowered terraces and brilliant markets. Each town and region varies in history, ambience and cuisine, and each dish is part of their heritage. Yet every village and every cook has a variation on such classics as bouillabaisse, ravioli, and ratatouille.

Provence and Nice have had an extraordinarily tumultuous history. Marseilles was founded by Greek settlers, but it was the Romans who settled the *Provincia Romana*, which was to become Provence. With its deep harbours, its Rhône river, Alpine mountains and Mediterranean shores, the area resisted the successive invasions of barbarians, Arabs and Franks until the sixteenth century, when it was securely annexed to France.

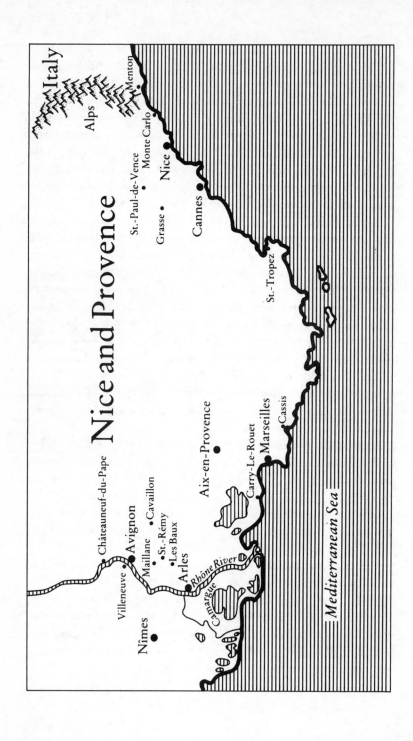

Though geographically close to Provence, Nice itself has a history that is, to a large degree, all its own. Like Marseilles, it was founded by Greek settlers and remained a Greek port until the first century, when the Romans formed the province of Alpes-Maritimes and made Nice its capital. During the next centuries the province was swept by barbarian tribes, and then by the Franks and Saracens. In the middle of the twelfth century Nice became a *ville de consulat* and was governed by four consuls, each of whom represented one class of society: a nobleman, a merchant, an artisan and a peasant. This form of government worked successfully for six hundred years. At the end of the eighteenth century the people of Nice, who had placed themselves under the protection of the Count of Provence, decided to join the House of Savoy. Both François I and Louis XIV attacked repeatedly, but it was not until 1792 that Nice became part of France. In 1814, however, when Napoleon was defeated, Nice again fell under the rule of the House of Savoy. Finally, in 1860, the population voted unanimously to once again become part of France, and it has been so ever since.

That Nice has assimilated its many foreign influences is evident in its cuisine. Settlers, invaders, Russian and European crowned heads and tourists all introduced new tastes, techniques and ingredients. The olive oil and wine came with the Phoenicians. The pasta and ravioli (originally of Chinese origin) came to Nice via Italy. The imaginative use of dried cod was probably inspired by the Portuguese. Stockfish was brought by the Norwegians, and couscous came from the Arabs' former North African colonies. Today this cookery, based on local products and on recipes that have been tested for so long, is a true link between farmers, artists, vinegrowers, shopkeepers and visitors.

For many years I have successfully adapted this southern French cuisine, improvising and altering recipes to combine the essence of Niçois and Provençal cooking with what is appealing and practical for the British cook.

The recipes in this book use a wide variety of fresh vegetables, fruits, herbs, seafood and reasonably priced meat, almost all of which are easily available in the average well-stocked market. Every week the vigilant buyer can find at least two or three perfectly crisp vegetables and as many interesting cuts of meat. In the last few years this spirited, heady cookery has become fashionable everywhere – olive oil, fresh and dried herbs, fish, vegetables, spices and fruit are the ingredients we all crave today. And because here there are no sacred rules or orders to follow, because the approach is flexible and resourceful and spontaneous, the dishes are totally unintimidating. Whether they are part of a dinner, a buffet, a picnic or the core of a luncheon, they evoke at first bite all the pungent and exuberant pleasures of Provence and the Riviera.

Each recipe is designed for six people, but be generous with your proportions, since many of the dishes are even better served cold or reheated the next day. As you will be happy to discover, several soups, hors-d'oeuvres, stews and gratins are based on a lunch or a dinner served the day before – an extremely economical way to cook. It is also a tangy, light and exceptionally healthy cuisine. The recipes contain little or no butter, cream or flour. Instead, the cuisine draws all its strength from the best of natural fresh ingredients and the verve with which they are prepared.

I hope you will come to make these recipes your own and to look upon them as confidences and delights shared with generations of lean, lively Niçois and Provençals, who long ago understood that what they enjoy also happens to be what is good for them.

Ingredients

All serious cooks consider their trip to the market the most delicate and decisive part of their culinary preparation. In Niçois and Provençal cooking the success of a meal depends on the quality of its basic ingredients. In Provence the shops and open-air markets are places of wonder. All the sinuous narrow streets in Antibes, Arles, Grasse and most Provençal towns lead to the market-place, which has a fountain in the centre, a few benches and some big plane trees all round it. In the afternoon children run about and adults play *pétanque* or sip *pastis*, but in the morning the whole square is the setting for the market. There are pyramids of fruit and vegetables, bunches of flowers standing in wide buckets, dozens of goat's cheeses, piles of breads, *bannettes, boules, fougasses.* Here the peasants have brought the small fruits of their labours: a few pounds of green vegetables picked a few hours ago, a basket of figs, a bowl of fresh eggs, a bundle of wild asparagus that were gathered between the olive trees, a couple of rabbits and ducks killed the night before, some cured olives, baskets of snails – some gathered in the fields and fed on rosemary and fennel, some gathered on the salty grass of Camargue.

In spite of Nice's extravagant vegetation and architecture, it is the irresistible market of the Cours Saleya that is the core of the city and truly defines best the whole region's contagious *joie de vivre*. In Old Nice, shops are like Ali Baba's cave: dark and carefully protected from the flies and bees by strips of coloured paper hung from the ceiling. They have large brown paper bags filled with pasta in strange shapes; cloth sacks of corn meal for *polente* and chick-pea flour for *socca* are on the floor. On the counter are enormous glass jars of anchovies in rough salt for *bagna cauda* and bowls of *pili pili* (little red peppers) for *rouille* and couscous. Whole dried codfish are soaking in tanks of fresh running water, ready for *brandade*. And on the shelves there are bamboo boxes of candied fruits, blue bottles of orange-flower water and cans of olive oil adorned with pictures of Niçoises wearing large straw hats and holding branches of fluffy mimosa. Clusters of sausages, bloodwurst and country hams sway from large hooks. There is pig's caul to wrap *caillettes* and lean salt pork coated with coarsely ground black pepper and wrapped in cheesecloth. There are barrels filled with green, purple and black olives.

The smells and colours of the French markets have a very special flavour, but most of what Niçois and Provençal cooking requires can be found in shops and supermarkets throughout Britain. Basic ingredients are not expensive. Try the two or three local shops to find where the vegetables are the freshest; where the butcher is the most cooperative, the specials are indeed special and the lean salt pork is the leanest; where you can count on genuine Gruyère every week; and where there is good olive oil and Spanish saffron. When you go shopping you must always concentrate on the essentials: unbleached flour, meat, fish, fresh vegetables, fresh fruits, good imported Gruyère or Parmesan cheese, garlic, olive oil (Spanish, Italian or French). For authentic items, you should explore the shops in Greek, Spanish and Italian neighbourhoods.

Of late there has been an increase in the number and variety of convenience foods. We are offered all kinds of brightly wrapped, vacuum-packed, chilled, frozen, dehydrated, processed foods and mixes full of additives. In the supermarkets the display of these 'time savers' may be so attractive that it seems hopeless to resist.

Of course, convenience foods are very expensive and they are neither nutritious nor very tasty. The excitement remains on the cover. So it is time to choose decisively and carefully and to share the Provençal quiet confidence in all the delights that come from good food. It is time to think of shopping for food as a serious undertaking. You must look, smell, touch, compare and carefully select all your ingredients. Take an early morning trip to the shops in your area and try to discover all the unusual foods available, then encourage your butcher, fishmonger and greengrocer to stock others for you. The following is a descriptive list of the basic Niçois and Provençal ingredients.

Fonds de Cuisine
Staples to have in your kitchen at all times

Anchovies: *les anchois*
Anchovies are used a great deal in Nice – in *bagna cauda, poulet en saupiquet, gigot d'agneau, poisson à la chartreuse*. It's best to buy them packed in salt as sold in Greek, Italian and Spanish markets; they keep well in the refrigerator. Before using the salt-packed variety, wash the fish thoroughly in cold running water. Cut along the back and pull out the bone; then remove the tail. If you can't find this type of anchovy, use the kind packed in oil and drain well on kitchen towels.

Bread: *le pain*
Stale bread, once a stand-by for the frugal cook, is now a traditional ingredient of many dishes in one of several forms: breadcrumbs, *croûtons* and *chapons*. Sometimes a slice is soaked in milk, which is squeezed out before the bread is used for a sauce or for stuffing. You can buy the so-called French or Italian bread, but home-baked bread is best. I prefer baking my own firm white bread with unbleached flour.

Breadcrumbs: *la panure, la chapelure*
Breadcrumbs are sprinkled on *farcis* and *tians*. The ready-made kind is uniformly bad; breadcrumbs simply have to be home-made.

To make a supply, either grate a few slices of stale bread or crumble them into a blender and blend at high speed for a few seconds. They will keep for at least two or three days in a jar and for three weeks in the freezer. When kept longer, they will become mouldy.

Chapons
These are strips (about 25 × 50 mm/1 × 2 in) of stale bread crust rubbed with a clove of garlic. They are added to salads such as *salade mesclun* and *salade niçoise*.

Cheese: *le fromage*
The traditional accompaniment for soups, *tians* and pasta in Nice was cheese made from goat's or sheep's milk. Nowadays Gruyère or Parmesan cheese is used instead. Keep a large wedge of each, tightly wrapped in waxed paper or a cling film recommended for that purpose, in the refrigerator to grate at the last moment. Never buy grated cheese; it will add no flavour to your dish.

Soft cheeses such as Caillé (a fresh goat's cheese that is sprinkled with olive oil and can be kept for weeks) or Brous (curdled cheese sprinkled with chopped garlic, pepper and brandy and kept in a closed jar) may not be available everywhere. I often buy ricotta or fresh curd cheese, although it is made with pasteurized cow's milk and not raw ewe's. I sprinkle it with orange-flower water and sugar and serve it as a light dessert that is very similar to the Brousse du Roves.

Chick-peas: *les pois chiches*
If you buy them dried, boil them with a bouquet garni and a few vegetables and then use them in soups, salads and hors-d'oeuvres. They are also widely available canned, which are infinitely quicker to prepare, although a little less firm and tasty.

Chick-pea flour: *la farine de pois chiches*
It is sold in some health-food and whole-food shops, and in some shops selling Indian or Middle Eastern foods. It is also called gram and *besan*. We make *socca* with it, as well as *panisses* and soups.

Couscous
This crushed grain is available in most health-food stores, some speciality shops and some supermarkets.

Corn meal: *la farine de maïs*
We make *polente* with it. Buy the stone-ground kind if possible.

Croûtons

We use them as a garnish for *brandade* and *poulet en saupiquet*, with *anchoïade* and with soups. To make them, cut slices of good, firm home-made bread in cubes or triangles and place in an oven at 180°C/350°F/Gas Mark 4 for 4 minutes. Turn them over, sprinkle with a little olive oil and bake 3 more minutes.

Dried salted cod: *la morue*

Dried cod can be kept in a dry corner of your kitchen or in the freezer. The dried whole fish (bone, skin and tail) requires about two days of soaking in cold water, with the water changed several times a day. Dried filleted cod requires an overnight soaking and four changes of water. Frozen fillets require only about four hours' soaking with four changes of water. Although not yet fashionable in Britain, it is healthy, full of protein, light, cheap, and will be the rage soon!

Always ask your fishmonger how long his particular dried cod-fish should soak and follow his instructions. For the tastier, drier kind, you will probably have to go to Italian, Spanish or Greek shops. Buy a great amount, since so many of Nice's light, tasty, inexpensive dishes can be made from it – *estockaficada, morue en raïto, aïoli* and so on. The Chinese *tai tze* salt-cod is very dry and perfect for *estockaficada*.

Flour: *la farine*

Always use unbleached flour, available in many supermarkets.

Gherkins: *les cornichons*

Used in hors-d'oeuvres, with *boeuf mironton* and in various sauces, they can be bought in speciality shops and some supermarkets. They are easy to make at home. Choose very small (about 50-mm/2-in long) cucumbers, all roughly the same size. Wash and dry carefully and place them in a bowl. Sprinkle with salt and let stand for twenty-four hours, tossing them from time to time. Place them in a jar with a few pickling onions, a few cloves, a garlic clove and a sprig of tarragon. Boil enough white wine vinegar to cover them and pour it over the vegetables. Let stand overnight. In the morning pour the vinegar into a pan and boil it again. Let the vegetables soak in it a second night. Repeat the boiling and soaking. The fourth day the gherkins are ready to use. Keep in a closed jar.

Nuts: *les noix: les noisettes; les pignons; les amandes*
Walnuts are used for sauces (*sauce aux noix*, for example) or biscuits (*les petits biscuits aux noix*). Pine nuts are used in *tourte de blettes* and are cooked with spinach. Almonds are used in ice cream and biscuits such as *soupirs aux amandes*. French bitter almonds are not sold in Britain, so I add some almond extract for the authentic flavour. Nuts can be purchased in every supermarket but are usually much cheaper and fresher bought by the pound in the ethnic markets. Always keep them frozen for freshness – they need no defrosting time.

Oil: *l'huile*
I usually use half peanut (or groundnut) oil and half olive oil for cooking and for mayonnaise and *aïoli*, since olive oil alone is too potent. For salad dressing and seasoning, of course, I use only olive oil. There are delicate yellow olive oils and heavy, green, fruity ones. Many good brands of imported olive oil are sold here. Experiment, then buy your favourite by the gallon, which is proportionately cheaper. Keep in closed dark bottles. Refrigerate if you use it slowly. (See pp. 270–72 for description of oils.)

Olives: *les olives*
The little black or dark purple olives of Nice are sold only in speciality shops. Use them unpitted. If you cannot find them, buy oil-cured black olives (available in Italian, Spanish and Greek shops, delicatessens and many supermarkets) and pit them, using an olive-pitter (*dénoyauteur*).

Parmesan cheese
Freshly grated Parmesan is sprinkled on *soupe au pistou, soupe de pêcheurs, pâtes aux oeufs, farcis* and numerous other dishes. Grate the cheese finely at the last minute so it is light and fresh. Never use the commercial grated Parmesan, which is dry and tasteless.

Pork caul, or lace fat: *la crépine*
This thin fatty membrane is sold in butchers' shops. If you cannot find it, substitute thin slices of streaky bacon. We use it for *caillettes* and to cover terrines.

Streaky bacon (unsalted): *le petit salé*
Sautéing in bacon is the essential first step in making stews and fish dishes, such as *loup farci*. Always choose the leanest and keep a large piece in the refrigerator. Most butchers sell joints of good streaky bacon; do not buy packages of sliced bacon. Try to find some that is free of nitrate and nitrite.

Vermouth
Dry white vermouth is good in sauces. Red sweet vermouth is acceptable for *raïto* sauces. Take a sip of your vermouth before using, since cooking intensifies its flavour – whether good or bad.

Vinegar: *le vinaigre*
Whether red or white, wine vinegar is available everywhere. Find one you like and keep a few bottles on hand. Or else make your own. In Nice we mostly use red wine vinegar.

Wine: *le vin*
I use hearty, simple red Burgundy to make stews, and either a dry white wine or a dry white vermouth for fish, lamb and chicken sauces. Always taste before using it. Keep a few bottles of your favourite wines in the kitchen for cooking.

Les Épices et les Aromates
Spices and flavourings

Anise seed: *les graines d'anis*
Anise has a flavour somewhat like that of liquorice. The seeds are used in pastry (*biscuits à l'anis*), with fish (*loup farci à la niçoise*) and with pork.

Basil: *le basilic*

Although there are some sixty kinds of basil, the two most common are sweet basil, with large leaves and a strong flavour, and bush basil, which has smaller leaves and is milder. Basil is easy to grow and can be frozen (in a plastic bag). You can make a purée of it with olive oil and grated cheese in a blender. This will keep for a month in the refrigerator covered with a little olive oil or it can be frozen. Add fresh crushed garlic to the purée at the time of using (garlic acquires an unpleasant taste when frozen). Basil goes well with aubergine (*caviar provençale*), pasta (*pâtes au pistou*), tomatoes (*salade niçoise*) and soup (*soupe au pistou*). It is an excellent garnish and can be mixed with fresh mint before sprinkling on vegetables. Basil finely chopped with anchovies is delicious on raw tomatoes, hard-boiled eggs and grilled fish.

Bay leaf: *le laurier*

Use it in stews (*daube d'Avignon*, ratatouille), soup (*aïgo bouido*), fish (*gigot de mer*) and rice (*riz aux herbes*).

Bouquet garni

This is a small bundle of herbs wrapped in a piece of cheesecloth and used to enhance the seasoning of soups, stews and the like. You can use 2 or 3 sprigs of parsley, a bay leaf and a sprig of thyme (or ¼ teaspoon of dried thyme); for a tastier bouquet garni, add a stalk of celery and a stalk of fennel. When the dish is ready, remove the bouquet garni.

Capers: *les câpres*

Capers are the buds of the caper bush. They are kept in vinegar or salt and used in hors-d'oeuvres, and with meat (*boeuf mironton, porc à la sauge et aux câpres*) and sauces (*sauce piquante*).

Cayenne pepper: *poivre de cayenne*

This strong red pepper is used in sauces (*rouille*, couscous sauce) and fish dishes.

Chives: *la ciboulette*

We use the narrow, long leaves, finely chopped, in omelettes (*troucha*), and with pasta (*pâtes à la verdure*) and vegetables (*févettes à la laitue*).

Cloves: *le clou de girofle*
We stick one clove in a large onion, sauté the onion on all sides and add it to *pot-au-feu* or chick-pea soup to give colour and flavour. Cloves also flavour *boeuf à la niçoise*.

Coriander: *la coriandre*
The round seeds of coriander look like peppercorns. This spice must be used with discretion because it is powerful. It is used in marinades and with pork, and is a must in hot sauce for couscous.

Cumin seed: *le cumin*
Quite a powerful spice, delicious with *capoun* and in couscous.

Curry powder: *le curry*
Used in *poulpe provençale* and *merlan aux moules*. Can be made at home by blending coriander, cumin and fennel seeds with cloves, cinnamon, mustard, ginger and peanuts.

Fennel: *le fenouil*
This is a marvellous savoury herb. The dried stalks of wild fennel are used to stuff grilled fish or to make a bed for cooking fish. They are used in soups (*soupe de pêcheurs, bourride*, bouillabaisse), in *court bouillon*, in pork dishes (*rôti de porc provençale*), and with snails (*escargots provençale*). However, it is quite difficult to find dried fennel stalks here, so I use fresh fennel or even dried fennel seeds. The taste and smell of lamb or fish barbecued over fennel or rosemary twigs are glorious. If you cannot find such twigs, sprinkle the meat with dried rosemary leaves and fennel seeds about an hour before grilling.

Garlic: *l'ail*
Since ancient times, when the Chinese, the Egyptians and the Hebrews discovered it, garlic has been used in both cooking and medicine. This potent, healthful vegetable is a staple of Provençal cuisine and, to a lesser degree, Niçois cooking. It is the base for *aïoli*,

rouille and fish dishes (*brandade, gigot de mer*), soups (*aïgo bouido*), meats (*gigot d'agneau à l'aillade*), *champignons provençale* and *caviar provençale*.

Choose large, plump garlic bulbs. Red garlic is tastier, stronger and keeps better. The white variety is milder, but as long as it is firm and fresh it is acceptable. Never use a clove of garlic that is soft, yellow or dark and has a green sprout in the centre.

Cooked garlic is very different from raw. Cooked slowly, it tastes sweet and nutty; sautéd whole, it is light and delicate. Raw garlic, minced or crushed, is potent enough to revive or enliven any dish. For guests fussy about their breath, offer bitter chocolate, lemon juice, or mint or parsley leaves after dinner.

Juniper: *le genièvre*
These little black berries are used to stuff birds (as in *chacha au genièvre*), to marinate game and to flavour *pot-au-feu provençale* and some pâtés. Juniper jelly is delicious on toast or mixed with a light herb tea instead of honey.

Lemon balm: *la mélisse*
This unusual mint makes a delicious cordial, *l'eau des Carmes*, and a tea that is supposed to cure indigestion.

Mint: *la menthe*
This is used chopped in *salade niçoise* (with or instead of fresh basil), *brochettes de Nice* and *pâtes à la verdure*. It is lovely as a garnish for *glace à la fleur d'orangers* and *tian de rhum*, or sprinkled on fruit salads. Brewed as a tea, it is supposed to rekindle an honest man's passion and a pretty woman's vigour!

Nutmeg: *les noix de muscade*
Buy whole nutmeg and grate what you need at the last moment with a sharp knife. Use in gnocchi, with vegetables (*papeton d'aubergines*), seafood and fish (*moules aux épinards, brandade*), and meat (*boeuf mironton*).

Orange-flower water: *l'eau de fleur d'orangers*
This flavouring is used in desserts (*glace à la fleur d'orangers*), with

vegetables (*épinards aux pignons*) and with fresh ricotta cheese. It is available here in chemists' shops.

Orange rind: *le zeste d'orange*
Use a potato peeler to pare only the thin orange-coloured rind and hang it in your kitchen to dry. (It's an essential in a well-stocked Niçois kitchen.) Use it in meat dishes (*boeuf à la niçoise, daube d'Avignon, estouffade, gardiane*) and in soups (*soupe de pêcheurs,* bouillabaisse).

Parsley: *le persil*
This is the most commonly used of all herbs. Italian parsley, flat-leaved, is the most savoury and will keep in a plastic bag in the refrigerator. Because parsley is rich in vitamins A and C, which heat destroys, add it, finely minced, at the last minute. Try to grow it (you might have a hanging basket in the kitchen), since there is constant use for it – sprinkled on black olives, in omelettes, in sauces, and in most meat and fish dishes. Always chop it as finely as possible with an *hachoir* (see Techniques and Tools, p. 21) so that it is almost a paste.

Pepper: *le poivre*
White pepper is made from the ripe berries of the pepper plant. Black pepper, made from the dried under-ripe berries, has a slightly stronger flavour than the white, but the major difference is colour – add white pepper to dishes that should have a pale colour and black to others. Peppercorns are sometimes added to a simmering liquid and then removed when the dish is done. For sprinkling, always use peppercorns to make freshly ground pepper. Red or pink peppercorns are pretty and tasty.

Rosemary: *le romarin*
This is a very strong herb, so use it cautiously. I enjoy cracking the dried needle-like leaves between my teeth, but if you do not, wrap them in a piece of cheesecloth to remove after cooking. Rosemary is used with lamb (*daube d'Avignon, brochettes de Nice, agneau à la niçoise*), soup (bouillabaisse) and fowl (*poulet en gelée*).

Salt: *le sel*

Gros sel (sea salt) is the very best and easily available. But kosher salt is also tasty. Since the amount of salt used depends on individual preference, I recommend tasting each dish at least twice to check the seasoning adequately.

Techniques and Tools

There are eight ways of cooking: boiling, steaming, roasting, grilling, sautéing, frying, stewing and braising (which means cooking in a closed pan with less liquid than when stewing). One can endlessly seek utensils to help one master each method, and with the proliferation of shops offering intriguing items, one can collect equipment for ever. But so far as traditional Provençal cooking is concerned, it requires no more than four pans: an earthenware *poêlon*, which has a handle; a *poêle*, or frying-pan; a *fait-tout*, a deep casserole made of cast iron, copper or earthenware, which can be tightly closed; and a *tian* for gratin dishes.

There are basically only two techniques in southern French cuisine: sautéing in oil, and simmering over a low heat. The first is quick and decisive – meat or vegetables are quickly seared over high heat in order to seal in the juices and therefore the natural flavour. The second method involves slow cooking, which tenderizes the meat and vegetables as they simmer in liquid in a covered pot or pan.

In addition, there are special techniques that I mention elsewhere in the book, such as making pasta and preserves, and I have chosen to describe these in connection with specific recipes.

The equipment needed to prepare my repertory of dishes is not very extensive. I have a plain functional kitchen, which looks and feels like a kitchen. It is honest and practical. My herbs are in glass jars and I never keep them more than a year. Sugar, flour and rice are in big Pyrex containers on an easy-to-reach shelf above the worktop. I keep vegetables and fruits in wide baskets. The grater, sieve, kitchen scissors, Mouli food mill and wire whisk hang on pegs on the wall. The mortar and pestle are within easy reach. I have an assortment of pretty baskets in which I serve *beignets*, fresh fruits and fried whitebait. I have cheerful earthenware dishes and bright paper napkins for *socca*, *beignets* and snails. I serve wine in glass jugs, water in earthenware jugs, and oil and vinegar in individual glass cruets.

The following is a list of the basic equipment in my kitchen that I use constantly in preparing Niçois and Provençal dishes.

Casserole: *la cocotte, le fait-tout*
The best of the cast-iron casseroles is the *doufeu* (which means gentle fire). It comes either round or oval and has a recessed cover, which I fill with water so that the stew bastes itself as it cooks. The evenly distributed heat makes it perfect for *boeuf à la niçoise, daube d'Avignon* and ratatouille.

Cheesecloth: *la mousseline*
Used to line a sieve before straining soups or sauces.

Chopping board: *la planche à hacher*
Narrow board with a handle (with a hole so that it can be hung in a convenient spot). I use it not only for chopping vegetables and meat, but also as an aid in slicing such foods as terrines so that each slice remains firm and intact – I hold the board perpendicular to the terrine resting on a platter or another board and press it against the terrine as I cut each slice.

Colander: *la passoire*
The three-legged stand makes this convenient for draining pasta and vegetables.

Conical sieve: *le chinois*
Made of strong aluminium mesh so you can purée food by pushing it through with a spoon or pestle.

Double boiler with a steamer: *la couscoussière*
This is primarily used to prepare couscous, but is useful for reheating meat, and for steaming fish and vegetables.

Frying-pan: *la poêle à frire*
I use this wide pan only for frying and clean it with paper towels and rough salt. Stainless steel pans are the best.

Gratin dish: *tian*
A somewhat shallow oval or square ovenproof dish made of earthenware, china or glass.

Garlic press: *le presse ail*
I use it to press garlic directly on to the dish I am preparing.

Kitchen scissors: *les ciseaux*
Snipping with scissors is still the best way to cut chives, basil, squid and cooked chicken livers.

Mincer and chopper: *le hachoir*
Curved stainless steel blade with two wooden handles. Perfect for mincing parsley, garlic and onion, it is also useful for chopping meat, salt pork, etc.

Mortar and pestle: *le mortier*
The traditional marble mortar with four round ears and its big wooden pestle are so expensive that I would advise the purchase of the widely available vitrified porcelain mortar and its matching porcelain pestle.

Mouli food mill: *la moulinette*
This wonderful machine has three interchangeable discs and is indispensable for making purées, sauces and soups. It gives more texture than a blender and, unlike a blender or food processor, it can retain such rough parts of food as fruit seed and fish skin. A food processor can be used instead if, where necessary, you strain the ingredients to remove these rough parts.

Multi-tiered steamer
This is an excellent investment, recommended for steaming all your vegetables to perfection.

Pepper mill: *le moulin à poivre*
Used to grind fresh peppercorns on dishes in preparation and on food at the table.

Rotary grater: *le mouli-fromage*
Has three cylinders for grating cheese, nuts and chocolate.

Salad maker: *le mouli-julienne*
Has five steel discs, which grate, shred and slice all vegetables and even chocolate. Of course, many people now use the electric version: the food processor.

Salad bowl: *le saladier*
The bowl should be of china or glass, not wood (garlic, vinegar and olive oil have lasting flavours that cling to wood). Glass is best because it gives the most appetizing effect. To evenly distribute the dressing, I gently toss the greens with my hands.

Saucepans: *les sauteuses*
Various sizes for boiling, sautéing and stewing, and one especially for sauces, made of copper or stainless steel and with low straight sides.

Skewers: *les brochettes*
The best kind is flat, not round. Skewered pieces of meat and vegetable will not twirl or slip off if you use two flat skewers to secure each row of them.

Stockpot: *la marmite*
This pot is used to prepare *pot-au-feu*, *pâtes aux oeufs*, *ravioli à la niçoise* and other similar dishes.

Tart pan: *la tourtière*
Used for *tourte aux noix et au miel* and *tourte de blettes*. It has a loose bottom for easy removal.

Terrine: *la terrine*
This type of casserole is made of porcelain or earthenware. It has a

lid that fits snugly and has a small hole that allows steam to escape. It is used with the lid for making *terrine de campagne* and without the lid for making *tians*. If you make pâtés often, it is well worth cutting a piece of plywood or cardboard to fit the dimensions of the terrine and wrapping it in aluminium foil. Put weights on top of it to press it down evenly.

Tongs: *les pinces*
Used for turning over pieces of meat or fish as you sauté them.

Wooden spoon: *la cuillère en bois*
The long handle is helpful in stirring food while it is cooking.

Les Soupes

Soups

Provence and Nice offer an abundance of delicious soups. They are pungent and fresh, and depend on the bounty of each season. Some constitute a whole meal in themselves: *pot-au-feu provençale, soupe au pistou*, bouillabaisse. Some, such as *aïgo bouido*, are light and cleansing. Although the ingredients are varied, there are only two ways to start a Niçois or Provençal soup. Either you sauté the meat or vegetables in olive oil, then add the liquid (broth, wine or water) or you put all the ingredients in boiling water to start with and then cook them together slowly over low heat.

Pistou is the only soup we eat cold as well as hot; all other soups are served hot. Most are served with *croûtons* or freshly grated Gruyère or Parmesan cheese and garnished with fresh herbs.

There are four types of soup:

- *Les soupes maigres* (or *potages de santé*), made with combinations of beans, courgettes, potatoes, squash, tomatoes, chick-peas, spinach, sage and garlic. Examples: *aïgo bouido, soupe de courges, soupe au pistou*.
- *Les soupes grasses*, made with meat and bones. *Pot-au-feu* is the classic example.
- *Les soupes au bâton* (so called because they were stirred with a stick), made with chestnut or chick-pea flour. *Fournade* is an example.
- *Les soupes de poissons*, made with fish or shellfish. Examples: *soupe de pêcheurs*, bouillabaisse, *bourride, soupe de moules*.

Always make these soups in generous quantities. They will keep two or three days in the refrigerator and some will freeze well. In any case, you will find them to be more than 'something to take the chill out of your children'.

Aïgo Bouido
Herb and garlic broth

This light and pungent soup is full of virtues. It is even said that *Aïgo bouido sauva la vido – Aïgo bouido* will save your life. It is the perfect soup to serve the day after a rich meal. For a more substantial version, you may add cheese, vermicelli or even egg yolks.

For 6 people

1.1 1/2 pt water
6 whole garlic cloves, peeled
2 50-mm/2-in pieces dried orange rind
2 bay leaves
5 fresh sage leaves, or ½ tsp dried sage
2 sprigs thyme, or 1 tsp dried thyme
115 g/4 oz vermicelli (optional)
salt
freshly ground pepper
1 tbsp olive oil

Heat the water in a large saucepan until it boils. Add the garlic, orange rind, bay leaves, sage and thyme, and boil for 20 minutes. Strain through a sieve.

Add the vermicelli if you wish, and cook it until it is soft – about 5 minutes. Turn off the heat. Add the salt, pepper and olive oil.

Variation
The broth may be prepared in a slightly different way: sauté garlic cloves in hot olive oil for 3 minutes; add the water, herbs and spices and, 10 minutes later, the vermicelli, and then cook for 5 more minutes.

If you want a richer soup, beat 4 egg yolks and pour in a little of the hot soup to warm them before adding them to the pot. Stir in 55 g/2 oz grated cheese and serve at once.

Bourride

A creamy garlic fish soup

This unctuous, savoury cream soup is a tradition in the south, from Marseilles to Monaco. Since either whiting and bass or cod are available year round, you may serve this soup in any season.

The chunks of fish are removed from the soup and served separately. I like to serve the fish as a second course after the soup, but most Niçois prefer having everything arrive on the table at the same time. Choose a bright crockery dish, since both the soup and the fish have a pale colour.

For 8 people (you must make this recipe for at least that many)

2 kg/4½ lb of three different fish in any proportions (choose among bass, whiting, haddock, cod, flounder, halibut)
1 whole leek, chopped
1 large onion, chopped
1 carrot, chopped
2 tbsp olive oil
340 ml/12 fl oz dry white wine
340 ml/12 fl oz water
3 50-mm/2-in pieces of orange rind

1 tsp dried fennel or anise
1 tsp thyme
2 bay leaves
salt
freshly ground white pepper
5 egg yolks
3 slices good white bread for making *croûtons* (p. 11)
450 ml/16 fl oz Aïoli (p. 71)
sprigs of parsley

Fillet the fish (do not discard the heads and bones) or ask the fish-monger to do it. Stew the leek, onion and carrot in the olive oil for about 15 minutes, or until they are soft. Add the fish heads and bones only, then the wine, water (more if necessary), orange rind, fennel or anise, thyme, bay leaves and salt. Bring to a boil and skim off the froth. Simmer uncovered for 30 minutes. Strain into a pot, pushing as many of the bits of fish through as possible.

Cut the fish fillets into 50-mm-/2-in-square pieces. Bring the soup stock to a boil, reduce to a simmer and put in the heavier pieces of fish first, adding the lighter, more delicate ones later. The whole cooking time should be about 6 minutes for the entire batch.

Meanwhile, warm a platter in the oven, set at the lowest tempera-ture. Place the fillets on the platter and pour a ladleful of warm broth over them. Seal with aluminium foil and keep the fish warm in the oven. Reserve the soup.

Prepare *aïoli* sauce. Put 8 tablespoons of this in a bowl and slowly add the egg yolks, stirring gently. Refrigerate the rest of the *aïoli* to use later. Prepare the *croûtons*.

Reheat the stock over a low heat. Beat half of it very slowly into the *aïoli*–egg mixture with a wooden spoon, then pour this mixture back into the rest of the soup (be sure the heat is low or the soup will curdle). Keep stirring and cook until the soup has thickened enough to coat a spoon, as with custard. When the soup has been reduced to a velvety texture, ladle it over the *croûtons* and serve as a first course.

As a following course, remove the foil from the platter of fish, garnish with parsley and serve with the bowl of chilled *aïoli*.

Variation
Serve the soup over both the fillets of fish and the *croûtons*, and pass the bowl of *aïoli* separately.

Soupe de Carottes
A delicate carrot soup

This light and refreshing soup is easy to prepare in any season. If you use big winter carrots, add a lump of sugar during cooking.

For 6 people

900 ml/1⅗ pt water	freshly ground black pepper
salt	1 tbsp olive oil
1 bay leaf	2 slices firm white bread for making
4 large or medium-sized carrots	*croûtons* (p. 11), (optional)
1 large potato	1 tbsp chopped parsley (optional)
1 large onion	

Bring water to a boil and add salt and bay leaf. Peel and slice the vegetables, then add them to the boiling water and simmer for 15 minutes. Pass through a Mouli food mill into a saucepan. Add salt and pepper (and sugar if desired), and check the seasoning.

Heat for 3 minutes. Sprinkle with olive oil and serve.

You may serve the soup on *croûtons* and sprinkle it with parsley at the last minute to add colour, but I like the very simple, unadorned version.

Soupe de Courges
Courgette or pumpkin soup

This is a light, delicious soup, whether it is made with courgettes in the spring or pumpkin in the autumn. Select very crisp vegetables, since the flavour of the soup depends on the freshness of the ingredients. Pumpkin is sweeter and thicker than courgettes, so you will need more salt, pepper and water for pumpkin soup.

For 6 people

1.25 kg/3 lb courgettes or a 1.25-kg/3-lb pumpkin
2 tbsp olive oil
4 large onions, chopped
1 garlic clove, peeled
140 g/5 oz cooked rice (4 tbsp, raw)
1 tsp sage

2–4 tsp salt
1–1½ tsp freshly ground black pepper
680–900 ml/1⅕–1⅗ pt water
1 tbsp raw olive oil
55 g/2 oz cheese, freshly grated
2 tbsp chopped fresh mint leaves or parsley

Peel and dice the courgettes or pumpkin (discard seeds). Heat the olive oil in a cast-iron saucepan, add the onions and cook them until they are transparent – about 5 minutes. Add the courgettes or pumpkin, and the garlic clove. Cook for 30 minutes more.

Add the rice, sage, salt and pepper. Pass the mixture through a Mouli food mill. Add enough water for the consistency you like and check the seasoning.

Add a dash of olive oil and a garnish of cheese and mint or parsley and serve piping hot.

Fournade
A creamy chick-pea soup

This is one of the simplest and most economical soups you can ever make. You can prepare it at the last minute. It is rather thick and should be stirred with a wooden spoon while cooking (in the mountains this kind of soup was called *soupe au bâton*). A great treat for children.

For 6 people

225 g/8 oz chick-pea flour
1.8 l/3⅕ pt water
salt
freshly ground white pepper
2 bay leaves

1 clove, or a pinch of ground cloves
a pinch of freshly ground coriander
4 tbsp olive oil

Combine the chick-pea flour and water in a large bowl, and beat with an egg beater until the mixture is fairly smooth. Pour into a saucepan and cook over medium heat. Add salt, pepper, bay leaves, clove, coriander and 2 tablespoons of the olive oil. Simmer, gently stirring, for about 10 minutes. The soup will quickly thicken. Add more water if you wish. Check the seasoning and add the remaining olive oil just before serving. This soup reheats well.

Soupe de Moules
Mussel soup

This light and delicately flavoured soup is one of the quickest and easiest to prepare.

For 6 people

275 kg/6 lb mussels, preferably small
1 l/1⅘ pt water
1 tbsp olive oil
1 garlic clove, unpeeled
1 large onion, minced

1 bouquet garni (p. 14)
salt
freshly ground white pepper
½ tsp saffron
115 g/4 oz fine vermicelli

Scrub the mussels thoroughly with a wire brush. Remove the beard with your fingers and place the mussels in a large bowl of cold water. Wait 2 minutes, then discard all the mussels that are open – they are not fresh.

Boil 115 ml/4 fl oz water in a heavy-bottomed saucepan and add the mussels. Cook them covered for 5 minutes, tossing from time to time with a slotted spoon. Turn off the heat. Place a piece of cheesecloth over a sieve and pour the mussel broth through it. Reserve the broth and the mussels.

Heat the olive oil in a large frying-pan. Crush the garlic clove with your fist on a board and add this, the onion and the bouquet garni to the oil. Cook for 5 minutes. Add salt, pepper and the mussel broth, and stir carefully for 5 more minutes. Add the saffron, crushing it between your fingers over the soup.

Pour this mixture into a large saucepan or stockpot and add 900 ml/1⅗ pt of *hot* water (using some to rinse the frying-pan). Bring to a boil and add the vermicelli. Cook for another 15 minutes.

Check the seasoning and add the mussels just before serving.

Soupe de Lentilles

Lentil soup

This is a hearty soup, perfect for a cold winter night. It seems to improve with each reheating, so make a good amount of it.

For 6 people

300 g/10½ oz dried lentils	1 tsp dried thyme
2 tbsp olive oil	2 bay leaves
1 onion, chopped	salt
1 tomato, peeled and quartered, or	freshly ground black pepper
75 g/2¾ oz drained canned	900 ml/1⅗ pt water
tomatoes	3 slices good white bread for
2 carrots, chopped	making *croûtons* (p. 11)
2 garlic cloves, peeled and crushed	1 tbsp sherry

Wash the lentils in cold water and drain in a sieve. Heat the oil in a heavy saucepan and cook the chopped onion until soft. Add the tomato, carrots, garlic, thyme, bay leaves, salt, pepper and lentils. Add water and bring to a boil. Cover and simmer 1 to 2 hours. Cooking time will depend on the size of the lentils (they should be tender but not mushy).

Prepare the *croûtons*, cutting them into 12-mm/½-in cubes. Place them in each soup plate or at the bottom of the soup tureen. Remove the bay leaves from the soup, add sherry to it and pour over the *croûtons*. Serve immediately.

Soupe de Pêcheurs
A rich fish soup

This great fish soup is the base for the renowned bouillabaisse, and is made of the cheapest possible ingredients: fish heads and bones. Those of bass, red snapper or whiting will make the best soup, since they are not oily. Either use the head and bones left over from a grilled fish dinner or ask for them at your fishmonger's, where you might get them for nothing.

You can use this recipe as a base and add crab, a whole firm fish, vermicelli, pasta or *croûtons*, and cheese to make it more substantial. Serve it with a chilled dry white wine.

For 6 people

1 snapper or bass fish head or 2
    whiting heads
1–2 fish backbones
salt
freshly ground black pepper
1 tbsp flour
2 medium-sized potatoes
2 medium-sized onions
7 tsp olive oil
2 fresh tomatoes, quartered, or 140 g/
    5 oz drained canned tomatoes
1 tsp thyme
3 50-mm/2-in pieces orange rind

1 bay leaf
1 ml/2⅖ pt water or 680 ml/1⅕ pt
    water mixed with 680 ml/1⅕ pt
    dry white wine
½ tsp Spanish saffron (do not use
    the powdered kind)
1 garlic clove, peeled and crushed
3 slices good white bread for
    making *croûtons* (p. 11)
55 g/2 oz Parmesan or Gruyère
    cheese, freshly grated
55 g/2 oz very thin vermicelli
    (optional)

Rinse and dry the fish head and bones. Sprinkle them with salt, pepper and flour and set aside. Peel and dice the potatoes. Peel and grate the onions or chop them finely.

In a heavy frying-pan, heat 6 teaspoons olive oil and add the onions. Sauté gently for 3 minutes, add the fish head and bones and sauté another 3 minutes. Add the potatoes, tomatoes, thyme, orange rind, bay leaf, salt and pepper, and cook for 5 minutes. Add the water or wine and water and bring to a boil. Simmer for 30 minutes.

Crush the saffron between your fingers over the soup. Cook the soup for another 2 minutes.

Place a Mouli food mill over a pan and pour two ladlefuls at a time of the soup mixture into it. Add broth whenever necessary. After the soup mixture is entirely ground, put it in a sieve over a large bowl and force it through with a pestle. Alternatively, blend the soup in a food processor and then strain it through a sieve. Discard the residue left in the sieve.

Reheat the soup over a medium heat. Add the garlic, 1 teaspoon olive oil, salt, and pepper to taste. Add more saffron if desired.

Cut the bread into triangles and make the *croûtons*. Serve the soup over *croûtons* sprinkled with the cheese.

Variation
If you want a more substantial soup, add the vermicelli 10 minutes before serving.

Soupe au Pistou
Vegetable soup flavoured with basil paste

Pistou refers to the paste of crushed garlic, basil, cheese, and olive oil that is added to a dish just before serving. This soup is enjoyed in Italy as well as in the South of France. The best time to prepare it is summer or autumn, when there is the greatest variety of fresh vegetables. However, since carrots, onions, cabbage, celery, dried white haricots and butter beans, and potatoes are available all year round, you can always make this soup if you keep *pistou* in the freezer.

This is a wonderful soup – strong in flavour, yet very light. It can be served hot or cold with equal success.

For 6 people

450 g/1 lb white haricot beans, fresh or dried	85 g/3 oz lean streaky bacon
	1 leek
225 g/8 oz fresh or frozen broad beans	½ head green cabbage
	½ head celery
225 g/8 oz French beans	1 tbsp olive oil
6 potatoes	1.8 l/3⅓ pt water
5 onions	2 bay leaves
5 carrots	a pinch of sage
3 medium-sized turnips or 1 swede	salt
5 courgettes, about 680 g/1½ lb	freshly ground black pepper

If you use dried white beans, parboil them for 30 minutes. Shell and blanch the broad beans if they are fresh. String the French beans or snap off both ends and cut into 25-mm/1-in pieces (put a handful at a time on a board and chop roughly with a large knife). Peel and dice the potatoes, onions, carrots and turnips. Dice the courgettes (unpeeled) and the bacon. Coarsely chop the leek, cabbage and celery.

Heat the olive oil in a large heavy-bottomed pan. Add the onions and cook over medium heat for 5 minutes, then add the bacon, potatoes, leek, carrots, sage and as much of the other vegetables as the pan will hold. Sauté for 5 more minutes.

Bring a large pot of water to a boil and add the contents of the pan, along with the rest of the vegetables, bay leaves and salt and pepper. Simmer uncovered for 40 minutes. Check the seasoning and continue cooking slowly for 1 hour more, or until the vegetables are just tender.

·············· Pistou* ··············

55–75 g/2–3 oz fresh basil, to taste	115 ml/4 fl oz olive oil
4–6 garlic cloves	a pinch of coarse sea salt or kosher salt
115–225 g/4–8 oz Gruyère, Parmesan or Romano cheese	

* You can double the amount of garlic or double the whole recipe, according to your taste. This recipe corresponds only to my own preferences.

While the soup is simmering, prepare the *pistou*. Rinse and dry the basil leaves, and shred them with kitchen scissors. Peel and crush the garlic cloves. Grate the cheese.

Place the garlic, basil and salt in a large mortar and pound vigorously with the pestle until you have a paste. Add the cheese, then the oil, stirring vigorously with the pestle until smooth. (A blender or food processor simplifies the process: put in the basil, cheese, garlic and olive oil and turn on high speed for a few seconds. Stop and stir with a spoon, then blend again. Do this two or three times until you have a smooth paste.)

Add the *pistou* to the soup a moment before serving and stir. You may want to serve the soup with a small bowl of grated Romano, Parmesan or Gruyère cheese.

Soupe de Petits Pois

Fresh pea soup

This is a refreshing hot-weather soup. Choose very fresh and smooth pea pods, because you will use the pods also for this soup.

For 6 people

680 g/1½ lb fresh peas	bouquet garni (p. 14)
3 slices firm white bread for making	water to cover
croûtons (p. 11)	a pinch of sugar
2 large onions	salt
3 carrots	freshly ground black pepper
55 g/2 oz lean streaky bacon	1 tbsp olive oil
2 tbsp peanut oil	

Wash the peas and shell them. Keep all the pods that are firm and green. Snap and pull each pod as you would tough celery fibres and discard the transparent linings. Prepare the *croûtons*, cutting them into triangles.

Peel and chop the onions, carrots and bacon. Heat the peanut oil in a cast-iron saucepan. Add the chopped ingredients, the bouquet garni, peas and pods. Cover with cold water and bring to a boil.

Reduce the heat and cook for 30 to 40 minutes. Add sugar and salt and pepper to taste.

Just before serving, remove the bouquet garni, add the olive oil, and garnish with the *croûtons*.

Variation

If you want a more elegant soup, purée it in a food processor or pass it through a Mouli food mill to make a fragrant, velvety *crème de petits pois*. Garnish it with *croûtons*, cut in cubes. Frozen peas are acceptable for this version of the soup.

Soupe de Pois Chiches à la Sauge
Chick-pea and sage soup

This is a hearty winter soup. For this recipe I always use canned chick-peas. They taste as good as dried ones and are infinitely more convenient.

For 6 people

2 onions	salt
2 carrots	1 tsp dried sage
1 tomato, fresh or canned	freshly ground black pepper
1 garlic clove	1.4 l/2⅖ pt water
5 heads soft round or iceberg	1 450-g/16-oz can chick-peas
lettuce (soft round is preferable)	3 slices firm white bread for making
4 tsp olive oil	*croûtons* (p. 11)

Chop the onions, carrots and tomato. Peel and crush the garlic clove. Rinse and chop the lettuce very finely.

Heat 3 teaspoons of the olive oil in a cast-iron frying-pan or enamelled casserole dish. Add the onions and sprinkle with salt. Add the carrots, garlic, tomato, lettuce, sage, pepper and water. Simmer for 25 minutes.

Drain and rinse the chick-peas under cold water, and add to the soup. Cook for 5 minutes, then pass the mixture through a Mouli food mill. Check the seasoning. Cut the bread into triangles and make *croûtons*.

Just before serving, add 1 teaspoon of olive oil to the soup and stir. Pour over the *croûtons* and serve immediately.

Les Hors-d'Oeuvres

Appetizers

In the Midi there is no cocktail hour. We may nibble on olives or toasted almonds with *pastis* (a liquorice drink served with iced water) or a chilled glass of herb-flavoured vermouth, but hors-d'oeuvres are served at the table and are part of the meal.

The French are highly conscious of the need for a delicate balance between the courses. The flavours and textures must complement each other. And in the South of France, with such a colourful array of fruits, vegetables and aromatic herbs, this is particularly important. Thus, before a hearty *boeuf à la niçoise* or *pot-au-feu provençale*, a light but tasty *anchoïade* might be served. Or a rich *terrine de campagne* might precede a vegetable main course such as *artichauts à la barigoule*.

However you compose your meals, remember always that they must be a feast for the eye as well as the palate. No hors-d'oeuvre, no matter how simple, should be served without a garnish, and the variety of what you can offer is as limitless as your imagination. As long as this first course is tasty, light and enticing, call it an hors-d'oeuvre.

You might prepare a basket of raw vegetables with a bowl of *bagna cauda*, *caviar provençale* or *aïoli* to dip them in, a platter of prosciutto ham surrounded by sections of a ripe melon, crisp pieces of *socca*, tomatoes filled with *sauce verte*, marinated sardines, yellow and red peppers sprinkled with garlic and parsley, raw whiting with wedges of lemon, or an assortment of raw oysters, clams and mussels garnished with lemon slices and buttered home-made bread. You may serve an endless variety of salads: raw fennel with vinaigrette sauce, warm chick-peas, cold mussels, and, of course, the queen of Niçois salads and hors-d'oeuvres, *la salade niçoise*.

Anchoïade
Anchovy and garlic spread

Here are two recipes for *anchoïade*, a spicy anchovy and garlic spread to be served on dry toast. The first is a powerful, concentrated version served hot; the second is creamy and served cold.

If possible, use the kind of anchovies packed in rough salt. If they are unavailable, use canned anchovies in oil, drained on kitchen towels.

For 6 people

············ Anchoïade I ············

20 anchovy fillets, rinsed and drained
2 garlic cloves, crushed
1 tbsp red wine vinegar or lemon juice
freshly ground black pepper
4 tbsp olive oil
6 slices good white bread or 12 slices French bread

Mash the anchovies in a mortar (or use a blender or food processor). Add the garlic, vinegar and pepper, and dribble the oil in very slowly so the sauce does not separate. Sprinkle the slices of bread with olive oil, place on a baking sheet and toast under the grill for 2–3 minutes, or until slightly crisp. Turn them over, spread them with the anchovy paste and return to the grill for 3–5 minutes. Cut each slice into 4 triangles and serve immediately while piping hot.

To garnish, you might sprinkle the triangles with crushed garlic and arrange them attractively on a platter with lemon slices, white and red radishes, chopped parsley or chives, and black olives.

············ Anchoïade II ············

24 anchovy fillets, rinsed and drained
2 garlic cloves, peeled
2 egg yolks
4 tbsp olive oil
freshly ground black pepper
6 slices good white bread

Mash the anchovies and garlic in a mortar. Add egg yolks and mix well. Very slowly beat in the oil and add pepper to taste. Sprinkle the slices of bread with olive oil and toast lightly under the grill for 2–3 minutes. Cut into triangles while they are still hot. Let them cool, then spread with the anchovy paste.

For garnishing, you might use chopped parsley or chives, a hard-boiled egg passed through a sieve, a grated onion, small black olives from Nice or sliced radishes.

Caviar Provençale
Aubergine, lemon, and garlic purée

This refreshing, piquant purée is served on toast as an appetizer. It also makes a wonderful dip: place it in half a scooped-out raw aubergine or in a brightly coloured bowl and surround it with 50-mm/2-in sticks of cucumber, fennel, celery and carrots, along with whole white radishes and cherry tomatoes, or with potato crisps. It is delicious served with a vermouth or chilled white wine.

For 6 people

3 aubergines (about 450 g/1 lb each)	salt
3 garlic cloves, crushed	freshly ground white pepper
70 ml/2½ fl oz olive oil	1 tbsp chopped onion or parsley or basil or anchovies
juice of 1 lemon	*croûtons* (p. 11)

Heat the grill and turn it down to low. Slice the aubergines in half lengthways. Place them 50 mm/2 in below the heat for about 50 minutes, turning once. When they become very soft, scoop out all the flesh (discard skins). Remove the seed strips and press the pulp through a Mouli food mill into a bowl. Add the garlic. Slowly beat in the olive oil, lemon juice, salt (a fair amount is needed, so taste to make sure) and pepper. Cover with cling film and chill.

To serve, sprinkle with chopped onion, basil, parsley or anchovies. Prepare triangular *croûtons* and arrange them around the bowl along with raw vegetables or potato crisps.

Citron, Courgette, Concombre, Oeuf et Tomate à la Tapenade

Lemon, courgette, cucumber, hard-boiled egg and tomato filled with a garlic, anchovy, olive, tuna and lemon-juice mixture

1 egg, hard-boiled, sliced in half lengthways
1 large tomato, sliced in half
1 cucumber, sliced in half lengthways
1 courgette, sliced in half lengthways
1 lemon, cut in half
1 garlic clove

2 anchovies
2 tbsp capers
2 tbsp canned tuna
6 fleshy black olives, pitted
3 egg yolks, raw
½ tsp thyme
juice of 1 lemon
2 tbsp chopped parsley
pepper

Remove the yolk from the hard-boiled egg and scoop out the pulp from the tomato, cucumber, courgette and lemon. Reserve the yolk.

Whirl all the remaining ingredients in the food processor to make the filling. Stuff the egg, lemon and vegetable halves with the filling and sprinkle with the egg yolk passed through a sieve. Chill.

Crudités et Bagna Cauda

Raw vegetables dipped in a 'warm bath' of garlic, anchovies and olive oil

This recipe has all the best qualities of Niçois cooking: it is fresh, colourful, easy to prepare and light. It is perfect for an outdoor buffet.

Choose among the vegetables suggested, but do not include any that are not tender and fresh – no frozen food.

cos lettuce, leaves separated
watercress, cut in 50-mm/2-in pieces
broccoli, only the peeled stalks
chicory, small, sweet whole leaves
celery hearts, cut in strips
cauliflower, florets separated

spring onions, whole or sliced lengthways
spinach, with stems
cucumbers, peeled, seeded and cut in strips
fennel bulbs, cut in strips
mushrooms, whole, with stems

radishes (white and red), whole,
    with leaves if possible
carrots, peeled and with some stem
    left on
courgettes, unpeeled and cut
    lengthways into 25-mm-/1-in-
    thick sticks
cherry tomatoes, whole

green peppers (small), seeded
    and quartered
baby purple artichokes, whole or
    cut lengthways
asparagus (preferably very small),
    pared
baby broad beans
Bagna Cauda (p. 72)

Wash, clean and prepare a variety of the vegetables listed. Arrange them attractively in a long, shallow basket or on an earthenware dish or several plates. Sprinkle with cool water, cover with foil and chill. Serve with *bagna cauda*, kept warm in an earthenware or chafing dish heated by a candle. Guests will dip the vegetables in the sauce, as with fondue.

Variations
Although *bagna cauda* is the sauce traditionally served, you will find that *crudités* are delicious with any of the following sauces: *Pistou* (p. 81), *Sauce Piquante* (p. 80), *Aïoli* (p. 71), *Rouille* (p. 84), *Sauce Ravigote* (p. 83), *Sauce Verte* (p. 86) or *Bagna Rotou* (p. 72).

Mousse d'Aubergines Froide
Aubergine dip

This pungent mousse is wonderfully versatile. You may fill halves of tomatoes with it or serve it as an appetizer in a brightly coloured bowl with sticks of cucumber, courgette and fennel for dipping. Since the mousse is so dull in colour, sprinkle it with parsley and always serve it in a colourful dish. You can mound it in an aubergine shell if you scoop the insides out of an aubergine in the recipe instead of using it whole, skin and all. The mousse is better made a day in advance and left in the refrigerator.

For 6 people

3 large (1.25-kg/3-lb) aubergines, unpeeled and sliced as thinly as possible
salt
2 anchovies
2 tbsp olive oil

2 onions, grated or very finely chopped
3 garlic cloves, crushed
freshly ground black pepper
2 tbsp parsley or basil, chopped
juice of ½ lemon

Sprinkle the aubergine slices with salt. Toss and let stand for 1 hour. Preheat oven to 190°C/375°F/Gas Mark 5. Wash the anchovies, fillet and cut them in small pieces. Rinse and dry the aubergine slices. Sprinkle with olive oil and bake in an oiled baking dish for 1½ hours, or until soft. Pass the aubergine through a Mouli food mill. (If you put the cooked aubergine and the chopped ingredients into a food processor, the texture will be more 'pasty', but the taste will be equally good.) Add the onion, garlic, anchovies and salt and pepper to taste (it should be highly seasoned). Chill.

Before serving, sprinkle on the parsley and lemon juice, and if you like, a few drops of olive oil.

Oeufs à l'Aillade

Hard-boiled eggs filled with garlic, capers and anchovies

This is made in a jiffy and is a flavourful way to stuff hard-boiled eggs. Boiled garlic cloves are mild and have an interesting texture.

For 6 people

6 eggs
10 garlic cloves, peeled
3 anchovies, filleted
3 tsp capers
3 tbsp olive oil
dash of red wine vinegar

salt
freshly ground black pepper
1 tbsp finely chopped parsley or basil
2 tsp cayenne pepper
sprigs of parsley or watercress

Place the eggs and garlic cloves in a saucepan of cold water, bring to a boil and cook for 10 minutes over medium heat. Peel the eggs and cut lengthways. Let the garlic cloves cool, then place them in a mortar. Add the anchovy fillets, capers and yolks of the hard-boiled eggs. Pound with the pestle and reduce the mixture to a paste. Slowly beat in the olive oil as you would for a mayonnaise. Add vinegar, salt, pepper and parsley or basil.

Fill the egg-white halves with the mixture and sprinkle with cayenne pepper (more for colour than for the taste). Garnish with parsley or watercress. Chill and serve.

Oeufs et Légumes à la Mayonnaise Orange

Hard-boiled eggs, tomatoes, cucumbers and courgettes filled with saffron mayonnaise

For 6 people

3 eggs, hard-boiled	225 ml/8 fl oz *Mayonnaise Orange*
3 large firm tomatoes, cut in half	(p. 78)
3 small, crisp cucumbers, peeled	mixture of chopped mint, basil and
3 small, crisp courgettes, peeled	parsley

Cut the eggs lengthways and remove the yolks. Scoop out some of the pulp from the tomato halves and turn upside down to let them drain (try to remove as much water and seeds as possible without wasting too much of the pulp). Cut the cucumbers and courgettes lengthways and remove seeds. Prepare the *mayonnaise orange*.

Fill the vegetable shells with the mayonnaise and sprinkle with chopped herbs and the yolks, which have been passed through a sieve. Chill. An attractive way to serve is to arrange the vegetable shells on a bed of watercress or lettuce leaves.

Note: You can also use *Sauce Verte* (p. 86) as a filling.

Pan Bagna

A Niçois sandwich

This sandwich is sold in the streets of Nice, like pizza in Italy, and may be one of the best you've ever tasted. It is prepared there with 75-mm-/3-in-thick round breads. Perfect for children and picnics. It is best prepared at least 1 hour before serving.

For each person

2 slices good French bread or whole-wheat bread, a bap or a lightly toasted hamburger bun
1 garlic clove, peeled
1 tbsp olive oil
about 1 tsp red wine vinegar
salt and pepper

½ onion, sliced
1 firm tomato, sliced (with skin)
3 white or red radishes, sliced
2 anchovy fillets, chopped
1 tbsp tuna (canned in oil or water)
a few leaves of basil or mint

Rub the bread with a peeled garlic clove. Sprinkle both slices of bread with olive oil, vinegar, salt and pepper, then pile all the other ingredients on one slice and crush the garlic clove on top. Cover with the other slice and weight the sandwich down for 2–3 minutes with a heavy plate so that the insides are pressed together (this is one sandwich that tastes best soggy).

Paniers et Barquettes au Thon et aux Anchois

Cucumbers, tomatoes and lemons filled with tuna, anchovies and capers

For any recipe where vegetables and fruits are filled with a sauce and served as a cold hors-d'oeuvre, make sure they are crisp and very fresh. Remove as little of the pulp as possible when you remove the seeds from such vegetables as tomatoes, courgettes and cucumbers. Always serve on a green bed – watercress or crisp lettuce.

For 6 people

3 eggs	juice of 2 lemons
6 anchovy fillets	4 tbsp olive oil
340 g/12 oz canned tuna (preferably	pepper
canned in oil; if canned in water,	salt
discard the water) or canned	3 large tomatoes
sardines	3 large lemons
85 g/3 oz capers	2 small, firm cucumbers

Hard-boil the eggs and let them cool. Peel and press them through a sieve into a bowl. Chop the anchovies, tuna (or sardines) and 75 g/ 2¾ oz capers, and press through the sieve into the same bowl. Stir in lemon juice and oil. Add pepper to taste before adding any salt. The mixture will have a coarse consistency. (All its ingredients can be put in a food processor and puréed, but it will lose in taste what it gains in smoothness.)

Cut the tomatoes in half and let them drain upside down. Cut the lemons in half and remove the insides; clean them with a very sharp knife so the shells will be completely free of pulp. Peel the cucumbers and cut them in half lengthways. Remove the seeds and drain them upside down.

Stuff the lemon and vegetable shells with the fish–egg mixture and top each shell with a few of the remaining capers. Chill until ready to serve.

Pissaladière
Onion tart

Whether you serve this crisp, light tart as a first course for a dinner or as the main offering for a light lunch or picnic, it is a simple but elegant dish to enjoy at any time of the year. In Nice there are many variations of the *pissaladière*. Each pastry shop, each market-place, each bakery, each home has its own version. Some have more crust, others have more onion purée; some are heavy with anchovies and olives, while others are mild and sweet. This version, which is my grandmother's, is the one I prefer, but feel free to adjust the seasonings to your own taste, since that is part of the tradition of this dish.

For 6 people

·············· Onion Purée ··············

12 (about 1.25 kg/3 lb) medium-sized yellow onions	1 bay leaf
	1 tsp thyme
2 tbsp olive oil	freshly ground black pepper
2 garlic cloves, peeled and crushed	½ tsp salt

Peel and finely chop the onions (since you must make a purée, it is important that the onions be chopped very finely). Warm the olive oil in a large frying-pan. Add the onions, garlic, bay leaf, thyme, pepper and salt (the salt draws water from the onions, preventing them from turning brown). Cover tightly and simmer gently *over the lowest heat* for 1–1½ hours, or until the onions have completely dissolved into a pale purée. Remove from heat and squeeze the onions gently to one side of the pan with a slotted spoon, drawing off the liquid, which you will use for the crust.

·················· Crust ··················

¼ tsp dried yeast	1 tsp salt
55 ml/2 fl oz lukewarm water	115 g/4 oz unbleached flour
liquid from onions (at least 1 tbsp – if there is not enough, add olive oil)	1 tsp olive oil

Dissolve the yeast in water in a large bowl. Let stand 5–10 minutes, preferably in a warm place. Stir in the onion liquid, salt and flour and mix well. Knead on a floured board for 20 minutes, or until the dough is soft and smooth. Place in a greased bowl and turn it over. Cover with a damp cloth.

Turn on the oven at 150°C/300°F/Gas Mark 2 for about 30 seconds. Put in the dough and turn off the heat. Let the dough rise there until it has doubled in bulk – about 1 hour. Punch it down. Sprinkle with olive oil and knead it in the bowl for 3 minutes. Re-cover with a damp cloth and let it rise again in the oven for 10 minutes. Remove the dough.

Preheat the oven to 190°C/375°F/Gas Mark 5. Oil a 200 × 330-mm/

8 × 13-in baking tray or a fluted round French tart pan. Roll out the dough with a rolling pin on a floured board and then, with your hands, stretch it along the sides of the pan so that the crust is 20 mm/¾ in high up the sides. Taste the onion purée to check for seasoning and spoon it into the crust.

················· Garnish ·················

6 anchovy fillets
1 tbsp olive oil
12–18 small black olives from Nice,
    or pitted, large oil-cured black
    ones, quartered

If the baking tray was used, arrange the anchovy fillets on top of the tart in a lattice pattern; if the French pan was used, arrange the fillets like the spokes of a wheel. Sprinkle the top with olive oil and bake for 1 hour, or until the dough has separated from the sides of the pan and is golden and crisp. Remove from the oven and dot with olives. This tart tastes best warm and reheats very well.

Plateau de Hors-d'Oeuvres Variés

A platter of cold appetizers

For an interesting hors-d'oeuvre you can assemble on a platter various dishes such as vegetable salads (fennel, tomato, chick-pea, French bean), shredded raw carrots (seasoned with olive oil, lemon and little black olives), marinated fish, rice salads, *brocoli au vin blanc* and *champignons en citronnette*. You can also present a colourful array of vegetables, lemons and hard-boiled eggs filled with delectable mixtures on a bed of watercress, such as:

Oeufs et Légumes à la Mayonnaise
    Orange or *à la Sauce Verte* (p. 44)
Paniers et Barquettes au Thon et aux
    Anchois (p. 45)

Tomates à la Brandade (p. 55)
Tomates et Courgettes au Caviar
    Provençale (p. 54)
Tomate à la Tapenade (p. 41)

Sardines au Vinaigre
Sardines marinated in red wine vinegar and spices

This vigorous hors-d'oeuvre can also be made with fresh anchovies, herring or smelts. It is better after two days in the refrigerator and will keep up to a week there.

For 6 people

1.25 kg/3 lb fresh sardines	1 tsp coriander seeds
1 fennel bulb, cut in sticks, or 3 tbsp fennel or anise seeds	half a nutmeg, freshly grated
	3 bay leaves
salt and freshly ground pepper	4 tsp salt
225 ml/8 fl oz red wine vinegar	a few sprigs of watercress or parsley
570 ml/1 pt water	
2 tbsp peppercorns	

Wash the fish and discard the heads. Fillet the fish (sardines may be left whole if they are small enough) and drain on kitchen towels. Put the fresh fennel between every two fillets or sprinkle the fillets with fennel or anise seeds. Season with salt and pepper and place the fish in a shallow baking dish.

Put the vinegar, water, peppercorns, coriander, nutmeg, bay leaves and salt in a saucepan. Bring to a boil, simmer for 5 minutes, then pour while hot over the fillets and let them cool. Cover and refrigerate.

To serve, carefully lift the fish with two spatulas on to a platter. Garnish with watercress or parsley.

Note: If there are any left-over sardines, dip them in a light batter (see *Beignets de Légumes*, p. 159) to make sardine fritters – delicious served with *Salade Mesclun* (p. 69).

Saussoun
Almond and fennel anchovy spread served with croûtons

An unusually refreshing spread on toast, a fine dip for raw vegetables and a fragrant sauce for *Pâtes aux Oeufs* (p. 200).

2–3 tbsp olive oil
140 g/5 oz finely chopped almonds
12 anchovy fillets, chopped
1 fennel bulb, chopped

2 leaves fresh mint or basil, finely
  chopped (optional)
6 slices firm white bread
fennel leaves, finely chopped

Using a mortar and pestle and adding a little olive oil, mash the almonds, anchovies, fennel and mint or basil to make a paste. Mash only a portion of these ingredients at a time, transferring each batch of paste to a bowl. Alternatively, put all these ingredients into a food processor and mix to a paste.

Toast the slices of bread under the grill, turn them over and sprinkle with a little olive oil and let them cool. Thickly spread the toasted bread with the paste and cut each slice in four triangles. Sprinkle with fennel leaves and serve.

Variation
If you use this sauce with warm pasta, add 3 tablespoons of olive oil to the sauce, stir and pour over the pasta.

Socca
Chick-pea flour pancake

Every morning the streets of Nice are full of men carrying large round trays of *socca* on their heads (wrapped with handkerchiefs) to the market-places and shouting '*Tout caud*' (It is hot). The fragrance of small pieces of *socca* wrapped in brown paper cones mingles with the smell of fresh fruits and vegetables to give the open-air market a truly wonderful atmosphere.

Socca is quick and easy to prepare at home. Chick-pea flour is sold in Greek, Spanish, Italian and Indian shops as well as some health-food and whole-food shops. Children love *socca* for snacks, and it is a delicious appetizer, cut in small pieces and wrapped in bright paper napkins to accompany a chilled rosé, vermouth or dry white wine.

For 6 people

75 g/2¾ oz chick-pea flour
3 tbsp olive oil
½ tsp salt
225 ml/8 fl oz water
freshly ground black pepper

Mix the flour, oil, salt and water in a bowl. Stir well and let stand for 1 hour (at room temperature or refrigerated).

Preheat oven to 200°C/400°F/Gas Mark 6. Oil a round, shallow pan and pour on the batter – it should be very thin, about 3 mm/⅛ in thick. Put the pan under a moderate grill as close to the heat as possible. After 5 minutes, sprinkle a little olive oil on the top and grill for 5–10 more minutes until it is crisp and golden, with the consistency of a thick crêpe or pancake. Sprinkle with salt and freshly ground black pepper. With a spatula, slide it on to a serving plate and cut it into 25 × 25-mm/2 × 2-in wedges. Serve on small plates with forks or on paper napkins – a bit messy, but so delicious.

Tapenade
Anchovy, olive, garlic and caper spread

This fragrant mixture can be served in many ways. Surrounded by raw vegetables or potato crisps, it is a delicious dip. Spread on thin *croûtons* (p. 11), it is a savoury spread. As a filling for raw tomatoes, it becomes *Paniers et Barquettes* (p. 45). Diluted with about 3 tablespoons of olive oil, it can be tossed with warm *Pâtes aux Oeufs* (p. 200) and become an interesting sauce.

For 6 people

85 g/3 oz fleshy black olives or oil-cured black olives,* pitted

6 anchovy fillets, cleaned, rinsed and drained

1½ tbsp capers

1 garlic clove, peeled and crushed

juice of 1 lemon

4 tbsp olive oil (possibly more)

freshly ground pepper

2 tbsp fresh basil, finely chopped (do not use dried basil)

Place the olives in a blender or food processor† with the anchovy fillets, capers, garlic, lemon juice, olive oil and pepper. Turn on high speed for a few seconds. Stir, and check if the mixture is too thick and needs more oil. Pour into a bowl and check the seasoning (if it is too salty, add ½ teaspoon of sugar). Add the basil. Cover with cling film and keep in the refrigerator until ready to use. It will keep for about ten days.

Terrine de Campagne
A hearty country pâté

A good terrine contains many textures and flavours. This one alternates three contrasting layers: the first consists of marinated strips of veal, chicken and ham; the second, chopped sautéd chicken liver; and the third, minced pork mixed with egg and seasonings. Terrines can, of course, be very rich and grand and their ingredients can include marrow, butter, cream, cognac, truffles, pistachios and goose or duck liver. This recipe is for a simple peasant terrine, lean and spicy, delicious served with sour gherkins, a tart green salad (dandelion, rocket, cos or watercress) and wine. It is excellent as the first course for a hearty winter meal or as the main course for a summer picnic or buffet.

The recipe is designed for a 1.5-l/2½-pt terrine with a lid, but you can substitute a loaf pan.

* If you use oil-cured olives, add 1 tablespoon or more of canned tuna oil to reduce the saltiness.

† You can use a mortar and pestle or a Mouli food mill, but I find a blender or food processor satisfactory, as well as time-saving, for this recipe.

For 8–10 people

1 onion, chopped
2 garlic cloves, crushed
1 bay leaf
3 sprigs fresh thyme, or 1 tsp dried
225 ml/8 fl oz dry white wine
1 tbsp brandy
6 peppercorns, crushed with a
    mallet
1 tsp salt
225 g/½ lb veal, cut roughly into
    100-mm/4-in strips
450 g/1 lb chicken breasts, boned
    and diced
3 slices ham or gammon

225 g/½ lb chicken livers
1 tbsp olive oil
225 g/½ lb minced pork or ham
225 g/½ lb streaky bacon, finely
    chopped
3 eggs
2 tbsp port or sherry
½ tsp dried thyme
2 tsp salt
450 g/1 lb caul or streaky bacon,
    cut in strips
2 100-mm/4-in slices streaky bacon
7 bay leaves
sprigs of parsley or watercress

Mix the first eight ingredients together. Marinate the veal, chicken and ham in this mixture overnight.

Sauté the chicken livers in olive oil until firm. Chop and set aside. In a bowl, mix the minced pork or ham, streaky bacon, eggs, port or sherry, thyme and salt. Line a terrine or loaf pan with three-quarters of the caul or bacon strips. Preheat the oven to 180°C/350°F/Gas Mark 4.

Assemble the pâté in the following order, packing down each layer: half of the pork or ham mixture, the marinated sliced ham, all the chicken livers, half of the liquid from the marinade, the marinated veal strips and chicken, and the remaining pork or ham mixture. Put 4 bay leaves on top and pour the rest of the marinade over the pâté. Seal completely with the remaining bacon strips. Seal with aluminium foil and place the terrine in a pan of hot water 40 mm/1½ in deep. Bake for 2 hours.

Remove from the oven and set 1–2.25 kg/2–5 lb of weights (stones, irons, tiles, etc.) on top of the foil-covered pâté.* Cover the entire surface with weights. This squeezes out the excess fat and juice so that the pâté will slice well and have the proper consistency. Refrigerate at least 5 hours.

---

* See the suggestion on p. 23, for making a board to fit the dimensions of the terrine to use with weights.

Remove the weights and gently lift out the pâté with two spatulas and place on a platter. Trim the fat – you may remove it all, if you wish – and cut a few slices of terrine with a big, sharp knife with the help of a chopping board (see technique for using this on p. 20). Cut 3 or 4 little clover shapes out of a slice of bacon with kitchen scissors and arrange them in a pattern, along with the remaining bay leaves, on the uncut part of the pâté. Surround the pâté with parsley or watercress.

This is delicious with a full-bodied red wine, a chilled dry white wine or a cool dry rosé.

Note: This pâté is a bit crumbly. To make it smoother, you can add more eggs, bacon and some bread, but it then becomes heavier and somewhat dull.

Tomates et Courgettes au Caviar Provençale

Tomatoes and courgettes filled with an aubergine, lemon and garlic purée

For 6 people

3 large or 6 small tomatoes
3 courgettes
225 g/8 oz *Caviar Provençale*
  (p. 40)

1 tbsp grated onion
1 tbsp finely chopped parsley

Cut the tomatoes and courgettes in half. Scoop out some of the pulp from the tomatoes and the seeds from the courgettes. Turn the courgette and tomato halves upside down and let them drain. Fill the vegetable shells with *caviar provençale* and garnish with onion and parsley.

To serve, arrange the stuffed vegetables on a bed of watercress or crisp lettuce leaves.

Tomates à la Brandade

Tomatoes filled with a dried-cod mousse

For 6 people

3 large or 6 small tomatoes
6 tbsp *Brandade* (p. 94)
2 tbsp chopped parsley

Cut the tomatoes in half and scoop out some of the pulp. Turn them upside down and let them drain. Fill the tomatoes with the *brandade* and sprinkle with parsley.

Arrange the stuffed tomatoes on a bed of watercress or crisp lettuce leaves, and serve.

Les Salades

Salads

In Nice salads can be served as an hors-d'oeuvre, an accompaniment or the main part of a meal. There are two kinds of salad: the cool, tart, crisp green salads, such as watercress, lettuce and dandelions, and the warm salads made with vegetables, rice, meat or fish.

The dressing is usually a simple vinaigrette. In a large glass or china bowl, a clove of garlic is crushed, and salt, red wine vinegar, and then the oil and freshly ground black pepper are stirred in.

Good red wine vinegar and pure olive oil (the Extra Vierge label means a pure oil extracted from the olives without the use of chemicals or heat) are essential to a good vinaigrette. You may make it thicker with mustard or the yolk of a hard-boiled egg by adding them first to the vinegar, and then thinning the mixture with the oil.

Vary the texture of your salads and work with whatever you have at hand – raw vegetables, cooked vegetables, left-over fish, shellfish, cooked meat, tuna, rice. Served warm, they will enhance the flavour of the vinaigrette. The whole spirit of southern French cooking is in such imaginative and highly flavourful mélanges.

Some salads will keep in the refrigerator. They can be life savers by making up for a dish ruined at the last minute. They are perfect for an improvised meal.

Salade Amère
Dandelion salad

You can pick dandelion leaves in the country, along roads, or buy them in some greengrocers in summer. Always pick the youngest, most tender leaves – when they are old they are tough and bitter.

For 6 people

40 young dandelion leaves
70 ml/2½ fl oz olive oil
2 tbsp red wine vinegar
2 garlic cloves, peeled and crushed
salt

freshly ground black pepper
1 egg yolk, hard-boiled
6–12 strips of stale bread crust for making *chapons* (p. 10)

Wash and dry the dandelion leaves. Wrap them in a towel and refrigerate for at least 20 minutes so they become cold and crisp.

Mix olive oil, vinegar, garlic, salt and pepper to make the dressing. Prepare the *chapons* and sprinkle a little dressing on them. Pass the yolk through a sieve.

Place the dandelion leaves in a salad bowl, pour the dressing over them and toss with your hands. Sprinkle the sieved egg yolk over the leaves and arrange the *chapons* around the edge of the bowl.

Asperges Vinaigrette
Warm asparagus dipped in vinaigrette

This appetizer is eaten warm – like *crudités et bagna cauda* – so that the full flavour of both the asparagus and the vinaigrette is enhanced. Each person should be served his or her own plate for mixing a little vinaigrette in which to roll the asparagus with the fingers.

For 6 people

24 asparagus
olive oil and red wine vinegar in small serving cruets

salt shakers
pepper mills

Wash and chop off the heavy ends of the asparagus. Pare with a vegetable peeler. Tie the stalks in two bundles and steam until tender, or cook in a large saucepan of boiling salted water for 10 minutes, making sure not to overcook (asparagus should be firm).

Remove the strings and serve on a folded napkin in a basket or on a platter, along with two or three sets of cruets, pepper mills and salt shakers set on a tray.

Salades Blanches

Warm bean, cauliflower and potato salads dressed with a spicy vinaigrette

The secret of these salads is that the sauce is added when the vegetables are warm. It is quickly absorbed and the salads steam with the powerful fragrance of olive oil, herbs, spring onions, anchovies and garlic.

Cauliflower or potato salad can be made in less than half an hour. If you use dried beans (white haricot beans, lentils or chick-peas) for a salad, you must let them soak overnight and then cook them the next day for about 1½ hours.

For 6 people

········ Dressing for All Three Salads ········

Simply mix and stir the following ingredients:

20 g/¾ oz parsley, finely chopped (reserve 2 tbsp for garnishing the salad)	1 tsp tarragon
	a few drops of Tabasco sauce
	3 garlic cloves, crushed
3 spring onions, finely chopped	1 tsp freshly grated nutmeg
6 anchovy fillets, chopped	1 tsp salt, or more, according to
70 ml/2½ fl oz olive oil	your taste
2 tbsp red wine vinegar	freshly ground white pepper

···················· Bean Salad ····················

450 g/1 lb dried white haricot beans or lentils or chick-peas	2 whole cloves
	bouquet garni (p. 14)
1.1 l/2 pt cold water	salt
2 carrots, sliced in half	2 tbsp chopped parsley or chives
2 onions, sliced in half	

Soak the white beans, lentils or chick-peas in a large bowl or saucepan of cold water overnight (read instructions on the package before soaking – they might require less time).

About 1½ hours before you are ready to serve this dish, place the beans in a large saucepan of water with the carrots, onions stuck with the cloves, and the bouquet garni. Bring to a boil. Add salt and cover. Simmer for 1–1½ hours. (The beans should be tender but retain their shape.) Meanwhile prepare the dressing.

Drain the beans. Discard the other vegetables and broth, or save them to use later for soup. Put the warm drained beans in a warm glass or earthenware bowl and pour the dressing over them. Toss gently and sprinkle with parsley or chives. Serve warm.

######## Cauliflower Salad ########

2 large heads cauliflower
2 tbsp parsley or chives

Rinse the cauliflower under cold water and cut out any bruised spots. Separate the florets and blanch them in salted water for 10–15 minutes. Do not overcook – they should remain crisp. Meanwhile prepare the dressing.

Place the warm cauliflower in a large glass or earthenware bowl and pour the dressing over it. Sprinkle with parsley or chives, toss very delicately and serve warm.

############ Potato Salad ############

8 large potatoes
2 tbsp parsley or chives

Boil the potatoes in a saucepan of salted water for 20 minutes or until tender. Meanwhile prepare the dressing.

Holding each hot potato with a kitchen towel or an oven mitt, peel them, then slice them 12 mm/½ in thick and place them in a warm shallow dish. Pour the dressing over them and sprinkle with parsley or chives. Toss gently and serve warm.

Brocoli au Vin Blanc

Blanched broccoli simmered in white wine and herbs

Broccoli is very popular in Nice and is often served in warm dishes. This chilled preparation may be part of your *plateau de hors-d'oeuvres variés*. It will keep in the refrigerator, covered with cling film, for a few days.

For 6 people

about 4 heads broccoli
water to cover
salt
115 ml/4 fl oz dry white wine
4 tbsp olive oil
5 spring onions, finely chopped

2 tbsp parsley, finely chopped
2 garlic cloves, crushed
juice of 2 lemons
2 tsp thyme
1 tbsp peppercorns

Wash the broccoli, pull off the leaves, cut off the tough base of the stems and pare the stems with a vegetable peeler. Blanch in a large pan of salted water for 10 minutes. Rinse under cold water and drain. Cut in 50-mm/2-in pieces.

Put the wine, olive oil, spring onions, parsley, garlic, lemon juice, thyme and peppercorns in a pan and simmer, covered, for 20 minutes. Add the broccoli and cook, uncovered, for 2 minutes more (the broccoli should be slightly crisp).

Check the seasoning and pour into a shallow dish. Serve at room temperature or slightly chilled.

Champignons en Citronnette

Sliced mushrooms with lemon and olive oil sauce

This tart, delicate dish can be part of a *plateau de hors-d'oeuvres variés*. It may accompany a roasted leg of lamb or a baked fish.

The mushrooms must be very fresh, firm, and cream-coloured. You can keep this dish, covered with cling film, for about a week in the refrigerator.

For 6 people

20 (about 680 g/1½ lb) 50-mm-/
   2-in-wide fresh mushrooms
115 ml/4 fl oz olive oil
juice of 2 lemons

salt
freshly ground white pepper
2 tsp finely chopped fennel leaves
   or parsley

Wipe the mushrooms carefully with a moist towel and cut off the tips of the stems. Slice the mushrooms as thinly as possible and place them in a bowl. Pour the olive oil and lemon juice over them, add salt and pepper to taste, and toss gently. Cover with cling film and chill for at least 3 hours.

Sprinkle with fennel leaves or parsley before serving.

Champignons en Marinade

Mushrooms marinated with lemon, bay leaves and garlic

This dish is best when prepared a day in advance.

For 6 people

140 ml/5 fl oz olive oil
115 ml/4 fl oz water
juice of 2 lemons
3 bay leaves

3 garlic cloves, peeled
5 black peppercorns
1 tsp salt
450 g/1 lb small fresh mushrooms

Bring everything *but the mushrooms* to a boil in a large, heavy saucepan. Simmer for 10 minutes. Strain carefully and put the stock back in the pan.

Wash the mushrooms and chop off the base of the stems but do not slice. Simmer them in the stock for 5 to 10 minutes, or until tender, and let them cool in the marinade. Cover and refrigerate for 1–2 days.

Serve chilled or at room temperature.

Salade de Haricots Verts

Warm French-bean salad with vinaigrette

This can, of course, be eaten cold as part of a *plateau de hors-d'oeuvres variés*.

For 6 people

2 tbsp red wine vinegar	1 garlic clove, crushed
salt	900 g/2 lb French beans
70 ml/2½ fl oz olive oil	20 g/¾ oz parsley, finely chopped
freshly ground black pepper	

Prepare the vinaigrette: mix the vinegar and salt, and add olive oil, pepper and garlic.

Snap off the tips of the beans and wash them in cold water. Steam or cook, uncovered, in boiling salted water for 15–20 minutes – do not overcook. Pour the beans into an earthenware bowl.

Add the vinaigrette and toss immediately. Sprinkle with parsley and serve.

Variation

I often boil 3–5 small new potatoes, unpeeled and quartered, along with the beans. The potatoes become quite mushy after absorbing the vinaigrette, so it is less elegant a dish, but so tasty.

Maïs en Salade

Sweet corn simmered in white wine, served cold

Everywhere in France, sweet corn is used for feeding animals, but in Nice it is prepared in many exciting ways for human enjoyment. We use it in *polente*, eat it cold with vinaigrette and with little shrimp, or prepared in the following manner (this dish looks lovely in a *plateau de hors-d'oeuvres variés*).

For 6 people

70 ml/2½ fl oz olive oil	salt
6 spring onions, finely chopped	2 bay leaves
2 garlic cloves, peeled and sliced in half	1 tsp thyme
	1 450-g/16-oz can sweet corn, drained
juice of 1 lemon	
1 tbsp peppercorns	115 ml/4 fl oz dry white wine

Heat the olive oil in a heavy-bottomed saucepan and add the spring onions, garlic pieces, lemon juice, peppercorns, salt, bay leaves and thyme. Cook on high heat for 5 minutes. Reduce the heat and add the sweet corn and wine. Simmer, uncovered, for 5 more minutes. Chill for at least 3 hours.

Salade Mélangée aux Noix

Mixed greens and walnut salad

For 6 people

2 tbsp red wine vinegar	55 g/2 oz coarsely chopped walnuts
1 tsp Dijon mustard	4 firm chicory, quartered lengthways
2 tsp salt	
70 ml/2½ fl oz olive oil	1 bunch watercress
1 tsp freshly ground black pepper	

Prepare the vinaigrette in a bowl: mix vinegar, mustard and salt, then add olive oil, pepper and walnuts.

Wrap the chicory and watercress in a tea-towel and refrigerate them. When ready to serve, put the greens in a salad bowl, pour the vinaigrette over them and toss gently with your hands.

Salade de Moules

Fresh mussels with herb vinaigrette

This is a perfect summer meal, light and enticing. Be sure to serve it with plenty of good bread and a cool, crisp white wine.

For 6 people

2.75 kg/6 lb mussels (there will be about 72, but only about 60 will be fresh)

340 ml/12 fl oz water

340 ml/12 fl oz dry white wine

3 bay leaves

70 ml/2½ fl oz olive oil

2 tbsp red wine vinegar

2 large onions, very finely chopped

20 g/¾ oz chopped Italian parsley

1 tsp chopped fresh tarragon or ½ tsp dried

2 tbsp capers or chopped French gherkins

freshly ground black pepper

salt

Scrub the mussels with a strong brush, remove the beards and leave the mussels in cold water for 10 minutes. Throw away all the mussels that are not firmly closed.

Bring the water, wine and bay leaves to a boil in a large, heavy casserole. Add the mussels and cook, tightly covered, over high heat for 4–6 minutes, shaking the pot two or three times so that the mussels cook evenly. When all the shells are open, remove the mussels with a slotted spoon and discard the shells. Boil the broth in the casserole to reduce it to about 115 ml/4 fl oz and strain it through wet cheesecloth. Check to make sure there is hardly any sand in the broth.

Combine the oil, vinegar, onions, parsley, tarragon, capers, pepper and salt (if mussels are excessively salty, use only a small amount), and toss with the cooled mussels. Add the mussel broth slowly and taste to check the seasoning. Toss well and chill for at least 1 hour. Check the seasoning again before serving.

Salade Niçoise

Vegetable, tuna, egg, anchovy and olive salad

This is the ultimate salad – a feast of feasts – eaten only in the spring or summer, when tender fresh vegetables are ripe and abundant. There are many adulterations of this salad – some of which use meat, left-overs and potatoes – but there is only one classic *salade niçoise*, and its ingredients are listed below. Use the freshest *raw* vegetables, never frozen or canned.

For 6 people

6 firm half-ripe tomatoes
1 cucumber, peeled and sliced
1 head soft round lettuce, each leaf
  cut in half
225 g/8 oz very young fresh broad
  beans
6 small purple artichokes, boiled or
  steamed and quartered
1 fennel bulb, sliced in 6-mm/¼-in
  strips
2 green peppers, seeded and sliced
6 small white onions or half a
  Spanish onion, thinly sliced
a handful of white or red radishes
  with stems
3 hard-boiled eggs, cut in half
  lengthways

10 anchovy fillets, cut in thirds
  (198 g/7 oz canned tuna in oil
  may be substituted)
a handful of small black olives,
  unpitted, or oil-cured big black
  olives, pitted
6–12 *chapons* (p. 10)
170 ml/6 fl oz olive oil
55 ml/2 fl oz red wine vinegar
salt
freshly ground black pepper
10 leaves fresh basil or mint,
  chopped
2 garlic cloves, peeled and crushed

Wash and quarter the tomatoes (do not peel them), salt lightly and let them drain upside down on a board for 10 minutes. Peel and slice the cucumber, drain on kitchen towels for 10 minutes. Prepare the other vegetables and the eggs, anchovy fillets and olives. Prepare the *chapons*.

To make the vinaigrette, mix the oil and vinegar, season to taste with salt and pepper, and add the garlic and basil or mint.

Arrange the vegetables, eggs, anchovy fillets and olives attractively on a shallow dish and surround with lettuce leaves and *chapons*. Pour the vinaigrette over everything and bring the dish to the table without tossing it. Just before serving individual portions, toss delicately but thoroughly.

Pois Chiches Marinés
Chick-peas simmered in white wine and herbs

Chilled, this pungent dish can be part of a *plateau de hors-d'oeuvres variés*. Served at room temperature, it can accompany plain meat or grilled fish.

For 4–6 people

3 tbsp olive oil	salt
5 small white onions, grated or very finely chopped	1 tsp peppercorns, roughly crushed
	115 ml/4 fl oz dry white wine
2 tsp thyme	juice of 2 lemons
1 garlic clove, peeled and crushed	1 450-g/16-oz can chick-peas

Heat the olive oil in a heavy-bottomed saucepan. Add the onions, thyme, garlic, salt and peppercorns and sauté for 5 minutes. Add the wine and lemon juice and bring to a boil. Reduce the heat and simmer for 5 minutes.

Drain and rinse the chick-peas. Add them to the pan and cook, uncovered, for 5 minutes over low heat.

Serve either at room temperature or chilled.

Pois Gourmands en Marinade

Mange-touts simmered in white wine

This dish can be served on a platter of hors-d'oeuvres and eaten cold. It is also a lovely accompaniment to cold fish, chicken or meats, and can be part of a buffet.

For 6 people

1.25 kg/3 lb fresh mange-touts (you may use frozen, but they are not as good)	juice of 2 lemons
	2 tsp thyme
	1 bay leaf
3 tbsp olive oil	115 ml/4 fl oz water
4–6 small onions, chopped	salt
2 garlic cloves, finely chopped	freshly ground black pepper
115 ml/4 fl oz white vermouth	

Snap off the stem ends of the mange-touts, pull out the strings and wash them carefully. Heat the oil in a large cast-iron saucepan and sauté the onions with the garlic. Cook until golden, then add the mange-touts, vermouth, lemon juice, thyme, bay leaf, water, salt and pepper. Wait until simmering begins, then cover and cook for 20 minutes, or until only a quarter of the liquid remains.

Remove bay leaves, pour into a bowl and refrigerate at least 30 minutes before serving.

Salade de Riz Variée

Rice salad with assorted meats and vegetables

This is a wonderful way to use left-over chicken, shellfish, fish, beef or vegetables. Be sure that the rice is fluffy, with each grain well separated.

For 6 people

200 g/7 oz raw rice
8 tbsp olive oil
340 g/12 oz chopped, cooked fish, chicken, beef, prawns, mussels, squid, slivers of fennel bulb, chopped green peppers or blanched peas
2 celery stalks (without leaves), diced

1 cucumber, peeled, seeded and diced
1 tsp Dijon mustard
2 tbsp red wine vinegar
2 tsp salt
freshly ground white pepper
1 head soft round lettuce

Cook the rice in a saucepan of boiling salted water. Drain well. Pour it into a bowl and add 2 tablespoons olive oil, tossing lightly with a fork until all the rice is well coated. Combine all the remaining ingredients except lettuce in a large bowl and toss gently with two forks.

Wash and dry the lettuce leaves. Scatter them on a shallow serving dish and mound the rice mixture on top. Serve at room temperature. (This can be prepared a day in advance and kept, covered with cling film, in the refrigerator.)

Tian Rouge

Cold red pepper and tomato gratin

This brilliant, layered gratin must be prepared at least 2 hours ahead of time so it can be served cold. It is most inviting on a hot day.

For 6 people

20 g/¾ oz Italian parsley, chopped	salt
8 g/⅓ oz fresh basil, chopped	freshly ground black pepper
1 tbsp dried thyme	1 tbsp capers
2–3 red bell peppers	2 tbsp breadcrumbs (preferably
2 tbsp olive oil	home-made)
6 large, firm tomatoes	

Preheat the grill to medium heat. Mix together the parsley, basil and thyme. Wash the red peppers, leaving the stems on. Brush them with oil and put under the grill close to the heat. Turn frequently with tongs until they are evenly blistered all over. Remove and wrap in a wet towel for 15 minutes. Peel off the skin under cold running water with a small sharp knife and discard stems and seeds. Dry and cut into 25-mm/1-in strips.

Preheat the oven to 200°C/400°F/Gas Mark 6. Wash the tomatoes and slice each into 4 round pieces. Oil an earthenware or enamel casserole dish and cover the bottom with a third of the tomato slices. Sprinkle with a quarter of the herb mixture and salt and pepper. Cover with a layer of half of the pepper strips. Repeat the layering until these ingredients are used up. Sprinkle the top with capers and breadcrumbs and dribble with olive oil. Bake for 20 minutes.

Chill well before serving.

Salade Verte
Fresh green salad with vinaigrette

You can choose from a variety of cultivated greens, such as:

Batavian endive	Little Gem lettuce
chicory	rocket
cos lettuce	soft round lettuce
endive	watercress
fennel	

or wild or semi-wild greens, such as:

> dandelion leaves
> lamb's-tongue lettuce
> purslane

Always follow the same process in preparing the greens: remove any wilted leaves; wash and dry the greens carefully; break into pieces with your hands; put leaves between tea-towels and refrigerate until ready to serve.

Prepare vinaigrette (p. 87). Put the greens in a large glass, china or earthenware bowl, add vinaigrette and toss *with your hands*. Add *chapons* (p. 10) and serve.

Variations
Salade de Noël, to accompany the Christmas turkey, is made with the tenderest celery leaves and the thick lower part of the stalks, a few fresh truffles and anchovy fillets, and seasoned with newly pressed olive oil.

Salade de Pâques, to accompany the Easter leg of lamb, consists of crisp round lettuce seasoned with vinaigrette and garnished with hard-boiled eggs quartered lengthways.

Salade Mesclun (from the Niçois *mescla*, to mix) is a strong, bitter, invigorating salad made with dandelion, rocket, lamb's-tongue lettuce, purslane and watercress seasoned with vinaigrette and garnished with garlicky *chapons*.

Lastly, you can, of course, prepare endless variations of *salades composées* (mixed greens) using such combinations as chicory and fennel bulbs or watercress, or chicory and round lettuce – all seasoned with vinaigrette.

Les Sauces

Sauces

French *haute cuisine* may boast about its three thousand sauces, but in Nice we do not want it said that '*la sauce fait passer le poisson*' (it is the sauce that makes the fish bearable). In our cuisine the ingredients must speak loud and clear, not smothered by heavy sauces that may drown their natural flavour. As Curnonsky, 'the prince of gastronomes', said, 'Cuisine is when food tastes of what it is.'

The other basic difference from *haute cuisine* is that Niçois and Provençal sauces are not based on butter, cream or flour but on oil and vegetables. Most of the sauces are cold, and accompany meat, fish and vegetables. They are used to fill halves of hard-boiled eggs and lemon, tomato and cucumber 'boats', and as dips to accompany a basket of *crudités* (trimmed raw vegetables).

The sauces can be grouped into those
- with a vinaigrette base;
- with a home-made mayonnaise base;
- with a tomato base;
- with special flavours, such as walnut sauce and anchovy butter.

These sauces are an essential part of Niçois cuisine because they are extremely versatile and can transform left-overs into hors-d'oeuvres, or simple dishes of vegetables into delightful feasts.

Aïoli
Garlic mayonnaise

This wonderful sauce has been called 'the butter of Provence', 'the soul of the South', 'cream of sun', and it is indeed as heady as it sounds. It can be served with a basket of raw vegetables and hard-boiled eggs or as part of an *aïoli monstre*, with snails, squid, dried cod, tuna and a splendid array of vegetables. In all cases, it is superbly invigorating. Only water should be served with this potent sauce, but a vigorous red wine is acceptable.

This is a sauce that cannot be made successfully in a blender or food processor. Mortar and pestle are as essential to *aïoli* as crisp, fresh garlic.

For 6 people

8–10 garlic cloves
2 egg yolks at room temperature
salt
340 ml/12 fl oz oil (half peanut and half olive oil) at room temperature
juice of 1 lemon
freshly ground white pepper

Peel the garlic cloves (make sure they are firm and without any green in the centre). Place the egg yolks in the mortar and slip a tea-towel under it to prevent it from slipping when you use the pestle.

Crush the garlic through a garlic press into the mortar. Add the salt and pound with the pestle until the garlic, salt and yolks have turned into a paste.

Slowly start pouring the oil in a steady flow, stirring constantly with the pestle. Keep stirring steadily until you obtain a thick, shiny, firm sauce. Add the lemon juice and pepper and stir for another minute. Cover and refrigerate until ready to use.

Note: If the *aïoli* curdles (that is, the oil and egg yolk separate), empty it into a bowl. Put a fresh yolk in the mortar, add 1 tablespoon of warm red wine vinegar or lemon juice and 1 teaspoon of mustard and stir vigorously. Then slowly add the curdled *aïoli*. Beat steadily until you have a smooth sauce. Add the lemon juice and pepper and beat for another minute.

Bagna Cauda

A warm 'bath' of anchovies, garlic and olive oil

This sauce is a delectable accompaniment to crisp raw vegetables (see *Crudités et Bagna Cauda*, p. 41). It can be heated and poured over room-temperature left-over slices of meat (from an abundant *pot-au-feu*, for instance) to make a zesty dish.

For 6 people

12 whole anchovies	2 garlic cloves
3 slices of bread, with crust removed	225 ml/8 fl oz olive oil
	½ tsp freshly ground black pepper
3 tbsp milk	15 g/½ oz butter

Wash the anchovies and fillet them; discard the backbones and tails. Place the bread in a bowl, pour the milk on it and mash it with a fork. Squeeze out the excess liquid and set aside.

Place the anchovy fillets in a mortar or bowl and mash them with a pestle or fork. Pass the garlic through a garlic press and add to the anchovy paste. Add the bread paste, and stir and pound. Slowly beat in the olive oil and pepper to make a smooth sauce.

Heat the butter in a small saucepan over a low heat. Add the anchovy-and-bread mixture. Heat gently while stirring, making sure not to let it smoke.

Pour into a flameproof pot and place over low heat. The guests will dip the vegetables in the warm sauce either with fingers or with a fork, as for fondue.

Bagna Rotou

A vinaigrette with anchovies, garlic and herbs

You may serve this cold sauce with a basket of trimmed raw vegetables, with left-over meat or shellfish, or with cooked warm or cold vegetables.

For 6 people

2 tbsp red wine vinegar
salt
6 tbsp olive oil
freshly ground black pepper
1 onion, grated
1 tbsp finely chopped basil

3 tbsp finely chopped parsley
4 anchovy fillets, chopped (canned
    either in oil or in rough salt)
2 garlic cloves, peeled and crushed
salt

Mix the vinegar and salt in a bowl. Add the oil and pepper, then the rest of the ingredients. Check the seasoning before serving.

Beurre d'Anchois
Anchovy butter

This is a traditional Niçois recipe for a sauce that is spread on grilled fish, such as red mullet and bass, or on grilled meat. It keeps well, refrigerated or frozen, and can transform a last-minute hamburger or boiled potatoes into a flavourful treat.

This recipe may lack Niçois integrity because it uses butter instead of the always favoured olive oil, but it is delicious.

For 6 people

12 whole anchovies (canned either
    in oil or in rough salt)
450 g/1 lb butter, softened at room
    temperature
juice of 2 lemons
freshly ground white pepper

Rinse the anchovies and fillet them; discard the backbones and tails. Cut the fillets into small pieces with scissors or a knife. Mash to a paste in a mortar and gradually add pieces of butter and lemon juice. When the paste is light and soft, add it to the rest of the softened butter and blend thoroughly. Add pepper and taste – you may wish to add more lemon juice or a good deal of pepper (as I do).

Roll the anchovy butter in the shape of a thick sausage about 50 mm/2 in in diameter. Wrap it in a piece of waxed paper and refrigerate or freeze until ready to use.

Note: Place a 12-mm-/½-in-thick slice of anchovy butter on a grilled fish, a slice of grilled meat, a lamb chop or a hamburger just before serving. Or sprinkle little pieces of it on boiled or sautéd potatoes; toss gently and serve at once.

Citronnette
A lemon and mustard vinaigrette

This is a lovely sauce to use with grilled fish or on delicate lettuce or a tender boiled artichoke.

For 6 people

1 tsp Dijon mustard
juice of 1 lemon
6 tbsp olive oil
freshly ground black pepper

½ tsp crushed fresh coriander
   leaves
salt

Place the mustard in a bowl and slowly beat in the lemon juice and then the oil until smooth. Add pepper, coriander and salt, stirring constantly.

Coulis
A warm tomato sauce

This tomato sauce is briskly cooked to avoid any bitter taste, and is delicious served with *Pâtes aux Oeufs* (p. 200), *Papeton d'Aubergines* (p. 181) or *Beignets de Légumes* (p. 159).

Poured into a jar and covered with 1 tablespoon of olive oil, it will keep for a week in the refrigerator.

For 6 people

2 onions, finely chopped	bouquet garni (p. 14)
2.25 kg/5 lb very ripe tomatoes	3 lumps sugar
2 tbsp olive oil	10 fresh basil leaves (omit if
2 garlic cloves, finely chopped	unavailable – do not use dried
20 g/¾ oz chopped parsley	basil)
1 tsp dried thyme, oregano or	salt
tarragon	freshly ground pepper

Squeeze the onions in a towel to remove excess moisture. Quarter the tomatoes and pass them through a Mouli food mill.

Heat the olive oil in a heavy-bottomed saucepan, add the onions, half of the garlic, the parsley, thyme and bouquet garni. Cook for 10 minutes, or until the onions are soft.

Place the tomato purée in a heavy-bottomed saucepan over a moderate heat. Add the sugar and simmer, uncovered, for 10 minutes. Pass through a sieve to get rid of the excess liquid.

Pour the thickened tomato purée into the onion-and-herb mixture and cook, uncovered, for 5 minutes. Remove from the heat and add the basil, the remaining garlic, salt and pepper. Discard the bouquet garni.

Variation
You may add 55 ml/2 fl oz of dry white vermouth to the sauce while it is simmering for the last 5 minutes.

Sauce Dorée
Tomato, vinegar and herb sauce

This tawny sauce is good with boiled meat, grilled fish, cold prawns or cold chicken. It will keep for up to two days in the refrigerator.

Makes 340 ml/12 fl oz (enough for 6 people)

225 ml/8 fl oz mayonnaise (p. 77)
115 ml/4 fl oz red wine vinegar
2 bay leaves
½ tsp nutmeg, freshly grated

2 tbsp tomato sauce (home-made, p. 86, or canned)
1 tbsp cognac
salt
freshly ground black pepper

Prepare the mayonnaise and set aside.

Pour the vinegar into a saucepan, add the bay leaves and nutmeg, and simmer for 5 minutes. Let it cool. Remove the bay leaves.

With a wire whisk, beat the vinegar, tomato sauce and cognac gradually into the mayonnaise. The mayonnaise will become softer, but it will regain its firmness when chilled. Add salt and pepper and chill.

This sauce needs lots of salt and pepper, so after the sauce has been chilled, check the seasoning before serving.

Sauce Jaune et Verte

A light vinaigrette with lemon, garlic and herbs

This fragrant cold sauce is wonderful with either warm or cold grilled fish. To serve fish cold, spoon the sauce over it while it is still hot – as it cools, the fish will absorb the sauce deliciously.

For 6 people

70 ml/2½ fl oz red wine vinegar
salt
140 ml/5 fl oz olive oil
freshly ground white pepper
3 large lemons, peeled with all membrane removed, and thinly sliced

20 g/¾ oz chopped parsley
15 g/½ oz chopped fresh tarragon or fresh basil, or 1 tsp dried
2 garlic cloves, peeled

Place the vinegar in a bowl, add the salt and stir. Add the oil, pepper, lemon slices, parsley and tarragon or basil. Crush the garlic cloves through a press into the bowl and stir.

Mayonnaise
The basic recipe

Home-made mayonnaise is so good and so easy to make that you can learn to make it *les yeux fermés* – that is, practically with your eyes closed. A blender or a food processor will, of course, make the task even easier. Mayonnaise can be used with cold meat, cold fish and vegetables, or as a dip. It is also the base of innumerable other sauces.

Makes 450 ml/16 fl oz

················ By hand ················

2 egg yolks
1 tsp Dijon mustard
450 ml/16 fl oz oil (half peanut, half olive oil)

about 2 tbsp lemon juice or red wine vinegar
salt
freshly ground pepper

Have all ingredients at room temperature. Slip a tea-towel under a small bowl to prevent it from sliding when you beat vigorously. Put egg yolks and mustard into the bowl and begin beating with a wire whisk. After a minute or so, slowly add the oil in a thin stream while continuing to beat. When the mayonnaise begins to thicken, you may add the oil a bit more rapidly, but always beat well after each addition. When the mayonnaise is firm, add the lemon juice, salt and pepper and beat well.

Cover with cling film and refrigerate. It will keep for about four days.

Note: If the mayonnaise curdles (the yolks separate from the oil), place a new yolk in another bowl, add 2 teaspoons mustard and stir well. Slowly add the curdled mixture, stirring constantly until it is firm and thick and silky. Add salt, pepper and half the juice of a lemon or less if you prefer thicker mayonnaise.

########## With a blender ···········

2 whole eggs
1 tsp Dijon mustard
juice of 1 lemon
450 ml/16 fl oz oil (half peanut,
    half olive oil)

1 tsp salt
freshly ground white pepper

Place the eggs, mustard, lemon juice and 1 tablespoon of the oil in
the blender or food processor. Cover and blend on low speed for 2
minutes. Still at low speed, slowly add the rest of the oil in a steady
flow. When the sauce has thickened enough, add salt and pepper.
Check and correct the seasonings. Pour into a bowl, cover with
cling film and refrigerate until ready to use.

Variations
The following recipes are essentially the basic mayonnaise with the
addition of special ingredients.

········ Mayonnaise Brune ········

225 ml/8 fl oz mayonnaise
2 whole anchovies, filleted, rinsed
    and chopped
2 tbsp finely chopped parsley

······· Mayonnaise Orange ·······

225 ml/8 fl oz mayonnaise
1–2 tsp curry powder or saffron
    powder (season to taste)

······ Mayonnaise Ravigote ······

225 ml/8 fl oz mayonnaise
2 hard-boiled egg yolks, passed
    through a sieve
1 tbsp chopped parsley
1 tbsp chopped chives
1 tsp capers
1 tsp dried tarragon

······ Mayonnaise Tartare ·······

225 ml/8 fl oz mayonnaise
2 tbsp chopped gherkins
2 tbsp chopped capers
2 tbsp chopped parsley

········ Mayonnaise Verte ·········

225 ml/8 fl oz mayonnaise
2 tbsp finely chopped parsley
2 tbsp finely chopped chives

Sauce à la Moutarde

A good vinaigrette with mustard and herbs

This is served with cold meat, mussels or boiled vegetables, such as artichokes, carrots, potatoes, green beans or cauliflower.

For 6 people

4 tbsp Dijon mustard
2 tbsp red wine vinegar
juice of 1 lemon
6 tbsp olive oil
salt

freshly ground pepper
1 tbsp finely chopped parsley
1 tbsp finely chopped mint, basil,
    tarragon or chives

Put the mustard in a bowl and, with a fork, slowly beat in the vinegar, lemon juice and olive oil. Keep stirring as you add salt, pepper and the herbs. Stir well.

Sauce aux Noix

A walnut, garlic and olive oil sauce

This is wonderful with freshly made *Pâtes aux Oeufs* (p. 200) or ravioli (made with squash, rice and cheese) or plain, boiled rice.

Make sure your walnuts are perfectly crisp and fresh (the best way to keep them is to freeze until ready to use).

For 6 people

55 g/2 oz walnuts, chopped
1 garlic clove, crushed
2 tbsp olive oil
2 tbsp warm water
salt

Place the walnuts in a mortar, add the garlic and pound with a pestle until you have a smooth texture. Stirring constantly, add the olive oil slowly and steadily. Add the warm water and the salt. The result should be a smooth sauce.

Sauce Piquante
A warm wine and vinegar sauce with tomatoes, shallots and gherkins

·········· Sauce Piquante I ··········

This is a rather rare item in Niçois cooking: a warm sauce. It is used with left-over meats or vegetables.

For 6 people

2 tbsp olive oil	1 garlic clove, crushed
4 shallots, chopped	salt
2 tbsp red wine vinegar	4 gherkins, chopped
70 ml/2½ fl oz dry white wine	40 g/1¼ oz capers
freshly ground pepper	
3 tomatoes, peeled and chopped, or	
225 g/8 oz canned	

Heat the oil in a heavy-bottomed saucepan and add the shallots, vinegar, wine and pepper. Boil for 5 minutes, then add the chopped tomatoes, garlic and salt. Cook over low heat for 15 minutes and remove from heat. Stir in the gherkins and capers.

········ Sauce Piquante II ········

This is a brisker version, which gives left-overs a new life. It is a good accompaniment for *Poche de Veau Farcie* (p. 139), and with any cold vegetables, meat or fish.

For 6 people

2 whole anchovies, filleted	2 tbsp red wine vinegar
1 onion	6 tbsp olive oil
1 garlic clove	3 tbsp parsley, chopped
a pinch of salt	freshly ground pepper

With a pair of kitchen scissors, finely cut the anchovies into a bowl. Grate the onion directly into the bowl and crush the garlic through a garlic press also into the bowl.

Dissolve the salt in the vinegar, then stir in the olive oil, garlic, anchovies, onion, parsley and pepper. Check the seasoning – it should be highly flavoured.

Pistou

Basil, garlic, olive oil and cheese sauce

Never use just-picked basil for this; let the fresh leaves rest for one day to lose some of their moisture. The proportions for this sauce are not definitive, as the pungency of the basil varies. Large leaves are stronger in flavour and the taste is influenced by where the basil was grown. Test to see what your basil is like and adjust the amounts of the other ingredients accordingly.

You can keep this sauce, covered with a little olive oil, in a jar in the refrigerator for months. You can also make a *pistou* base (using basil, parsley and a little oil) without completing the sauce and freeze it flat in a tight plastic bag; when you need it, you can break some off and add the garlic and cheese.

For 6 people

75–140 g/3–5 oz day-old basil leaves (preferably the large-leaved variety) finely shredded with kitchen scissors	freshly ground black pepper
	3 garlic cloves, peeled and crushed
	55 g/2 oz freshly grated Parmesan
20 g/¾ oz chopped parsley	or Gruyère cheese
1 tsp salt	170 ml/6 fl oz olive oil

Mortar and pestle method

Put a little of the basil, parsley, salt, pepper, garlic and cheese in the mortar. Pound to a smooth paste; do a little at a time to make the pounding easier – it will take about 15 minutes to make it all into paste. Slowly pour in the olive oil, mixing well. If the consistency is too thick, add more olive oil.

Blender method

Place a third of all the ingredients except the cheese in the blender and blend at high speed. Stop and scrape down the sides now and then. When the purée is smooth, put it in a bowl or refrigerator jar and purée the rest in two more batches. Add the cheese (this must be freshly grated in order to give the proper texture to the sauce, which becomes too smooth when made in the blender).

Sauce Raïto

A warm tomato, wine and onion sauce

A variety of fish can be simmered in this fragrant sauce: dried cod, whiting, fresh cod, halibut and monkfish. Since the traditional *vin cuit* is hard to prepare, here we have replaced it with a sweet red vermouth or a rich red wine.

For 6 people

2 tbsp olive oil
3 onions, finely chopped
450 ml/16 fl oz good red sweet
    vermouth or red wine (taste
    carefully)
225 ml/8 fl oz water
4 fresh tomatoes, or 285 g/10 oz
    canned, chopped
6 cloves garlic, peeled and crushed
2 tsp thyme

2 tsp oregano or savory
3 bay leaves
salt
freshly ground pepper
85 g/3 oz unpitted little black olives
    from Nice, or pitted oil-cured
    Greek or Italian olives
2 tsp chopped capers
2 tbsp chopped parsley
3 tbsp chopped gherkins

Heat the olive oil in a heavy-bottomed saucepan, add the onions and cook slowly for 20 minutes until soft. Add the vermouth or wine and the water. Stir and boil for 5 minutes, then add the tomatoes, garlic, thyme, oregano or savory, bay leaves, salt and freshly ground pepper. Reduce heat and simmer, uncovered, for 1 hour. It should be quite thick.

Remove from the heat. Discard the bay leaves and pass the mixture through a Mouli food mill. Check the seasonings (the sauce should be pungent) and correct them if necessary. Add the olives, capers, parsley and gherkins and cook for an additional 5 minutes.

Note: Check your red vermouth before using it. A good red wine is often better in a *raïto* sauce than a mediocre red vermouth. I prefer red wine myself.

Sauce Ravigote
Vinaigrette with gherkins, capers and onions

This is a good sauce to serve with cold chicken, turkey, prawns, mussels, vegetables or beef.

For 6 people

a pinch of salt
2 tbsp red wine vinegar
6 tbsp olive oil
freshly ground pepper
3 tbsp finely chopped chives,
    parsley, or tarragon

1 onion, peeled and grated
2 gherkins, finely chopped
2 tbsp capers

Dissolve the salt in the vinegar. Stir in the olive oil, pepper, herbs, onion, gherkins and capers.

Rouille

A thick cayenne pepper and garlic sauce

For 6 people

················ Rouille I ················

4 garlic cloves
2 tsp cayenne pepper or Tabasco
    sauce to taste
1 slice good white firm bread,
    preferably home-made, sprinkled

with a little milk, then squeezed
    to a paste
4 tbsp olive oil
salt
freshly ground white pepper

Peel the garlic cloves and press them through a garlic press into a mortar. Add the cayenne pepper or Tabasco sauce and the bread paste. Stir with a fork or pestle and slowly add the oil. Season with salt and pepper, correct the seasoning and pour the sauce into a bowl. Cover and keep in the refrigerator until ready to use.

················ Rouille II ················

4 garlic cloves
salt
2 egg yolks
225 ml/8 fl oz olive oil

½ tsp saffron
1 tsp cayenne pepper
juice of half a lemon (optional)

Make sure all ingredients are at room temperature and the garlic cloves are firm and crisp.

Peel the garlic cloves and crush them through a press into the mortar. Pound with the pestle, sprinkle with salt and pound some more – after a few minutes the garlic should turn into a paste. Add the yolks; the mixture will become sticky. Add the oil slowly, stirring constantly, as in making mayonnaise. When the sauce is firm, add the saffron, cayenne pepper and salt to taste. If you find it too heavy, add the juice of half a lemon before serving and stir.

This sauce can be kept for 24 hours in the refrigerator covered with cling film.

Note: You may use a blender or food processor to make the sauce, but first crush the garlic cloves and salt in the mortar and pound into a smooth paste. Put 2 *whole* eggs in the blender and a little more salt if you think it's needed (the sauce should be heavily seasoned). Cover and blend at high speed for 30 seconds. Add the garlic paste. Cover again and blend for about 1 minute and then start pouring in the oil very slowly while blending at high speed. When the sauce is smooth and firm, remove from the blender and add cayenne and saffron. Check the seasoning – you may want to add more salt.

Sauce Tartare
A vinaigrette with hard-boiled eggs, mustard and gherkins

This lovely sauce has a rich texture and is wonderful served with cold fish or left-over beef. It can also be used to fill hard-boiled-egg and tomato halves.

For 6 people

10 g/⅓ oz chopped basil or mint or parsley
55 g/2 oz chopped *cornichons* (see gherkins, p. 11)
3 hard-boiled eggs
1 tbsp Dijon mustard

140 ml/5 fl oz olive oil
juice of 1 lemon or 2 tbsp red wine vinegar
55 g/2 oz capers
salt
freshly ground pepper

Place the herbs and *cornichons* on kitchen towels or a tea-towel and squeeze them well to extract as much moisture as possible. Peel the eggs and remove the yolks.

Place the yolks in a large bowl, mash, add the mustard and stir. When the mixture is smooth, slowly add the oil, beating constantly. When the sauce is firm, add the lemon juice or vinegar. Sieve the egg whites. Stir into the sauce the gherkins, capers, salt, pepper and egg whites.

Note: This sauce cannot be made in a blender or food processor because its essence is its rough texture. A blender would turn it into a paste.

Sauce Tomate

A raw tomato sauce

This delicious cold sauce is light and fresh – superb with cold dishes.

For 6 people

2.25 kg/5 lb ripe tomatoes, peeled
2 large onions, quartered
2 garlic cloves, peeled
3 tbsp chopped fresh basil

3 tbsp coarsely chopped parsley
3 tbsp olive oil
salt
freshly ground pepper

Put half of the tomatoes in a blender or food processor with half of the onions and 1 garlic clove. Blend at high speed for 5 minutes and pour into a large bowl. Put the remaining tomatoes, onion and garlic clove in the blender, along with the basil, parsley and oil. Blend for 5 minutes, then add it to the first batch in the bowl. Season with salt and pepper, stir well and refrigerate covered with cling film (the oil will rise to the surface, so stir well before using). The sauce will keep for four or five days.

Sauce Verte

Spinach, anchovy and caper sauce

This is an unctuous but refreshing sauce, delicious with cold meat or grilled fish. You may also fill tomato or courgette halves with it for *plateau de hors-d'oeuvres variés* (see *Oeufs et Légumes*, p. 44).

The blender is a great help for this recipe. Covered with cling film, the sauce will keep for two or three days in the refrigerator.

For 225 ml/8 fl oz sauce (enough for 6 people)

140 g/5 oz frozen spinach or 280 g/
   10 oz fresh spinach
1 thin slice bread
1 hard-boiled egg, sliced in half
6 anchovy fillets, rinsed and
   chopped
115 ml/4 fl oz olive oil

2 tbsp red wine vinegar
salt
freshly ground black pepper
1 tbsp finely chopped *cornichons*
   (see gherkins, p. 11), or whole
   capers

Blanch the frozen spinach or cook and drain the fresh spinach, let it cool and squeeze it with your hands to remove excess moisture. Put it in a blender or food processor.

Add a little water to the bread, then squeeze it so that you have about 2 tablespoons of bread paste. Add this to the blender. Add the egg, anchovies, olive oil and vinegar. Blend at high speed, stopping from time to time to scrape down the sides. In 3–4 minutes you should have a very smooth sauce.

Pour the sauce into a bowl and add salt and pepper to taste. Add the *cornichons* or capers and chill.

Vinaigrette

Olive oil and red wine vinegar sauce

This is a basic sauce made in a second and with all kinds of interesting additions possible. Don't add herbs. Don't keep it in the refrigerator. The ingredients are always at hand, so only prepare what you need for the moment.

For 6 people

a pinch of salt
2 tbsp red wine vinegar
6 tbsp olive oil
freshly ground black pepper

Dissolve the salt in vinegar and beat in the oil very slowly. Add pepper and stir. Check to see if it is seasoned enough.

To this basic recipe you may add any of the following:

1 garlic clove, peeled and crushed
1 tsp Dijon mustard (mix with vinegar first and stir well)

2 tbsp chives or parsley or basil or mint, finely chopped with kitchen scissors
1 onion, grated

Les Poissons

Fish

Fish has always been the base of Nice's cuisine. It used to be abundant, varied and reasonably priced. Caught at dawn, sold early in the morning, sprinkled with herbs and cooked over a rosemary-scented wood fire, it was a usual dish to enjoy at lunch.

The situation has changed. Although the rocky coast, cut by gulfs and bays, is still a perfect habitat for a rich variety of fish, each with its distinctive colour, shape, texture and taste, problems of distribution and pollution plague the Riviera. The traditional fishing boats bringing loads of sardines, anchovies, squid, bream, fresh *rascasses* and *loups* to sleepy little harbours every morning are no longer the sole purveyors. Eighty per cent of the fish sold in Nice markets now comes from the Atlantic, the English Channel or even farther away. I have seen *daurades* from Argentina, *baudroie* from Scotland, *merlan* from Denmark.

It is important that the cardinal rules for buying and cooking fish be respected at all times. Learn how to choose fresh fish. Know what fish you enjoy and demand it if your fishmonger does not stock it regularly. Never overcook a fish. Enhance its flavour, but don't camouflage it. In Nice tradition has taught every cook the qualities to enhance, the shortcomings to deal with in almost any fish. A coarse, oily fish is blanched in *court bouillon* or boiled to get rid of its fat before herbs and spices are added. A dull fish rests in a highly flavoured marinade before it is cooked. Above all, fish is selected with the greatest care. The skin must be smooth and tight around the body, the gills very red, the whole fish straight and firm, the eyes shiny and dark, never bloodshot.

Some fishmongers offer fresh catches but relatively little choice. They tend to stock only the most easily sold items, such as prawns, plaice, cod, and sole. A trip to the wholesale market will show you what is good and available every day. So the first thing to do is to select a fishmonger who takes his business seriously, and then convince him you'll be a steady customer for squid, monkfish, whiting, mussels and whitebait.

All the fish I use in the following recipes are easy to find here and have the qualities required by Mediterranean cuisine.

Anchovies: *les anchois*
The best kind to buy is the preserved variety kept in rough salt in a tin or glass jar. Niçois cooking uses this type widely in *pissaladière, salade niçoise, anchoïade, bagna cauda, mousse d'aubergines* and many other dishes. You will need large quantities, so buy them in large cans.

Bass: *le loup*
This superb fish successfully replaces bream (*daurade*). It is abundant all year round. Delicious in *loup farci à la niçoise* or grilled with fennel, it can also be cooked with mussels or served cold with *rouille, aïoli,* or *mayonnaise verte*. It is a staple of Niçois cuisine.

Monkfish: *la baudroie, la lotte*
This is an unimposing name for a wonderful fish. The French name is *lotte*, but in the South we call it *baudroie*. In Nice we prepare it with baked vegetables, boiled in bouillabaisse, or combined with mussels. It is light, delicate, firm and virtually boneless.

Dried salted cod: *la morue*
Dried cod, which is so popular in Mediterranean countries, is the base for *brandade, estockaficada, tian de morue, beignets de morue* and *morue à l'aïoli*.

It is sold in three forms, but filleted dried cod is the most common. It should soak overnight before it is cooked (see Ingredients, p. 11). The whole fish, opened, is drier, requiring two days' soaking, and tastier – ideal for *morue en raïto, capilotade* or *estockaficada*. Then there is the Chinese whole cod (tail, fins, skin and bones), dried and salted until it is 'wooden'. This type of cod is the closest thing to Nice's stockfish, superb for *estockaficada*; it requires at least three days of soaking and changing the water about six times.

Dried cod is very nutritious and quite inexpensive, and keeps well. It has a pungent, fresh, unique taste. Always choose a plump dried cod, the thicker the better. Stock up when you find it – it keeps well. The part near the tail is the thickest. To desalt the cod, cover it with cool water, skin side up, and change the water often. Always check to see if it has desalted enough by eating a little piece raw before cooking.

Mussels: *les moules*
About two hours before the mussels are to be cooked, scrub them with a strong wire brush and pull the beard off each one. Rinse the mussels in a colander and put them in a basin of cold water. After half an hour, toss out any that are open (they aren't fresh) or any that are unusually heavy (they are full of sand). Rinse again under cold water and put back in the basin for another half hour of cold-water soaking to cleanse further and reduce saltiness.

Sardines: *les sardines*
Sardines are delicious grilled with a sprinkling of lemon juice or red wine vinegar.

Squid: *les tautennes, les suppions*
There are all kinds of imaginative and delicious recipes in Nice for this delicacy. We call it poor man's lobster, but it is a rich man's delight, too. It is very inexpensive, and is sold perfectly cleaned, tender and fresh. Filled with spinach and rice, cold in salads, added to fish soup or *salade de riz*, sautéd with tomatoes and white wine, simmered with tomatoes and herbs, it is a delicacy nobody can afford to ignore.

Tuna: *le thon*
Fresh tuna is available all year round. Fresh tuna *à la chartreuse* or cooked with tomato is a rich, wonderfully tasty dish.

Whitebait: *la petite friture*
These fish are very small (about 50 mm/2 in long and 6 mm/¼ inch wide), and are delicious simply floured, fried in deep fat and eaten sprinkled with lemon juice or red wine vinegar.

Whiting: *le merlan*
This is a delicate, inexpensive fish, which is served in a variety of ways in Nice: baked, boiled, accompanied by mussels or in soup. Try to buy the largest ones, for they have more flesh for the money.

Court Bouillon
Stock for cooking fish

We will deal with four kinds of *court bouillon* here. The first one is for a fish that is somewhat bland, such as whiting, bass or cod, or has been kept on ice. The second is for freshwater fish (trout and the like); the third is for large fish (salmon, halibut, tuna, cod or monkfish); and the fourth is for very delicate fish, such as sole or flounder. All these versions of *court bouillon* can be kept frozen, so make a large amount to put in small containers and keep it ready for later use.

When you cook your fish, always make sure there is enough *court bouillon* to cover it. Place the fish on a rack in the fish cooker, then cover it with *court bouillon*. Place a few lettuce leaves on top of the fish. Bring to boiling point, reduce the heat and simmer for as long as you need to (the classic rule is 8–10 minutes for each 450 g/ 1 lb of fish once the boiling point has been reached).

·········· Court Bouillon I ··········

A *court bouillon* made with fish heads and bones and vegetables and wine. This fish stock will improve a dull fish or one that has been kept on ice.

For 6 people

900 g/2 lb fish heads and backbones, roughly broken in pieces	1 tsp thyme
	bouquet garni (p. 14)
	225 ml/8 fl oz dry white wine
3 onions, chopped	2.25 l/4 pt water
1 carrot, chopped	salt
the white part of 1 leek, chopped, or an additional onion, chopped	freshly ground pepper

Place the fish heads and bones in a saucepan. Add the onions, carrot, leek, thyme, bouquet garni, wine and water. Bring to a boil and simmer for 40 minutes. Add salt and pepper before removing from heat. Pass through a sieve lined with a piece of cheesecloth, forcing through as much liquid as you can.

######## Court Bouillon II ########

A *court bouillon* made with vinegar to be used with freshwater fish such as pike, trout and carp. The moisture of the flesh must be maintained, so do not wash the fish or remove the scales. Do not gut the fish in the usual way by slitting the belly; instead, make a small hole either in the stomach or the head and pull out the entrails, and then dry carefully with cheesecloth.

For 6 people

450 ml/16 fl oz red wine vinegar	bouquet garni (p. 14)
2.25 l/4 pt water	10 peppercorns
3 carrots, chopped	salt
3 onions, chopped	

Place all ingredients except peppercorns in a large saucepan and bring to a boil. Simmer for 1 hour. Add the peppercorns (to eliminate bitterness). Cover and remove the stock from the heat. Let it cool, then pass it through a sieve lined with cheesecloth.

######## Court Bouillon III ########

A *court bouillon* made with white wine. This is for large fish – salmon, halibut, tuna, monkfish, cod. Follow the recipe for *Court Bouillon II*, using white wine instead of vinegar.

········ Court Bouillon IV ········

A *court bouillon* made with milk. This is for very delicate fish, such as sole or flounder. Its lightness enables the fine flavour of the fish to stand out.

For 6 people

450 ml/16 fl oz milk
1.8 l/3⅓ pt water
3 carrots, chopped
3 onions, chopped

bouquet garni (p. 14)
salt
10 peppercorns

Place all ingredients except peppercorns in a large saucepan. Bring to a boil and simmer for 1 hour. Add the peppercorns. Cover and remove from the heat. Let it cool, then pass through a sieve lined with a piece of cheesecloth.

Brandade
Hot dried-cod mousse

This dish is part of the traditional 'lean dinner' on Christmas Eve. The delicious, fluffy mixture is served warm in a thin puff-pastry shell called *vol-au-vent* or garnished with crisp *croûtons* and truffles; or served cold, simply stuffed in tomato halves and garnished with little black olives.

Traditionally, the cod was crushed in a marble mortar with the milk and oil to form a smooth paste, which became creamy-white when heated. I use an electric blender – a much quicker and simpler process, which *charcuteries* always favour!

Serve with a tart salad of rocket, dandelion or watercress.

For 6 people

680 g/1½ lb dried cod
2 garlic cloves
1 potato, boiled and quartered
225 ml/8 fl oz milk at room
    temperature
225 ml/8 fl oz olive oil at room
    temperature

juice of 1 lemon
½–1 tsp freshly grated nutmeg
freshly ground white pepper
salt (may not be needed)

Let the cod soak overnight in the sink or a large basin of cold water. Change the water four to five times. Taste a bit of cod to check if it has desalted enough.

When the cod has been adequately soaked, place it on a board. Remove the skin, bones and all the loose pieces with your hands and a small, sharp knife. Then place the cod flesh in a pan of cold water to cover and bring to a boil. Just as the water starts to simmer, remove from the heat and let it cool. Drain.

Peel the garlic cloves and crush with a press into the blender. With your hands, flake the fish in small pieces into the blender. Add the potato and pour in half of the milk and half of the olive oil. Turn to low speed for 1 minute. Stop and stir with a long-handled wooden spoon. Blend for 2 more minutes at high speed. Put the blender on low and slowly but steadily start pouring in alternately the rest of the milk and oil, stopping from time to time to stir with the spoon. This blending should take about 8 minutes.

When all the milk and oil are incorporated, blend at high speed for 2 minutes. The paste will be fluffy and white and quite smooth. Spoon it into a saucepan. Add the lemon juice, nutmeg and pepper. Taste before adding any salt. Cook over a low heat, stirring gently, for 5 minutes or until just warm.

Ways to serve *brandade*

Place the *brandade* in a warm shallow dish, surround with *croûtons* (p. 11) and decorate with sliced truffles or black olives. Or stuff tomato halves with cold *brandade* and garnish with chopped basil. Or stuff six puff-pastry shells with warm *brandade* and place in a moderate oven for 15 minutes, then sprinkle with sliced truffles or chopped olives. Or use as a filling for an omelette: make an omelette and when the first side has set, spread some *brandade* in the centre, fold the circle in half and cook for 2 minutes more; sprinkle with chopped black olives before serving.

Capilotade

Dried cod stewed in a sweet vermouth and tomato sauce

This is another dish traditionally served on Christmas Eve. Like the *brandade* and *estockaficada*, this should be served with a strong green salad (dandelion, rocket, watercress, or chicory). Not the least of the joys of this dish is that it takes about 10 minutes to prepare.

For 6 people

900 g/2 lb dried cod
3 tbsp olive oil
2 large onions, chopped
2 garlic cloves, peeled and crushed
1 tbsp unbleached flour
115 ml/4 fl oz sweet red vermouth or *Vin Cuit* (p. 249) or good red wine

55 g/2 oz chopped *cornichons* (see gherkins, p. 11) or 25 g/1 oz capers
salt (optional)
freshly ground black pepper
3 tbsp chopped Italian parsley

Soak the cod in a large bowl of water or in the sink for several hours or, if it is hard as wood, overnight (follow directions on the package). Change the water three or four times. Taste a piece to be sure it is not too salty; if it is, soak the fish for another hour or so. Drain and chop the cod into large pieces.

Heat 2 tablespoons of the olive oil in a large frying-pan. Fry the pieces of cod for 3 minutes on each side. Remove with tongs or a slotted spoon and set aside.

Add the remaining tablespoon of olive oil and gently cook the onions over a low heat until they are soft. Stirring constantly, add the garlic and flour to the onions. Stir in the vermouth and *cornichons* or capers and simmer, uncovered, for 5 minutes. Put the cod back in the pan. Check for seasonings – you may want to add some salt and/or pepper – and cook for a few more minutes.

Serve in a brightly coloured shallow dish, sprinkled with chopped parsley.

Variation

You may omit the flour and add the pulp of 3 chopped tomatoes to thicken the sauce.

Escargots à la Provence
Snails simmered in herbs and wine

Throughout France snail hunting, *la chasse aux escargots*, is one of the children's favourite pastimes. Snails are gathered right after a rainfall in wire baskets and kept there or in cages for two weeks, and are fed only flour or chaff so that their systems are purged of all the unpleasant slime. Before cooking they are rinsed in vinegar or water. In Marseilles entire meals of snails, *caracolades*, are served, and in market-places cooked snails are often sold as snacks in paper cones. Snails can also be the base of an omelette.

In the South of France there are two kinds of snail: *les blanquettes*, which are whitish and plump, and *les petits gris* (*cantareu* in Nice), which are striped grey and white and served with *aïoli monstre* or a strong tomato and red pepper sauce. Here is a Provençal recipe that can be used for either kind. For a main course, double all the ingredients. In Provence peasants eat snails with a straight pin, but here snail dishes and forks can be bought to set a more elegant table.

As an appetizer for 6 people

2 tbsp olive oil	freshly ground black pepper
3 dozen canned snails	225 ml/8 fl oz dry white wine
2 shallots, finely chopped	½ tsp fennel or anise seed
2 garlic cloves, peeled and crushed	bouquet garni (p. 14)
2 tbsp chopped Italian parsley	2 tbsp breadcrumbs (preferably
salt	home-made)

Heat 1 tablespoon of the olive oil in a large frying-pan. Add the snails but not the shells. Sauté them for 2 minutes over a medium heat, tossing with a wooden spoon. Add the shallots, 1 crushed garlic clove, 1 tablespoon parsley, and salt and pepper. Cook 2 more minutes, stirring gently. Add the wine, fennel and bouquet garni. Cover, reduce the heat and simmer for 10 minutes. Remove snails with a slotted spoon. Reserve snails and wine sauce.

Preheat the grill. Place the empty snail shells in a baking dish and put a snail and 1 teaspoon of wine sauce in each shell. Sprinkle on each snail some breadcrumbs, crushed garlic, parsley and olive oil. Grill for 3 minutes. Serve immediately with plenty of French bread and a dry white wine.

Variation

Simply sauté the snails with herbs and garlic and serve as is, *comme ça*. Or serve them with hot tomato sauce or *aïoli*.

Estockaficada
Dried-cod and vegetable stew

This highly seasoned super fish stew made of dried cod has a place of honour in Nice: one of the most renowned culinary clubs of the city has borrowed its name. The club meets once a month to chat and taste a new interpretation of *estockaficada*.

'Stockfish' means fish that is literally 'as dry as a stick'. The name 'stockfish' (hence the term *estockaficada*) was originally applied to the dried cod brought to Nice by Norwegian sailors in exchange for olive oil and fresh vegetables.

To buy a substitute for stockfish, try to find the hardest, driest cod available (Italian and Spanish groceries are the most likely to have it), or buy the Chinese *tai tze*. Since it keeps for ever, keep a good amount in your kitchen ready for use.

In Nice the advice is to let the stockfish sit in a running creek for two days. Depending on the dryness and saltiness of the cod you buy, the soaking time can vary from one to two days.

Estockaficada is much better reheated after the cooked fish has marinated for a few hours in its pungent sauce. It freezes well.

For 6 people

900 g/2 lb dried cod	2 tsp thyme
115 ml/4 fl oz olive oil	2 tsp savory
5 garlic cloves, finely chopped	freshly ground black pepper
5 large onions, finely chopped	340 ml/12 fl oz dry white wine
3 bell peppers (green, yellow or red) seeded and sliced into 25-mm/1-in strips	8 potatoes, sliced 12 mm/½ in thick
	85 g/3 oz olives (unpitted black olives from Nice or pitted oil-cured black olives)
8 tomatoes, fresh or canned, quartered	4 tsp chopped parsley
2 bay leaves	olive oil in small cruets

If you use the very dry cod, let it soak in the sink in cold water or a large saucepan for two days and change the water four times. If you use the kind of cod most fishmongers carry, one night of soaking is enough. In any case, always check with the fishmonger on how long his particular cod needs to be soaked, and always taste before cooking it to see that it is tasty but not oversalty.

When the cod has been properly soaked, remove the tail, skin and bones with your fingers. Shred the flesh with your fingers and let it marinate for a few hours in a dish covered with a layer of the olive oil (save the oil for using later in this recipe).

Heat 2 tablespoons of the olive oil (or more, if necessary) from the marinade in a *doufeu* or heavy-bottomed saucepan. Add the cod and sauté it, turning it over once with tongs or a wooden spoon, for 5 minutes. Add 1 tablespoon of the olive oil, then the garlic, onions, peppers, tomatoes, bay leaves, thyme, savory, pepper and wine. Simmer, covered, in the pan for 1½ hours. Add the potatoes and cook, uncovered, for 20–30 minutes more.

Just before serving, add the olives and parsley. Check the seasoning once more (it must be highly peppered). Place the cruets of olive oil round the dinner table so that each person can crush his or her potatoes in the sauce and add a dash of olive oil to the dish.

Gigot de Mer

Fish baked with onion, aubergines, courgettes, peppers and white wine

This 'leg of lamb from the sea' is so called because slices of garlic are stuck into the fish the same way they would be for roast leg of lamb – *gigot d'agneau* – before the fish is baked on a bed of ratatouille. You may use thick slices of haddock, fresh cod or monkfish or a whole large whiting, striped bass or red snapper. It is a remarkably easy yet delicious dish imbued with the flavours of vegetables, garlic and white wine. *Riz aux Herbes* (p. 206) perfectly complements the taste of *gigot de mer*, and a green tossed salad concludes the meal happily. Serve with a chilled dry white wine.

For 6 people

2 large aubergines
salt
2 tbsp olive oil
4 onions, chopped
4 green peppers, diced
4 courgettes or 2 cucumbers, diced
freshly ground white pepper
1 2.25–2.75-kg/5–6-lb whole fish
    (red snapper or whiting or
    bass),* or about 2.25 kg/5 lb
    fillets (haddock, cod or

monkfish), sliced 35 mm/1½ in
    thick
2 garlic cloves, slivered
2 bay leaves
1 tsp thyme
4 lettuce leaves
225 ml/8 fl oz dry white wine or
    dry white vermouth
2 tbsp finely chopped basil or
    Italian parsley

Peel and dice the aubergines into 12-mm/½-in pieces, toss with salt and drain in a colander for 30 minutes. Squeeze out as much moisture as possible with kitchen towels. Heat the olive oil in a heavy frying-pan. Add about a quarter of the chopped onions and the green peppers, courgettes and aubergines. Sprinkle with salt and pepper and simmer for 20 minutes, stirring from time to time and adding more olive oil if the mixture begins to stick to the pan. (This step can be done in advance.)

---

* Ask your fishmonger to remove the head and backbone but to save the bone. The dish will have a better flavour if you add the bone during the baking, placing it between the two fillets. It should be removed, of course, before serving.

Heat the oven to 190°C/375°F/Gas Mark 5. If you are using whole fish, make 6-mm/¼-in slits in the skin and insert the garlic slivers as you would in a leg of lamb. For thick slices of fish, insert the garlic between the rings of muscle – two or three per slice.

Place the fish in an oiled baking dish. Sprinkle with the remaining chopped onion and the bay leaves, thyme, salt and pepper. Cover with the lettuce leaves, pour in the wine and bake for 15 minutes.

Lift the whole fish out of the dish with two spatulas and discard the lettuce. Scrape the cooked onions into the aubergine mixture and put a part of this into the baking dish to make a bed. Lay the top half of the fish skin side down on the vegetables. Place the bottom half on top, skin side up. If you are using slices of fish, simply lay them on top of the aubergine bed. Put 2–3 tablespoons of the vegetables over the fish and the remainder around it. Bake for another 15 minutes, or until the fish is opaque and flakes easily. Serve immediately, sprinkled with the basil or parsley.

Note: Sprinkled with olive oil, this dish is delicious served cold the next day.

Loup Farci à la Niçoise
Bass stuffed with tomatoes, olives and mushrooms

Although this is called *loup farci*, the colourful stuffing is not cooked with the fish but added just before serving. It is a delight to the eye and an uncommon pleasure to the palate. Indigenously Niçois, it is delicious served with *Gnocchi* (p. 196), *Riz aux Herbes* (p. 206) or *Courgettes Râpées* (p. 165).

This recipe makes six very generous portions, but any left-overs (plus the raw fish head that has been saved) can be used for *Soupe de Pêcheurs* (p. 32).

For 6 people

.... Fish ....

2 tbsp fennel or anise seed	½ tsp freshly ground white pepper
2 tsp Dijon mustard	3 bay leaves
1 2.75-kg/6-lb bass, filleted, and its backbone	1 tbsp olive oil
salt	3 lettuce leaves (round, iceberg, or endive)

Preheat the oven to 180°C/350°F/Gas Mark 4.

Mix the fennel or anise seed and mustard. Make six evenly distributed 12-mm/½-in slits in the fish and put a dab (about the size of a pea) of the mixture in each cut. Sprinkle the fillets with salt and pepper.

Place one fillet skin side down in an oiled baking dish, put the bone on it and lay the other fillet on top, skin side up. Lay the bay leaves on the fish and sprinkle with olive oil. Cover with lettuce leaves and bake for 40 minutes.

.... 'Stuffing' ....

2 tbsp oil (half olive oil, half peanut oil)	680 g/1½ lb tomatoes (fresh or canned), chopped
85 g/3 oz finely chopped lean salt pork or streaky bacon	225 ml/8 fl oz dry white wine
3 onions, finely chopped	85 g/3 oz small black olives or pitted oil-cured olives
450 g/1 lb mushrooms, finely chopped	20 g/¾ oz finely chopped parsley
3 garlic cloves, finely chopped	salt
	freshly ground white pepper

Heat the oil in a large frying-pan. Add the pork, onions, mushrooms and garlic and sauté for 5 minutes. Add the tomatoes and wine and simmer, uncovered, for 30 minutes to reduce the liquid. This should be a *fine* mixture. Add the olives, parsley, salt and pepper. Cover and keep warm.

Using two spatulas, gently place the whole fish on a warm platter. Remove the lettuce and bay leaves. Carefully lift the top fillet and place it skin side down next to the other fillet. Remove the bone (save it for making soup) and pour the 'stuffing' down the middle of the fillets. If fish slices are used, simply pour the 'stuffing' over them.

Loup Grillé au Fenouil

Grilled fish with fennel, lemon juice and olive oil

A grilled fish should be moist inside, crisp outside and fragrant all over. In Nice *loup de mer*, *dorades*, *pageots* and *rougets* are brushed with olive oil, stuffed with dried fennel branches and cooked over wood fires sprinkled with dried herbs. Often, since they have been caught that very morning, they are neither gutted nor scaled. This is a simple but perfect way to eat fresh fish.

Bass, bream and red mullet are delicious prepared with fennel seed and a little savory and grilled, if it is not possible to have a wood fire. You may want to place two thin slices of *Beurre d'Anchois* (p. 73) over each fish just before serving or to pass a bowl of *Sauce Jaune et Verte* (p. 76), *Rouille* (p. 84), *Aïoli* (p. 71), *Sauce Citronnette* (p. 74), *Sauce Dorée* (p. 75, *Sauce Tartare* (p. 85) or *Sauce Verte* (p. 86) to spread on the grilled fish. Serve the fish with *Riz aux Herbes* (p. 206) *Courgettes Râpées* (p. 165), *Pommes de Terre à l'Ail* (p. 183) or *Champignons Farcis* (p. 164).

For 6 people

6 450-g/1-lb fish or 3 larger fish (sea bass, bream, red mullet), with their heads and tails left on	3 tbsp savory or oregano
	fresh fennel stalks
6 tbsp fennel seed	2 tbsp olive oil
juice of 1 lemon	12–15 vine leaves or lettuce leaves
salt	1 bunch parsley or watercress
freshly ground pepper	2 lemons, sliced

Clean and dry the fish. Cut a few slashes on the sides of each fish with a sharp knife (to allow it to cook evenly, to prevent it from curling as it cooks and to let the flavour of the herbs penetrate it).

Sprinkle the inside with fennel seed, lemon juice, salt, pepper and savory, and rub the outside with the same ingredients. Stuff the fish with fresh or dried fennel stalks. Sprinkle olive oil over both sides of each fish and wrap loosely with vine or lettuce leaves, which will protect the fish from the heat for a few minutes and keep the flesh moist; as the fish grills, the leaves will crumble away.

If the fish are small and thin, put them on a wire grill. If you have larger fish, use the fish-shaped wire baskets, which will hold them securely and allow proper cooking.

When your wood or charcoal fire is ready (with a fine bed of embers), sprinkle on it a pinch of dried herbs, then place the wire basket over it and cook the fish for about 10 minutes on one side. Turn them over and cook the other side for 10–15 minutes more. The entire cooking time will vary between 20 and 30 minutes, according to the thickness of the fish. The flesh will flake easily and become opaque when cooked.

Place the fish on a warm serving platter and surround with watercress or parsley and sliced lemons.

Merlan aux Moules

Whiting, mussels and vegetables baked in a light curry sauce

This is a very pretty, very light dish. The curry and lemon give a pungent flavour to the vegetable mixture. It is an easy dish to prepare, and since whiting and mussels are available all year round, it is a truly reliable stand-by. Always choose the largest whiting possible, but a 1–1.25-kg/2–3-lb fish will do. I like this dish served alone, but you may make it more important by serving it with *Riz aux Herbes* (p. 206), *Purée de Légumes* (p. 184) or *Fenouil Braisé* (p. 169). A chilled dry white wine would be lovely with this.

For 6 people

1 1.8–2.25-kg/5-lb or 2 1.25-kg/3-lb whiting	2 onions, finely chopped
salt	juice of 1 lemon
freshly ground white pepper	2 bay leaves
1.25 kg/3 lb mussels	6 lettuce leaves (round or iceberg)
115 ml/4 fl oz dry white wine	1 tsp curry powder (or more if you prefer)
2 tbsp olive oil	2 tbsp chopped fresh basil or parsley
2 carrots, finely chopped	

Fillet the whiting, remove the head and bones (which can be saved for making soup). Rinse and dry the fillets with kitchen towels and sprinkle with salt and pepper.

Scrub the mussels with a wire brush, pull out the beards with your fingers, and place the mussels in a large bowl of cold water for 10 minutes. Discard the mussels with open shells.

Heat the wine in a heavy-bottomed saucepan. Add the mussels and cook for 4 minutes, shaking the pan once. When they are cool, remove them from their shells and set aside. Pass the stock through a sieve covered with a piece of cheesecloth and reserve it.

Put 1 tablespoon of the olive oil in a frying-pan. Add the carrots and onions and cook for 15 minutes.

Place half of the carrots and onions in an oiled baking dish and lay the whiting on top. Salt and pepper the fish and sprinkle it with 1 tablespoon of olive oil and the lemon juice. Put the bay leaves on top, spread the rest of the carrots and onions on the fish and cover with the lettuce leaves.

The dish may be prepared up to this point and kept in the refrigerator until the next day, when it can be baked and finished. In that case, cover the mussels and whiting with cling film and put the mussel stock in a jar.

About an hour before serving, preheat the oven to 190°C/375°F/Gas Mark 5. Place the dish of whiting in the oven and lower the setting to 180°C/350°F/Gas Mark 4. Bake for about 40 minutes.

Ten minutes before the whiting is done, boil the mussel stock in a saucepan for 10 minutes. Stir in the curry powder, add the mussels, and when the stock starts to boil again, cover and remove from heat.

Lift the fillets on to a warm serving platter with two spatulas. Discard the bay leaves and lettuce. Spoon the vegetables round and over the fish. Pour the mussels and the stock over the whole dish. Check the seasoning – it should be quite spicy. Sprinkle with basil or parsley and serve.

Note: You can use the left-overs from this dish for *Soupe de Pêcheurs* (p. 32) or *Salade de Riz Variée* (p. 67).

Merlan Magali

Whiting and mussels in white wine sauce

This lovely dish shows a curious combination of influences – the egg sauce obviously comes from the north of France, and the oregano adds an interesting southern touch to the delicate flavour of the whiting.

Serve with boiled new potatoes or *Riz aux Herbes* (p. 206) and chicory salad or *Salade Mesclun* (p. 69).

The recipe calls for a large whiting, which may seem a bit excessive, but you can make *Salade de Riz Variée* (p. 67) with the left-overs.

For 6 people

1 1.8–2.25-kg/4–5-lb whiting	freshly ground white pepper
1.8 kg/4 lb mussels	2 egg yolks
115 ml/4 fl oz dry white wine	juice of 1 lemon
1 onion, finely chopped	1 tbsp flour
1 carrot, finely chopped	15 g/½ oz butter
1 tbsp olive oil	1 tsp oregano
bouquet garni (p. 14)	3 tbsp chopped Italian parsley, plus
salt	2 sprigs

Scrub the mussels with a metal or strong nylon brush and remove the beards. Set the mussels in cold water for 10 minutes. Discard any opened mussels.

Heat the wine in an earthenware dish or a *doufeu*. Add the mussels, cover and cook for 5 minutes, tossing gently with a spoon. Cool. Take out the mussels and discard the shells. Strain the stock through a piece of cheesecloth spread over a sieve and reserve.

Preheat oven to 190°C/375°F/Gas Mark 5.

Spread the onion and carrot in a deep baking dish and add the oil and bouquet garni. Lay the fish on top, season with salt and pepper and bake for 25–30 minutes. Peel off the fish skin with a knife and discard it.

Blend the egg yolks and lemon juice in a small bowl. In a heavy-bottomed saucepan, blend the flour and butter over low heat. Add the mussel stock while stirring gently with a wooden spoon over low heat. Remove from heat and add the oregano and egg–lemon mixture. Heat the sauce for 1 minute, adding the mussels. Cover and remove from heat.

Place the whiting on a warm serving platter and pour the mussels and sauce over it. Before serving, sprinkle with chopped parsley and put a sprig of parsley at each end of the dish.

Morue et Légumes Cuits sur Braise
Dried-cod and vegetable barbecue

This is associated with an old Provençal custom. On Sunday nights fathers were responsible for dinner and this was one of their treats. They would light a fire with the help of all the children, then the whole family would sit around the fireplace and chat while the cod and the vegetables sizzled on the grill.

The dish was sometimes prepared with unsoaked dried cod, but cooked that way it is too salty for my taste.

For 6 people

900 g/2 lb dried cod
12 small potatoes, unpeeled and washed
6 small white onions, peeled
6 garlic cloves, unpeeled

1 bottle good olive oil
1 bottle red wine vinegar
salt
peppercorns in a pepper mill

Soak the cod for several hours or overnight in cold water, changing the water according to the instructions on the package. Drain the cod and cut the fillets in half.

Light a fire and wait until the flames are out and the wood or charcoal is glowing. Place the potatoes and the onions on a fine-meshed grill. Add the cod and the garlic cloves. After 15 minutes turn the potatoes over with tongs (do not turn the cod – it might fall apart) and cook until all the ingredients are tender, about 20–30 minutes.

Place all the ingredients on a warm platter and pass it around with the cruets of oil and vinegar, the salt shaker and the pepper mill. Each person will peel his or her potato and garlic clove, and the seasoning will be done individually.

Serve with a cool rosé and a *Salade Mesclun* (p. 69) or *Salade Amère* (p. 57).

Moules aux Épinards
Baked mussels filled with spinach and mushrooms

Delicious and quite dressy as a first course. If it is your main course, double the proportions.

For 6 people

900 g/2 lb (about 24) mussels
115 ml/4 fl oz dry white wine or
   water
1 tsp thyme
2 tbsp olive oil
1 large onion, chopped
12 mushrooms, chopped
1 tsp freshly grated nutmeg
2 tbsp chopped parsley

salt
freshly ground black pepper
285 g/10 oz frozen spinach or 570 g/
   1¼ lb fresh spinach, cooked,
   drained and chopped
2 tbsp breadcrumbs (preferably
   home-made)
lemon juice

Scrub the mussels and remove the beards. Soak them in cold water for 10 minutes, then discard all those that are opened or too heavy. Place the mussels in a large saucepan with the wine or water and thyme. Cover and cook for 5 minutes, or until the shells have opened. Cool. Discard half of the shell of each mussel.

Preheat oven to 190°C/375°F/Gas Mark 5. Heat 1 tablespoon of the oil in a heavy-bottomed saucepan. Add the onion and mushrooms. Cook for 5 minutes, add the nutmeg, parsley, salt and pepper, and cook for 5 more minutes. Check to see if the seasoning is right. Add the spinach and remove from heat.

If the mussels are unusually large, cut them into two or three pieces with kitchen scissors. Put a mussel or a piece of mussel in each shell and spoon the spinach stuffing over it, then smooth the top with your fingers. Sprinkle breadcrumbs and a little olive oil on each. Arrange the stuffed mussel shells on a large baking dish with

115 ml/4 fl oz of water at the bottom (to prevent sticking), and bake for 15 minutes. Sprinkle with lemon juice just before serving.

Note: Some people add 2 eggs to the stuffing to bind it, but I prefer the looser version given here.

Moules de Pêcheurs
Steamed mussels with mayonnaise and mustard, served cold

This is a tart and invigorating dish. It can be prepared in advance, and is dressy enough to be either the first course of an elegant dinner or the main attraction of a lunch. Serve with a crisp white wine.

For 6 people

2.25 kg/5 lb mussels (about 60 mussels)
2 large onions, chopped
5 tbsp water
about 1 tsp salt
2 garlic cloves, chopped
freshly ground black pepper

1 egg yolk
170 ml/6 fl oz oil (half olive oil, half peanut oil)
1 tbsp Dijon mustard
juice of half a lemon
20 g/¾ oz finely chopped Italian parsley

Scrub the mussels under cold water with a stiff brush and remove the beards. Let the mussels stand for 10 minutes in cold water and discard the mussels that either have open shells or are very heavy.

Put the onions in a large frying-pan with the water, salt, garlic and pepper. Boil, covered, for 10 minutes. Add the mussels and cook, covered, for 4 minutes, stirring occasionally. Remove the mussels with a slotted spoon and discard the shells. Strain the liquid through a piece of cheesecloth spread over a sieve.

Prepare the sauce with the egg yolk, oil, mustard and lemon juice (for instructions, see *Mayonnaise*, p. 77). Add almost all the parsley, then slowly stir in 2–3 tablespoons of the mussel broth. Pour the sauce over the mussels, sprinkle with the remaining parsley and chill.

Nu et Cru

Sliced raw fish with lemon and parsley

This fascinating dish is one of the quickest and simplest to prepare. It can be served as an hors-d'oeuvre, but, if you double the proportions, it can be the main part of a summer meal, followed by a vegetable dish and a light dessert. Prepare it the day before, then chill it. It needs no last-minute preparation and will be ready to serve when you need it.

For 6 people

1 900-g/2-lb whiting, filleted	2 tbsp chopped chives
salt	freshly ground white pepper
juice of 2 lemons	2 tbsp olive oil
3 tbsp chopped parsley	2 tbsp chopped capers

Skin the fillets and dry them with a kitchen towel. With a sharp knife, cut them into 6-mm/¼-in strips. Put them on a plate and cover with salt. Cover and refrigerate overnight. The next day, taste a little of the fish and if it is too salty, rinse it under cold water. Dry with kitchen towels and place on a plate. Sprinkle with lemon juice, parsley, chives, pepper and olive oil. Cover with cling film and chill for about 4 hours.

Check the seasoning. Add pepper if needed, and sprinkle with capers.

Omelette de Moules

Mussel omelette

One of the lightest and tastiest luncheon dishes, it is also one of the easiest to prepare. Served with a tossed salad and followed by a light dessert, it makes for a lively and inexpensive meal you can prepare all year round.

For 6 people

900 g/2 lb mussels	salt
8 eggs	freshly ground pepper
2 tbsp chopped parsley	2 tbsp olive oil

Scrub the mussels and remove the beards with your fingers. Place the mussels in a bowl of cold water for 10 minutes. Discard all the mussels that have opened and place the rest in a heavy-bottomed saucepan in 5 tablespoons of water. Cover and cook for about 5 minutes, tossing once. Remove from heat and let cool. Discard the shells and place the mussels in a bowl. With a pair of kitchen scissors, cut each mussel into two or three pieces.

Beat the eggs in a large bowl. Add the mussels, parsley, salt and pepper.

Heat the olive oil in a frying-pan. Add the omelette mixture and cook for a few minutes, shaking gently. Slide the omelette on to a warm dish and sprinkle with a little olive oil.

Poisson à la Chartreuse
Baked fish and vegetables in white wine

This is a delicious way to cook a strong fishy fish (such as fresh tuna or cod) – a variation on a recipe created by the monks of La Grande Chartreuse. Fresh red tuna is not always easy to find, but swordfish, cod and halibut are usually available and lend themselves to this preparation. Serve this with a light tossed salad and a dry white wine.

For 6 people

1.25 kg/3 lb fresh red tuna (or halibut, cod or swordfish), cut in a thick slice as for a fish steak	2 onions, sliced thin
	freshly ground black pepper
	3 garlic cloves, finely chopped
boiling water to cover	½ tsp fennel seed
salt	200 g/7 oz sorrel leaves, chopped (optional)
1 lemon, cut in half	
12 anchovy fillets, cut in half	4 leaves round or cos lettuce, blanched and cut in strips
3 tbsp olive oil	
2 carrots, sliced thin	225 ml/8 fl oz dry white wine

Blanch the slice of tuna in a saucepan of boiling water with salt and the lemon halves for 5 minutes and drain it. Because the fish has been cut crosswise, the flesh will have concentric rings. Make small cuts between these rings with a knife and insert the anchovies.

You can prepare this much in advance. Cover with cling film and refrigerate until ready to cook. (The carrots, onions and blanched lettuce can also be cut and kept covered and refrigerated.)

Heat the olive oil in a heavy-bottomed pan and add the carrots and onions. Lay the fish on them, sprinkle with salt and pepper, and cook over medium heat for 10 minutes. Gently turn the fish over with two spatulas. Add the garlic and fennel seed. Cover with the sorrel and lettuce leaves and simmer for 10 minutes more. Add the wine and cook over low heat for 20–30 minutes. Check the seasoning.

Place the fish in the centre of a warm platter. Pile the carrots and onions at one end of the dish, the sorrel at the other end and lettuce along the sides. Pour the juices over the fish and vegetables and season again with a little salt and pepper.

Poisson aux Champignons

Baked fish and mushrooms in white wine

This delectable, light dish is very easy to prepare. The delicate, subtly flavoured sauce is thickened only by the cooked onions, so make sure you mince or grate them very fine.

I like to serve this dish by itself, followed by a green tossed salad. But if you want a more substantial meal, *Courgettes Râpées* (p. 165) or *Riz aux Herbes* (p. 206) are good accompaniments.

Choose a large, firm fillet of bass, red snapper, fresh cod, haddock or monkfish. This dish is highly seasoned but not rich, and the lettuce or sorrel infuses the fish with moisture and flavour.

For 6 people

1.8 kg/4 lb fish fillets or trimmed slices	900 g/2 lb fresh mushrooms, sliced 6 mm/1¼ in thick
freshly ground white pepper	salt
1 tbsp savory	225 ml/8 fl oz dry white wine
3 tbsp oil (half olive and half peanut oil)	3 lettuce leaves (round, Batavian endive or iceberg) or chopped sorrel leaves*
1 tbsp cognac (optional)	
450 g/1 lb white or yellow onions, grated or finely chopped	220 g/7 oz sprigs of parsley

Dry the fillets with kitchen towels. Sprinkle with pepper and savory and set aside. Heat 2 tablespoons of the olive oil in a baking dish that covers two burners on the cooker. If you use a very delicate fish, you may prefer to bake it in the oven at 190°C/375°F/ Gas Mark 5 for about 40 minutes instead of cooking it like this. Add the fish and sauté for 2 minutes. Turn over gently with two spatulas and cook for 5 minutes. Remove from the stove. Add cognac, if you have it on hand, and light it. Set aside.

Heat 1 tablespoon of the olive oil in a heavy-bottomed frying-pan. Add the mushrooms and onions and sauté for 10 minutes. When the vegetables are limp, add salt, pepper and the wine and continue cooking. Gently lift the fish on to a platter. Add its juices to the onion–mushroom mixture. Wash and oil the baking dish and place half of the mixture in it. Gently lay the fish on this bed and cover with the rest of the mixture. Spread the lettuce leaves (or sorrel sautéd in 1 tablespoon olive oil) on top and cook over a low heat for 40 minutes. (When you can easily prick a needle through to the bone, it is done.) Remove the lettuce leaves.

Sprinkle the fish with salt and pepper and serve surrounded with sprigs of parsley on a large warm platter.

* If you have neither of these on hand, use aluminium foil instead.

Poisson au Court Bouillon
Cold poached fish

This is served throughout the South of France in the summertime. It makes a superb buffet dish surrounded by colourful vegetables and a variety of cold sauces. The best fish for this dish are the large, firm kinds, such as red snapper, striped or sea bass, whiting and salmon.

For 6 people

Court Bouillon (p. 92)
1 2.5-kg/5-lb fish (people tend to
    eat more when it's cold)
white wine or water if needed
salt
freshly ground white pepper
2 hard-boiled eggs, sliced
    lengthways
10 cherry tomatoes

8 sprigs rocket or watercress or
    basil
2 small bunches Italian parsley
2 lemons, sliced
8 black olives
2 tbsp capers
1 bowl of each sauce: *Rouille*
    (p. 84), *Aïoli* (p. 71), *Pistou*
    (p. 81), *Sauce Verte* (p. 86)

Prepare the *court bouillon* (this takes at least 2 hours).

Clean the fish and lay it on the cheesecloth in a pan with sides as high as the fish is thick. Be sure the cloth hangs over the sides so you can pick up the fish when it's ready. Cover the fish with *court bouillon* (if there isn't enough, add white wine or water). Fold the edges of the cloth over the fish. Simmer on top of the cooker for 45 minutes. (A rule of thumb is 10 minutes per 25 mm/1 in of the measurement across the widest part of the fish.)

Let the liquid cool. Gently remove the fish with two spatulas, using the cloth to hold it together, and let it drain on a platter. Remove the cloth and peel off the visible skin. Blot the fish with a tea-towel and sprinkle with salt and pepper.

Arrange the eggs, tomatoes and rocket or watercress or basil to surround the fish. Decorate the head with bunches of parsley on each side and place lemon slices, olives and capers on top of the fish.

Serve at room temperature or chilled. Offer a variety of sauces; the fish will seem to be several different dishes.

Poisson en Papillotte
Baked fish with shallots

You may use any large, firm fish for this dish: red snapper, bass, whiting or cod. The lettuce leaves will keep it moist during the baking. You may serve this with *Céleri Paysanne* (p. 163), *Févettes à la Verdure* (p. 171), *Riz aux Herbes* (p. 206) or *Pommes de Terre aux Herbes* (p. 183).

For 6 people

2 tbsp white or red wine vinegar
140 g/5 oz shallots, finely chopped
1 2.25-kg/5-lb bass
salt
freshly ground black pepper
2 tsp thyme

1 tbsp olive oil
1 bay leaf, cut in half
4 lettuce leaves (round, Batavian
    endive or iceberg)
3 tbsp chopped Italian parsley

Heat the vinegar in a frying-pan and cook the shallots gently for 5 minutes, or until soft.

Preheat oven to 180°C/350°F/Gas Mark 4.

Clean and dry the fish. Sprinkle salt, pepper and thyme inside and outside. Spread the shallots and vinegar inside the fish and rub the outside with olive oil. Place the bay leaf on top and cover with lettuce leaves. Wrap in aluminium foil and seal the folded edges. Put in a large baking dish and bake for 40 minutes. Remove the foil and lettuce, sprinkle the parsley on top and serve.

Poisson Mariné
Cold grilled fish marinated with vegetables

This is a delectable way to serve fish in summer – perfect for a buffet or a luncheon, followed by a tossed lettuce salad and a dessert. The fish needs to marinate for five days but is otherwise very easy to prepare and none of the ingredients are exotic. Offer a cool crisp white wine with this.

For 6 people

6 small fish (sardines, bass or whiting) or 1 large 2.25-kg/5-lb fish (whiting or red snapper)	1 celery stalk, chopped
	5 tbsp finely chopped parsley
	1 whole clove
salt	1 tsp thyme
900 ml/1⅗ pt wine vinegar	3 bay leaves
1 large onion, chopped	freshly ground pepper
1 carrot, chopped	4 tbsp olive oil
2 shallots or 2 small white onions	2 lemons, sliced

Fillet the fish and rinse and dry them. Sprinkle heavily with salt and cover with cling film. Refrigerate for 3 hours.

Meanwhile, prepare the marinade. Heat the vinegar in a heavy-bottomed pan and add the onion, carrot, shallots, celery stalk, 3 tablespoons of the parsley, clove, thyme, bay leaves and pepper. Bring to a boil and simmer for 30 minutes. Remove from heat and let it cool.

Preheat the grill. Rub the fillets with a kitchen towel to remove the excess salt. Place under the grill for 3 minutes on each side. Remove the skin with a sharp knife and place the fillets side by side in a shallow dish. Pour the cold marinade over them, cover with cling film and refrigerate.

After three days, discard the marinade and cover the fillets with olive oil. Leave them, covered with cling film, two days longer in the refrigerator.

Using two spatulas, place the fish on a platter. Sprinkle 2 tablespoons of parsley on top and garnish with slices of lemon before serving.

Poisson en Raïto

Fish stewed in a vegetable and red wine sauce

The preparation *en raïto* means the fish is first fried in a little olive oil, then slowly cooked in a sauce consisting of red wine (or red vermouth), tomatoes and herbs. You can use a variety of fish for this, but make sure all skin is removed and the fillets are trimmed and completely boneless when you add them to the sauce: *raïto* is thick and will camouflage any bones, and you don't want any unpleasant surprises as you bite into the fish.

You can serve this substantial dish with *Fenouil Braisé* (p. 169), *Gnocchi* (p. 196), *Tout-Nus* (p. 207) or *Riz aux Herbes* (p. 206), along with a watercress or chicory salad and a full-bodied red wine.

For 6 people

6 medium-sized whiting or mullet, filleted, or 1 1.25-kg/3-lb piece of halibut, fresh cod or haddock, cut in a slice 35 mm/1½ in thick
2 tsp thyme
4 tbsp olive oil
3 large onions, chopped
450 ml/16 fl oz red wine
4 tomatoes, peeled and quartered, or 285 g/10 oz canned, quartered

6 garlic cloves, peeled and crushed
3 bay leaves
2 tsp savory
salt
freshly ground black pepper
12 little black Niçois olives, unpitted, or 6 black oil-cured olives
55 g/2 oz capers
2 tbsp chopped parsley

Sprinkle the fish fillets or slices with 1 teaspoon of the thyme. Heat 3 tablespoons of the olive oil in a frying-pan and cook the fish 3 minutes on each side, turning delicately with a spatula. (Instead of frying, you can bake the fish in the oven at 180°C/350°F/Gas Mark 4 for 30 minutes.) Let it cool and then carefully remove the skin with a sharp knife.

Heat 2 tablespoons of the olive oil in a heavy-bottomed pan, add the onions and stir for 2 minutes. Add the wine and simmer for 10 minutes, then stir in the tomatoes, garlic, bay leaves, 1 teaspoon of the thyme, savory, salt and pepper. Cook, uncovered, for 30 minutes.

Purée the mixture through a Mouli mill into a bowl. Put half of the purée in a wide pan or baking dish. Place the fish on it, sprinkle with salt and pepper, and cover with the rest of the purée. Cook, uncovered, over medium heat on top of the cooker for 20 minutes.

Add the olives and capers, check the seasoning, and cook for 5 minutes. Transfer to a warm serving dish and sprinkle with parsley.

Poulpe Provençale
Octopus cooked in a tomato and white wine sauce

Along the Mediterranean coast and in the Orient octopus and squid are considered delicacies. It would surprise many to know that much of the canned 'lobster' sold in France is rumoured to be octopus. In any case, *le homard du pauvre* is simply delicious. It should be served with a robust dry white wine.

For 6 people

900 g/2lb fresh octopus	2 garlic cloves, crushed
2.7 l/4¾ pt water	1 tsp thyme
3 tbsp olive oil	225 ml/8 fl oz dry white wine
70 ml/2½fl oz cognac	salt
2 medium-sized onions, chopped	freshly ground black pepper
5 large tomatoes, chopped	2 tbsp chopped parsley
bouquet garni (p. 14)	1 garlic clove, finely chopped
a pinch of Spanish saffron (not the powdered kind) or curry powder	

Wash the octopus under running water. Make sure the fishmonger has removed the ends of the tentacles, eyes, ink bag and intestines. Soak the octopus for 3 hours in cold water, changing the water twice.

Bring the water to a boil in a large saucepan and scald the octopus in it three times, counting to three each time. Then cut the octopus into 35-mm/1½-in cubes with a large knife or kitchen scissors and dry thoroughly.

Heat 2 tablespoons of the olive oil in a heavy frying-pan, add the octopus and toss for a few minutes. Reduce the heat, cover and simmer slowly for 30 minutes. Put the octopus in a bowl.

Pour the cognac into the frying-pan, swishing it round, and scrape the bottom of the pan. Pour this liquid over the octopus in the bowl. Add the remaining olive oil to the frying-pan and gently cook the onions and tomatoes for 15 minutes. Add the octopus with its juice, the bouquet garni, saffron (or curry powder), crushed garlic, thyme, wine, salt and pepper. Simmer, covered, for 1 hour, or until tender. Remove the octopus from the sauce.

Sprinkle the octopus with parsley and finely chopped garlic and put it in the centre of a crown of rice. Serve the sauce separately in a bowl.

Sardines Grillées
Grilled fresh sardines with parsley and garlic

This is an incredibly easy way to prepare fresh sardines, and to my taste one of the best. It will take about 10 minutes from start to finish. If you cannot grill them over an open fire, a regular grill will do. Serve this alone as an hors-d'oeuvre or with *Salade Mesclun* (p. 69) or *Salade Amère* (p. 57) and *Riz au Safran* (p. 207).

For 6 people

24 small sardines, cleaned but left whole with their heads	freshly ground pepper
	3 tbsp finely chopped parsley
salt	3 garlic cloves, finely chopped
2 tbsp flour	1 tbsp olive oil
juice of 2 lemons	

Preheat the grill. Rinse and dry the sardines between kitchen towels and sprinkle them with salt and flour. Place them in a shallow baking dish and put them 50 mm/2 in from the grill flame for 2 minutes. Using two spatulas, turn them over on the other side. If you feel they are too small and fragile to turn over, let them cook 2 minutes longer on the same side.

Using two spatulas, carefully place the sardines on a warm platter. Sprinkle them with lemon juice, salt, pepper, parsley, garlic and olive oil and serve.

Variation
If the sardines are large, you may want to treat them more elaborately. Stuff them with chopped cooked spinach and lay them on a gratin dish. Sprinkle with breadcrumbs and a little oil and grill for 5 minutes. Sprinkle with lemon juice before serving.

Suppions aux Légumes
Squid with mushrooms and peppers

Cooked squid is light and tender. It acquires an entirely new flavour when simmered with vegetables and white wine. Served with lettuce, bread and cheese, this dish makes a rich meal. It reheats beautifully.

For 6 people

900 g/2 lb squid
2 tbsp olive oil
4 medium-sized onions, chopped
450 g/1 lb mushrooms, thinly sliced
2 yellow or red bell peppers, seeded and cut into 12-mm-/½-in-thick strips

3 garlic cloves, peeled and crushed
1 bay leaf
1 tsp thyme
225–450 ml/8–16 fl oz dry white wine
salt
freshly ground black pepper
3 tbsp chopped Italian parsley

Wash and dry the squid. Cut it into 12-mm/½-in slices with heavy kitchen scissors. Heat the olive oil in a large frying-pan. Sauté the onions, mushrooms and peppers, and add the garlic, bay leaf, thyme, wine, salt and pepper. Simmer, uncovered, for 40 minutes, adding more wine if the vegetable mixture becomes too thick. Remove the bay leaf. Sprinkle with parsley and serve.

Suppions Farcis
Squid stuffed with spinach and cheese and simmered in wine

Filled with a delicate mixture of spinach, cheese and herbs and simmered in a tomato and wine sauce, squid makes not only a light and tasty dish but an inexpensive one as well.

Don't choose the smallest squid, as they would take too long to fill. Serve with *Riz aux Herbes* (p. 206), a green tossed salad and a dry white wine.

For 6 people:

········ Squid and Stuffing ········

1.25 kg/3 lb rather large squid, cleaned	freshly ground pepper
2 tbsp olive oil	2 egg yolks
2 medium-sized onions, chopped	55 g/2 oz grated Gruyère or Parmesan cheese
1 tsp savory	570 g/20 oz frozen spinach, cooked, drained and chopped
1 tsp freshly grated nutmeg	
salt	

Wash the squid and drain on kitchen towels. Cut off the tentacles (reserve the bodies) and chop them with kitchen scissors. Put them in a frying-pan, add the olive oil, onions, savory, nutmeg, salt and pepper, and cook slowly for 10 minutes. In a large bowl, beat the egg yolks, and add the cheese, spinach, tentacles and the cooked onions. Check the seasoning and set aside.

Put some stuffing on each squid and close with a cocktail stick or tie with string. (Cocktails sticks are easier to remove than string, but choose whichever you find more convenient.) The squid will shrink as they cook, so they must not be too full.

You can prepare this much in advance. Cover with cling film and set aside in the refrigerator until ready to use.

················ Sauce ················

2 tbsp olive oil	2 tsp savory
3 medium-sized onions, chopped	1 tsp thyme
4 fresh tomatoes or 365 g/13 oz canned, chopped	½ tsp Spanish saffron, crumbled
225 ml/8 fl oz dry white wine	about 1 tsp salt
2 bay leaves	freshly ground pepper
	3 tbsp chopped parsley

Heat the olive oil in a *doufeu* or a large cast-iron saucepan, then add the stuffed squid. Cook for 5 minutes over medium heat, reduce the heat and turn the squid over with a pair of tongs. Add the onions, tomatoes, wine, bay leaves, savory, thyme, saffron, salt and pepper. Simmer, covered, for 20 minutes, then remove the cover and cook for 35 minutes. Check the seasonings (this dish must be highly seasoned). Add more saffron, salt and pepper, if necessary. Remove the bay leaves.

Serve in a warm shallow dish. Protect your hand with a tea-towel or an oven mitt and remove the cocktail sticks or string. Sprinkle with parsley. If some of the stuffing escapes into the sauce, put the sauce through a sieve before pouring over the squid.

Note: Rice is sometimes added to the filling for a more substantial dish.

If you have left-over filling, you can use it for *Tout-Nus* (p. 207) or *Tian d'Épinards* (p. 188), or to replace the chicken liver in *Caillettes de Nice* (p. 131).

Suppions à la Niçoise
Squid simmered in tomatoes and white wine

Squid are excellent served with *Riz au Safran* (p. 207), *Pâtes aux Oeufs* (p. 200), *Pâtes à la Verdure* (p. 202) or as a hot first course with French bread and a green tossed salad.

This dish is also good served cold as a first course or as part of a buffet, and can be successfully reheated by adding a tablespoon of olive oil before serving.

For 6 people

900 g/2 lb squid (the smaller the better)
3 tbsp olive oil
2 large onions, finely chopped
3 tomatoes (fresh or canned), quartered
2 garlic cloves, peeled and crushed
225 ml/8 fl oz dry white wine
bouquet garni (p. 14)

1 bay leaf
salt
freshly ground black pepper
1 tsp Spanish saffron (do not use the powdered kind)
85 g/3 oz small black olives or oil-cured large
3 tbsp chopped Italian parsley

Rinse the squid in cold water and pat dry. Cut them into 12-mm/½-in slices with kitchen scissors.

Heat 2 tablespoons of the olive oil in a large frying-pan and sauté the pieces of squid for 5 minutes, turning them frequently. Remove them with a slotted spoon and set aside in a bowl. Add the remaining olive oil and cook the onions and tomatoes slowly for 10 minutes. Put the squid back in and cook for another 5 minutes. Add the garlic, wine, bouquet garni, bay leaf, salt, pepper and saffron (crush it between your fingers as you sprinkle it on). Cover and simmer over low heat for 40–45 minutes. Add the olives and cook, uncovered, for 10–15 minutes. Check the seasoning and discard the bay leaf. The squid should be tender and moist.

Place the squid on a warm dish and sprinkle with parsley before serving.

Thon Provençale
Fresh red tuna cooked with vegetables and white wine

In this hearty dish the tuna is first marinated in vinegar, then simmered with wine and vegetables until it has absorbed all their flavour. If tuna is not available you can substitute swordfish or halibut. Serve with *Riz aux Herbes* (p. 206) or, if you want some green vegetables with it, with *Épinards aux Pignons* (p. 167) or *Courgettes Râpées* (p. 165).

For 6 people

1 1.25-kg/3-lb piece fresh red tuna, cut 35 mm/1½ in thick and skinned
115 ml/4 fl oz red wine vinegar
2 tbsp olive oil
2 garlic cloves, peeled and crushed
2 large onions, sliced
3 carrots, sliced
2 tomatoes, quartered, or 140 g/ 5 oz canned, drained

salt
freshly ground pepper
3 bay leaves
1 lemon, sliced
170 ml/6 fl oz dry white wine (add more if necessary)
20 g/¾ oz finely chopped Italian parsley or basil

Marinate the fish in the vinegar for 2 hours, adding enough cold water to cover it.

Put the olive oil in a large shallow baking dish. Add the garlic, onions, carrots and tomatoes and lay the tuna on top. Sprinkle with salt and pepper and arrange the bay leaves and lemon slices on top of the fish. Add the wine.

Place the baking dish over two burners on top of the cooker and simmer, uncovered, over low heat for 40 minutes (30 minutes for swordfish and halibut) or bake at 180°C/350°F/Gas Mark 4 for 40 minutes.

Turn the slices of fish over with two spatulas. Cover and simmer for another 20–30 minutes (swordfish and halibut require less time, so start checking after the first 10 minutes). If the tuna absorbs all the liquid before the end of the cooking time, add more wine at any point to keep it from going dry.

Remove the bay leaves and lemon slices. Purée the vegetables through a Mouli food mill. Place the fish on a warm serving platter and spread the vegetable purée over it. Sprinkle with parsley or basil and serve.

Les Viandes

Meats

Some people from northern France find Nice's cooking to have 'not enough meat and too many bones', but the frugality of this cuisine is balanced by the imagination with which it deals with inexpensive cuts of meat. Since meat was never plentiful in the South, every part of the animal is treated with respect.

Choose your meat carefully: beef should be bright red; lamb, dark pink. Trim it well and use seasonings with care. The heady *boeuf à la niçoise*, the vigorous *gardiane*, the pungent *poulet en saupiquet* rely on inexpensive materials – but God is in the details.

Most of the meat recipes here are better the next day. Many freeze well and left-over dishes are the basis for delicious preparations such as *boeuf mironton, tians, salade de riz variée, farcis, ravioli à la niçoise, capoun*, so be generous with your proportions.

Beef: *le boeuf*

In Provence in the past, beef was a rare commodity because the land was better suited to raising goats and sheep – animals that could climb the steep hills and manage on any grass they could find. So even today beef is seldom eaten rare in large hunks; the grilled steaks covered with herbs and barbecued are newcomers to the repertory of southern French cooking.

Beef is mostly prepared *mijoté*, carefully simmered with onions, carrots, orange rind and herbs, and moistened with wine.

Chicken: *le poulet*
We usually sauté chicken in olive oil, deglaze it with white wine or tomato sauce, then simmer it with herbs or vegetables and garlic. Sometimes after I have rinsed and dried the chicken, I let it marinate in oil and herbs so the flavour can penetrate the meat before it is cooked.

Lamb: *l'agneau*
This meat is widely used simmered with thyme, rosemary, garlic and white wine. The leg or shoulder is usually roasted with slivers of garlic or anchovies inserted in it and sprinkled with olive oil. Or it may be stuffed with red tuna, hard-boiled eggs and herbs, and served with a purée of garlic.

Pork: *le porc*
Because British pork is less flavourful than its French counterpart, it will benefit from the Provençal use of sage, fennel and anise seed, white wine and vinegar. Trim it carefully so you start with a reasonably lean meat.

Agneau à la Niçoise
Lamb and vegetables simmered in white wine and herbs

Curiously enough, garlic – often used with lamb – is not an ingredient in this delicate stew. The turnips enhance the flavour of the lamb and the fresh baby broad beans add a substantial texture. Serve with a chilled dry white wine. You may like this with *Polente* (p. 203), *Gnocchi* (p. 196), *Riz aux Herbes* (p. 206); or a *Purée de Légumes* (p. 184), but it is a very complete dish in itself.

For 6 people

1.8 kg/4 lb lamb shoulder or leg, cut into 35-mm/1½-in cubes	2 onions, sliced
1 tsp rosemary	2 carrots, sliced
1 tsp thyme	3 turnips, quartered
2 tsp salt	2 tomatoes, chopped, or 140 g/5 oz canned tomatoes
freshly ground black pepper	3 celery stalks, chopped
510 g/18 oz baby broad beans (fresh or frozen)	2 bay leaves
2 tbsp olive oil	450 ml/16 fl oz dry white wine
85 g/3 oz chopped lean streaky bacon	3 tbsp finely chopped fresh parsley or mint

Dry the lamb with a kitchen towel and sprinkle with rosemary, thyme, salt and pepper. (If you add a few bones to the pot, the dish will be less elegant but even tastier.) Blanch fresh or frozen broad beans for 5 minutes and drain. Set aside.

Heat the oil in a *doufeu* or cast-iron saucepan and add the bacon. Reduce the heat and add the lamb. Sauté for a few minutes until the lamb is browned on all sides, then add the onions, carrots, turnips, tomatoes, celery and bay leaves. Cook, stirring well, for 5 minutes. Add the wine, cover and cook over a low heat for 1 hour or until the lamb is tender. Add the beans and cook uncovered for 5 minutes more.

Sprinkle with the parsley or mint and serve in a preheated shallow dish.

Boeuf Mironton *
Boiled beef baked in vinegar and caper sauce

This crisp, golden gratin is one of the favourite Niçois ways to use left-over beef. In Provence they use what is left of their *pot-au-feu*.

Serve with a chilled dry white wine or a rosé, since the dish is not as strong as its ingredients may suggest.

---

* The word *mironton* is thought to have originated in the eighteenth century and the more commonly used variant *miroton* is a corruption.

For 6 people

2 tbsp olive oil

2 onions, finely chopped

2 tomatoes, chopped, or 140 g/5 oz
  canned, drained

2 tbsp beef stock or water

1 tsp red wine vinegar

1 garlic clove, peeled and crushed

1 bay leaf

½–1 tsp freshly grated nutmeg

4 tbsp chopped parsley

salt

freshly ground black pepper

6–8 slices or 510 g/18 oz chopped
  cooked beef

2 tsp capers

20 g/¾ oz breadcrumbs, preferably
  home-made

Preheat the oven to 190°C/375°F/Gas Mark 5. Oil a baking dish.

Gently heat 1 tablespoon of the olive oil in a cast-iron frying-pan and cook the onions over low heat for about 5 minutes. Add the tomatoes and cook 5 minutes more. With a wooden spoon, stir in the beef stock and vinegar to make a smooth sauce. Add the garlic, bay leaf, nutmeg, parsley, salt and pepper. Simmer, uncovered, for 10 minutes.

Remove the bay leaf and pour half of the sauce into the oiled baking dish. Put the slices of beef and the capers on the sauce and pour the rest of it over them. Sprinkle with breadcrumbs and the remaining olive oil. Bake 30 minutes.

Variation

If you have any of this dish left over, you can prepare *croquettes de boeuf ménagère*. Add 3 potatoes, boiled and mashed, and 1 egg to 170 g/ 6 oz of the beef mixture. Mix well with your hands, check the seasoning, and make little balls the size of an egg. Roll the balls in flour and fry in oil. Serve with *Coulis* (p. 74).

Boeuf à la Niçoise
Marinated beef simmered with tomatoes, wine and spices

Although this takes two days to prepare, it is well worth the effort. This Niçois version of the classic *boeuf bourguignon* is superb. The orange rind, herbs, garlic and olives give it a fresh and distinctive flavour. Be generous with your proportions because this dish is not only delicious the day after, but its left-overs are the basis for *Ravioli à la Niçoise* (p. 204).

Serve this with *Pâtes aux Oeufs* (p. 200), *Gnocchi* (p. 196) or plain boiled potatoes – nothing too emphatic. If it is served cold, a perfect accompaniment would be *Salade Verte* (p. 68).

For 6 people

1 1.25–1.8-kg/3–4-lb boneless rump or round of beef
salt
4 tbsp olive oil
3 large onions, chopped
1 carrot, sliced
1 celery stalk, chopped
680 ml/1⅕ pt red wine
1 garlic clove, peeled
bouquet garni (p. 14)
freshly ground black pepper
1 tbsp olive oil
85 g/3 oz diced lean streaky bacon
2 garlic cloves, peeled and crushed

6 small white onions, peeled
2 tomatoes, chopped
1 small piece pork rind
2 tsp thyme
1 whole clove
rind of 1 small orange (or 4 50-mm/2-in pieces of rind)
6 carrots, sliced
85 g/3 oz small Niçois black olives or pitted oil-cured olives
2 tbsp finely chopped parsley
115 g/4 oz freshly grated Parmesan or Gruyère cheese

Trim the beef to remove fat and gristle and cut into 50-mm/2-in cubes. Rub the beef with 1 teaspoon of salt and set aside in a large bowl.

Heat 3 tablespoons of the olive oil in a large cast-iron frying-pan. Add the chopped onions, carrot and celery and sauté gently for 5 minutes. Stir in the wine, garlic clove, bouquet garni, salt and pepper and cook for 20 minutes. Let the liquid cool before pouring it over the meat. Cover the marinade and refrigerate overnight.

The next day, remove the meat from the marinade with a slotted spoon and dry with kitchen towels.

Heat the remaining olive oil in a *doufeu* or cast-iron saucepan. Sauté the bacon gently for 5 minutes, add the beef cubes and cook for 10 minutes, using tongs to turn them so that they brown evenly on all sides. Add the crushed garlic and cook for 10 minutes. Add the small white onions, tomatoes, pork rind, thyme, clove, orange rind, salt and pepper, and the marinade. Scrape the bottom of the pan with a spoon, reduce the heat and simmer, covered, for 2 hours. Then add the carrots and cook for 30 minutes (do not overcook – the carrots should be firm).

Refrigerate for 24 hours and then remove the fat, which will look like a sheet of wax. Discard the bouquet garni and the pork and orange rinds. Add the black olives and sprinkle with parsley and cheese. Serve with a red Burgundy.

Brochettes de Nice
Lamb heart and kidney skewered with vegetables

Lamb kidneys are not difficult to find, but hearts may have to be specially ordered at your butcher. Both kidney and heart freeze well. This recipe also works well with shoulder of lamb, but it won't be as interesting.

Serve with *Pommes de Terre à l'Ail* (p. 183), *Riz aux Herbes* (p. 206), *Tomates Provençale* (p. 189) and a green tossed salad.

For 6 people

6 lamb kidneys, cut in 50-mm/2-in cubes	6 very firm tomatoes, quartered
3 lamb hearts, cut in 50-mm/2-in cubes	3 large green bell peppers, cut in 50-mm/2-in pieces
85 g/3 oz lean streaky bacon, cut in 25-mm/1-in squares	3 tsp dried rosemary
	2 tsp thyme
6 tiny white onions, peeled and cut in half	salt
	freshly ground black pepper
24 mushroom caps (save the stems for other use)	3 tbsp olive oil
	12 sprigs fresh rosemary (if available)

Place the kidneys, hearts, bacon and vegetables in a large bowl and sprinkle with dried rosemary, thyme, salt, pepper and olive oil. Marinate for at least 1 hour. If kept for several hours, cover with cling film and refrigerate until ready to cook.

Preheat the grill.

Using *flat* skewers (two for each brochette, to make sure the ingredients are securely held), string the brochettes, alternating meat and vegetables and placing sprigs of fresh rosemary in between if you have some. Preferably start and end with an onion half or a piece of green pepper. Place brochettes over a deep pan and grill for 5 minutes. Baste, turn on the other side, and grill for 15 minutes. Check the tenderness of the heart and kidney by piercing them with a fork, and cook for 5 minutes more if necessary.

Remove the brochettes from the grill. Pour the wine into the pan and scrape up the coagulated juices with a spoon. Pour into a saucepan and heat on top of the cooker for 2 minutes. Put the brochettes on a bed of watercress or parsley or on a bed of *Riz aux Herbes* (p. 206) and pour the juices over them. Sprinkle with salt and pepper just before serving.

Caillettes de Nice
Crisp spinach, chicken liver and rice balls

Caillette means little quail, and that is what these plump balls look like. The crispy *caillettes* are usually served warm at Christmas time and cold as an hors-d'oeuvre in summer. They are wrapped with caul, the veil-like membrane taken from the pig's abdomen. If caul is unavailable, use very thin strips of streaky bacon. *Caillettes* are especially popular with children and are perfect for a buffet.

For 6 people

680 g/1½ lb chicken livers
salt
freshly ground black pepper
2 tbsp unbleached flour
3 tbsp olive oil
1 onion, chopped
680 g/1½ lb lean fresh pork, chopped
140 g/5 oz cooked rice
20 g/¾ oz chopped parsley

570 g/1¼ lb frozen spinach, or 1.1 kg/2½ lb fresh spinach, cooked and chopped
2 garlic cloves, peeled and crushed
1 tsp thyme
2 eggs, slightly beaten
12 75 × 75-mm/3 × 3-in pieces of caul (or slices of streaky bacon)
6 leaves fresh sage

Sprinkle the livers with salt, pepper and flour and set aside. Heat 1 tablespoon of the olive oil in a large frying-pan and cook the onion for 10 minutes or until it is transparent. Remove with a slotted spoon and put into a bowl. Add 1 tablespoon of olive oil to the pan and sauté the chicken livers for 5 minutes, tossing with a wooden spoon. Remove from the pan and, when cool enough to handle, chop them with kitchen scissors and add to the onion. Sauté the chopped pork in the same frying-pan and add this to the bowl of sautéd onions.

Preheat the oven to 200°C/400°F/Gas Mark 6.

Mix the liver, onion, rice, parsley, pork, spinach, garlic, thyme, eggs, salt and pepper in a large bowl. With your hands, shape this mixture into balls about 35 mm/1½ in in diameter (the balls will shrink a little when they cook). Wrap each ball in caul (or streaky bacon) and place in an oiled baking dish. (You can keep the balls up to two days in the refrigerator.) Stick a sage leaf on top of each ball, sprinkle with the remaining olive oil and bake for 30 minutes. Serve hot or cold.

Variations

Instead of shaping it into balls, bake the mixture in a terrine for 45 minutes. As it cools, cover the entire surface with a piece of foil-covered wood or cardboard, put something heavy on top and leave it for 3 hours to squeeze out the fat. Refrigerate. Slice the terrine holding a chopping board against the end so it can be cut without crumbling.

Another version of this dish, very popular near Grasse, is made with an equal amount of sliced pork liver and sliced pork lung, sprinkled with sage, chopped parsley, salt and pepper. Tight rolls are made of the liver and lung, then tied with string and cooked slowly in dry white wine. They are served warm or kept throughout the winter in a large jar covered with lard, to be eaten cold as an hors-d'oeuvre.

Canard comme à Nice
Stuffed duck roasted with tomato, white wine and olives

This is a wonderful way to give zest to duck. Serve with *Céleri Paysanne* (p. 163), *Tian de Navets Rosés* (p. 188), *Papeton d'Aubergines* (p. 181) or a *Purée de Légumes* (p. 184).

For 6–8 people

················ Stuffing ················

285 g/10 oz frozen spinach,
blanched, drained and chopped,
or 570 g/1¼ lb fresh spinach,
cooked, drained and chopped
140 g/5 oz cooked rice
20 g/¾ oz finely chopped parsley
2 garlic cloves, peeled and crushed
50 g/1¾ oz chopped chicken livers

2 duck livers, chopped
2 eggs, beaten
1 tsp savory
1 tsp thyme
2 bay leaves
salt
freshly ground black pepper

Combine all ingredients and set aside.

·········· Duck and Sauce ··········

2 1.8-kg/4-lb ducks
salt
freshly ground black pepper
2 tbsp olive oil
2 onions, finely chopped
4 tomatoes (fresh or canned),
quartered

225 ml/8 fl oz dry white wine
3 garlic cloves, peeled
2 tsp thyme
3 bay leaves
85 g/3 oz olives
6–8 sprigs parsley

Preheat oven to 230°C/450°F/Gas Mark 8. Pull out the loose fat inside the ducks. Dry the ducks carefully and season both inside and out with salt and pepper. Fill them with the stuffing and sew or skewer the skin over the opening. Truss the legs and wings, place in a roasting pan and prick them all over with a sharp fork to allow the fat to escape. Place the pan, uncovered, in the middle of the oven and cook for 30 minutes. Remove and discard all the fat. Return to the oven and lower the heat to 190°C/375°F/Gas Mark 5.

Meanwhile, heat the olive oil in a heavy-bottomed saucepan, add the onions and cook for 5 minutes. Add the tomatoes, half of the wine, the garlic cloves, thyme, bay leaves, salt and pepper. Cook, covered, for 20 minutes over low heat. Add the olives and set the sauce aside.

Again discard the fat in the pan and turn the ducks over on the other side. Pour the sauce over them and lower the heat to 180°C/ 350°F/Gas Mark 4. Cook for 50 minutes. (The entire cooking time is about 1¾–2 hours.)

Place the ducks on a warm platter. Add the remaining wine to the sauce in the pan and scrape up the bottom of the pan while cooking for 2 minutes over high heat.

To serve, scoop out the stuffing and mound it in the centre of a warm serving platter. Carve the ducks, arrange the pieces around the stuffing, and spoon the sauce over them. (There will be very little sauce, as the duck will have absorbed most of it while cooking.) Garnish with parsley.

Note: The ducks can be prepared in a slightly different way, which may be more convenient for you. Sprinkle them with salt and pepper, prick them all over with a fork, and roast at 190°C/375°F/ Gas Mark 5 for 1½ hours. After they are roasted, stuff them and refrigerate them, and the following day reheat with the sauce. The ducks will be drier but equally tasty.

Estouffade
Lamb and beef stew

This is a simple, delicious stew. It can be made *à la fortune du pot*, so meat proportions can vary according to what you have on hand. *Estouffade* means that all meats are smothered with herbs and tomatoes in a covered *doufeu*. In this unexpected combination all the ingredients complement each other. Marinate the meats overnight before cooking.

You can prepare this dish a day or so in advance, since it always seems to taste better when reheated. It also freezes superbly. Serve with *Pâtes aux Oeufs* (p. 200), *Pâtes à la Verdure* (p. 202),

Gnocchi (p. 196), *Févettes à la Verdure* (p. 171) or *Céleri Paysanne* (p. 163), along with a green salad (lettuce, watercress, chicory or rocket) and a hearty red wine.

For 6 people

680 g/1½ lb chuck or bottom round of beef, cut into 50-mm/2-in cubes, plus bones
680 g/1½ lb neck or shoulder of lamb, cut into 50-mm/2-in cubes
1 onion, quartered
115 ml/4 fl oz dry white wine
1 tbsp olive oil
2 bay leaves
2 tbsp unbleached flour
2 tbsp peanut oil
3 onions, finely chopped
85 g/3 oz chopped lean streaky bacon

1 tsp savory
bouquet garni (p. 14)
3 50-mm/2-in pieces orange rind
2 garlic cloves, finely chopped
225 ml/8 fl oz stock, water or white wine
salt
freshly ground black pepper
3 tomatoes, chopped, or 115 g/4 oz canned
85 g/3 oz small black olives from Nice or pitted oil-cured olives
2 tbsp finely chopped parsley

Put the beef and lamb in a large bowl, add the quartered onion, wine, olive oil and bay leaves. Marinate overnight.

Drain the beef and lamb and spread them out on kitchen towels to dry. Sprinkle with flour.

Heat the peanut oil in a *doufeu* or heavy-bottomed pan. Add the finely chopped onions, cook gently for 5 minutes, and remove with a slotted spoon. In the same pan, brown the meat on all sides, turning with tongs, and add the sautéd onions, bacon, savory, bouquet garni, orange rind, garlic and the marinade liquid. While stirring, scrape the bottom of the pan. Add stock or water or wine, salt and pepper, and bring to a boil. Reduce the heat and cook, covered, for 1½ hours, or until the meat is tender. Add the tomatoes and cook, covered, for 1 hour. Skim off as much fat as possible (or refrigerate overnight and lift off the hardened fat). Discard the bouquet garni and orange rind. Add the olives, sprinkle with parsley and serve.

Daube d'Avignon

Lamb, vegetable and herb stew

This hearty dish does not need an expensive cut of lamb or rare fresh vegetables, yet it is very special. It must marinate overnight before cooking. It freezes well and reheats beautifully, so make a generous amount. Serve with a fresh mixed green salad and a robust white wine.

For 6 people

1 1.8-kg/4-lb lamb shoulder, cut into 50-mm/2-in cubes	1 tsp salt
3 carrots, thickly sliced	freshly ground black pepper
3 onions, chopped	170 g/6 oz dried white haricot beans
5 tbsp olive oil	55 g/2 oz chopped lean streaky bacon
1 tbsp rosemary	3 garlic cloves, chopped
2 tsp thyme	450 ml/16 fl oz dry white wine
2 bay leaves	2 tbsp chopped parsley
3 50-mm/2-in pieces orange rind	

Place the lamb (and bones if you have them – they will give additional flavour), carrots, onions and the olive oil in a large bowl. Sprinkle with the rosemary, thyme, bay leaves, orange rind, salt and pepper and refrigerate overnight. Soak the beans overnight in 710 ml/1¼ pt of water.

The next day, cook the beans (see instructions on the package for cooking time) until tender. Heat 3 tablespoons of the marinade oil in a heavy-bottomed pan (preferably a *doufeu*). Add the bacon, half of the carrots and onions from the marinade, the garlic, and the lamb. Sprinkle again with salt and pepper and cover with the rest of the carrots and onions. Add the wine. Reduce the heat and simmer, covered, for 2 hours, or until very tender. Remove the bay leaves and orange rind. Add the beans and check the seasoning. Simmer for 5 minutes.

Serve in a warm shallow dish sprinkled with parsley.

Fausses Grives

Pork liver filled with juniper and garlic

This is delicious served with *Pommes de Terre aux Herbes* (p. 183) or *Purées de Légumes* (p. 184).

For 6 people

6 slices pork liver, cut 8 mm/⅓ in thick
2 tsp juniper berries, crushed
salt
freshly ground pepper
6 pieces of caul or thinly sliced streaky bacon

2 tbsp mixture of peanut and olive oil
6 garlic cloves, peeled
115 ml/4 fl oz dry white vermouth

Dry the liver with kitchen towels and sprinkle with juniper berries, salt and pepper. Roll up each slice, wrap with caul or bacon, and secure it with half a cocktail stick or tie with a piece of string.

Heat the oil in a heavy-bottomed pan. Add the liver rolls and garlic cloves and sauté for 2 minutes. Turn the rolls with tongs and reduce the heat. Sprinkle with salt and pepper, add the vermouth and cook, uncovered, for 30 minutes. Serve on a warm platter.

Gigot d'Agneau à l'Aillade

Leg of lamb with garlic sauce

This recipe embodies all the flavours of Provence. It can be served with haricot beans, red kidney beans, *Pâtes aux Oeufs* (p. 200), *Gnocchi* (p. 196), *Tomates Provençale* (p. 189), *Céleri Paysanne* (p. 163), *Févettes à l'Ail* (p. 170), *Fenouil Braisé* (p. 169), *Carottes Paysanne* (p. 162), *Épinards aux Pignons* (p. 167), *Pommes de Terre aux Herbes* (p. 183) or a crisp green salad. It is traditionally served at Easter with a green salad garnished with hard-boiled eggs and followed by little 'pâtés' of marrow of beef.

For 6 people

1 2.25-kg/5-lb leg of lamb	salt
6 garlic cloves, slivered	freshly ground black pepper
12 anchovy fillets, chopped	12 garlic cloves, peeled
3 tbsp olive oil	115 ml/4 fl oz dry white wine
1 tsp rosemary	2 tbsp chopped parsley or mint
1 tsp thyme	

Make slits in the lamb and insert a sliver of garlic and a piece of anchovy in each incision. Rub the lamb with 2 tablespoons of the olive oil, rosemary, thyme, salt and pepper. Let it stand for 1–2 hours.

Preheat the oven to 220°C/425°F/Gas Mark 7. Place the meat on a rack in a roasting pan and cook, uncovered, for 20 minutes. Reduce the heat to 180°C/350°F/Gas Mark 4 and cook for 40–45 minutes for medium-rare lamb.

Heat the remaining olive oil in an iron frying-pan and cook the garlic cloves slowly for about 10 minutes, or until they are soft (do not let the edges become crisp). Set aside in a small bowl.

Remove the lamb from the roasting pan. Pour the wine into the pan, scrape the bottom well and boil the wine over a high heat to reduce it. Add the garlic cloves to the reduced liquid. Mash well with a fork and add salt and pepper to taste.

Slice the lamb and sprinkle with pepper. Spoon the sauce over it and sprinkle with parsley or mint.

Note: Left-over lamb can be used to make Nice's shepherd's pie. Finely chop it, along with some parsley and garlic; cover with mashed potatoes, then sprinkle with Parmesan cheese and olive oil and bake for 15 minutes.

Gardiane
Lamb and potatoes stewed with garlic and orange rind

Orange rind, garlic and white wine enliven the flavour of this very simple stew. You can use a variety of cuts, but I find lamb shoulder the best. Serve with *Céleri Paysanne* (p. 163), *Fenouil Braisé* (p. 169) or a plain *Salade Amère* (p. 57) and a dry white wine, well chilled.

For 6 people

1.25 kg/3 lb lamb shoulder
1 tbsp thyme
salt
freshly ground black pepper
4 tbsp olive oil
225 ml/8 fl oz dry white wine
4 onions, thinly sliced
8 potatoes, cut in half lengthways
    and then into slices 12 mm/½ in
    thick

4 garlic cloves, peeled and
    quartered
2 50-mm/2-in pieces orange rind
2 bay leaves
85 g/3 oz little black olives
2 tbsp finely chopped parsley or
    fennel leaves

Trim the lamb of all fat, bone and gristle. Cut into 50-mm/2-in cubes and sprinkle with thyme, salt and pepper.

Heat 2 tablespoons of the olive oil in a heavy-bottomed frying-pan. Add the lamb and sauté for 5 minutes. Sprinkle with salt and pepper, cook for 15 minutes and set aside in a bowl. Put the wine in the pan, scrape up the bottom and pour into the bowl of lamb. (You can prepare this much ahead of time and cover with cling film until ready to use. Or you can prepare the whole dish in advance and at serving time reheat over a low heat for 10 minutes.)

Heat the remaining olive oil in the frying-pan. Add the onions, potatoes, garlic, orange rind and bay leaves, and cook for 5 minutes. Add the lamb and the liquid. Cook, covered, for 40 minutes or until the lamb is tender (add more wine if necessary). Check the seasoning.

Remove the bay leaves and orange rind. Five minutes before serving add the olives. Garnish with parsley or fennel and serve.

Pietsch (Poche de Veau Farcie)
Breast of veal stuffed with vegetables and simmered in white wine

This is a spectacular dish whether it is served hot or cold. The long simmering in wine and vegetables enlivens the delicate flavour of the veal, and the stuffing, which consists of spinach, broad beans and peas, is light, fresh and very pretty.

For 6–8 people

1 large breast (about 3 kg/7 lb) of
  veal or 2 small (1–1.8 kg/2–4 lb)
  breasts sewn together
85 g/3 oz finely chopped lean
  streaky bacon
450 g/1 lb peas (fresh or frozen),
  cooked
450 g/1 lb frozen broad beans,
  cooked
140 g/5 oz cooked rice
900 g/2 lb frozen or 1.8 kg/4 lb
  fresh spinach, cooked, drained
  and chopped
3 garlic cloves, finely chopped
55 g/2 oz grated Parmesan or
  Romano cheese
20 g/¾ oz finely chopped parsley

4 eggs, beaten
1 tsp thyme
½ tbsp freshly grated nutmeg
salt
freshly ground pepper
3 tbsp olive oil
2 carrots, chopped
2 onions, chopped
1 leek, chopped
2 celery stalks, chopped
2 tomatoes (fresh or canned),
  chopped
450–680 ml/¾–1⅓ pt dry white
  wine
2 bay leaves
3 tbsp chopped parsley

Ask the butcher to prepare the breast for stuffing by making a pocket. Check to see that all the little rib bones have been removed. Reserve the bones.

In a large bowl, mix the bacon, peas, broad beans, rice, spinach, garlic, cheese, parsley, eggs, thyme, nutmeg, salt and pepper. Check the seasoning and stuff the breast or breasts with the mixture (do not overstuff). Use a needle and thread to sew up the opening. (The stuffed breast will look like a plump cushion.) Set aside.

Heat 2 tablespoons of the olive oil in a large heavy-bottomed pan or a large baking dish that you can place over two burners on top of the cooker. Add the carrots, onions, leek, celery, tomatoes and the breast bones (soup bones may be substituted). Sauté for 5 minutes, then remove all the ingredients with a slotted spoon. Add the remaining olive oil and put the veal in the pan. Cook over a high heat for 15 minutes to brown on both sides.

Make a layer of half the vegetable mixture, including the bones. Lay the veal on top and cover with the remaining vegetables. Add the wine and bay leaves. Cover and cook on top of the cooker for 2 hours or in the oven at 190°C/375°F/Gas Mark 5 for 2½ hours. Baste twice. During the first half hour check to be sure there is enough liquid (if too dry, add some wine). Uncover the pan for the last 1½ hours of cooking.

When the veal is cooked, place it on a chopping board, but leave the vegetables and liquid in the pan in the oven or over a low heat. Pull out the thread from the veal. With the help of a plate or, better, a wooden board with a handle (*planche à hacher* – see Techniques and Tools, p. 20), keep the stuffing together while you cut the veal in 12-mm/½-in slices. Arrange the slices on a warm platter and sprinkle with salt and pepper. Cover and keep warm in the oven.

Skim the fat from the liquid. Pass the liquid through a Mouli food mill, along with the vegetables, into a bowl. Discard the bones. Correct the seasoning. Pour over the sliced veal and sprinkle with parsley before serving.

Note: If you serve the veal cold, slice it when it is cold – it will be easier. Serve with a bowl of *Sauce Piquante* (p. 80).

Pot-au-Feu Provençale
Boiled beef, lamb and vegetables

The Provençal version of *pot-au-feu* requires lamb, garlic and chick-peas. It may even include chicken feet to thicken the stock a bit. The rich stock should always be prepared a day in advance so that the fat will congeal on top and can be removed completely. Left-over *pot-au-feu* provides the base for several other dishes: *Boeuf Mironton* (p. 127), *Tian de Boeuf aux Légumes* (p. 151), *Capoun* (p. 161) and *Salade de Riz Variée* (p. 67), so be generous with your proportions. Serve with a hearty red wine.

It is said that one must be at least thirty years old to enjoy fully this simple dish.

For 6–8 people

10 carrots
1 large yellow onion
2 garlic cloves, peeled
2 cloves
4 leeks
1 head celery
900 g/2 lb beef short ribs or flank,
    tied with string to stay intact
    while cooking
900 g/2 lb beef shank
900 g/2 lb lamb (shoulder, shank
    or left-over leg)
1 veal knuckle
2 chicken feet (optional)
salt
bouquet garni (p. 14)

10 juniper berries
10 peppercorns
8 small white onions
3 turnips
6 small potatoes
6 slices firm white bread for making
    triangular *croûtons* (p. 11)
115 ml/4 fl oz vinaigrette (p. 87)
1 large beef marrow bone (or 4–5
    small ones)
2 tbsp coarse sea or kosher salt
freshly ground black pepper
4 tbsp chopped parsley
570 g/1¼ lb canned chick-peas
2 tbsp *cornichons* (p. 11)
Dijon mustard

Peel 1 carrot, the yellow onion and garlic cloves and leave them whole. Stick 2 cloves in the onion. Trim the leeks and celery stalks (reserve the heart).

Bring a large saucepan of water to a boil. Add the three pieces of meat, the veal knuckle and chicken feet (if you have them). Boil, skim off the surface fat, add salt and skim again. Add the clove-studded onion, carrot, celery, leeks, garlic cloves, bouquet garni, juniper berries, peppercorns and salt. Reduce the heat and simmer for 2 hours. Cool and refrigerate overnight.

The next day remove the layer of fat from the stock (and discard the chicken feet if they were added). Remove the celery, bouquet garni and clove-studded onion. Bring the stock to a boil. Peel the white onions, turnips, the remaining carrots and potatoes and leave them whole. Add to the stock the celery heart, turnips and carrots. Reduce the heat and simmer for 10 minutes. Add the onions and potatoes and simmer for about 15 minutes. (Cooking time will depend on the size of the vegetables; check frequently to see if they are tender.)

Prepare the *croûtons* and vinaigrette.

Put the meat on a platter, untie the string and slice it. Arrange the meat slices attractively and surround with the vegetables. Cover with foil and keep warm in a turned-off oven.

Add the marrow bone to the stock and cook for 10 minutes, then remove it. Use a slender knife to scrape the marrow out of the bone, chop it and sprinkle with coarse sea or kosher salt.

Strain the stock and reheat to serve as the first course. Line individual soup bowls with the *croûtons* and place a piece of marrow on top of each *croûton*.

For the main course, remove the platter of meat and vegetables from the oven, sprinkle with salt, pepper and parsley, and pour a ladleful of hot stock over it. Pass around small bowls of chick-peas (heated in a separate pan), *cornichons*, coarse sea or kosher salt, Dijon mustard and vinaigrette.

Note: You can use the left-over lamb for *Farcis à la Niçoise* (p. 167). Serve the left-over beef with *Aïoli* (p. 71), in a *tian* or in a cold salad with potato or rice.

The left-over vegetables can be a lovely first course: slice them and serve chilled or lukewarm with a vinaigrette and some chopped *cornichons*.

Porc à la Sauge et aux Câpres
Pork with sage, capers and white vermouth

Sage is a wonderful accompaniment for pork; it is not only savoury, but is thought to help the digestion.

This dish is delicious served with *Gnocchi* (p. 196), *Céleri Paysanne* (p. 163), *Pâtes aux Oeufs* (p. 200) or *Fenouil Braisé* (p. 169) and a rosé or dry white wine. Try to use fresh or recently dried sage leaves.

For 6 people

1.25 kg/3 lb pork loin or shoulder	4 tbsp finely chopped Italian parsley
2 tsp salt	or fennel leaves
freshly ground black pepper	2 tsp thyme
4 tbsp olive oil	115 ml/4 fl oz dry white wine
2 onions, chopped	115 ml/4 fl oz dry white vermouth
4 tsp sage	55 g/2 oz capers
2 bay leaves	sprigs of parsley or fennel leaves

Trim the fat and bones from the pork and cut it into 50-mm/2-in pieces 25-mm/1-in thick. (You may use the bones to add flavour.) Sprinkle the pork with salt and pepper.

Heat the olive oil in a *doufeu* or a heavy-bottomed saucepan. Sauté the pork on all sides for 5 minutes. Reduce the heat and add the onions, sage, bay leaves, parsley, thyme and more salt. Add the wine. Cover and cook very slowly for 1½ hours, checking to be sure the pork is not dry (add a little water if necessary). Remove the meat and set aside in a warm, covered dish. Add the vermouth to the pan juices while scraping the bottom of the pan. Add the capers, put the pork back in and reheat for 5 minutes. Remove the bay leaves and serve on a warm platter garnished with parsley or fennel leaves.

Poulet aux Artichauts

Chicken sautéd with artichokes and white wine

The artichokes give this very simple dish a rich, pungent flavour, but they must be very fresh, small and young. This is delicious served with *Courgettes Râpées* (p. 165), *Pommes de Terre à l'Ail* (p. 183), *Tomates Provençale* (p. 189), *Févettes à l'Ail* (p. 170) or *Carottes Paysanne* (p. 162).

Wine goes very poorly with artichokes, but a dry white wine may be acceptable if it is well chilled.

For 6 people

6 young artichokes	freshly ground black pepper
juice of 1 lemon	6 chicken breasts, boned and split
4 tbsp olive oil	2 tsp thyme
salt	225 ml/8 fl oz dry white wine

Cut the artichokes in half lengthways, remove the tough outer leaves and the choke, and cut off the stems. Soak them in water and lemon juice for 30 minutes.

Heat the olive oil in a heavy frying-pan. Drain the artichokes and fry them over a medium heat for 30 minutes. Sprinkle with salt and pepper. Remove from heat and set aside in a covered dish.

Sprinkle the chicken breasts with thyme. Reheat the oil in which the artichokes were cooked and brown the chicken on all sides. Reduce the heat and cook for 10 minutes. Add the artichokes and cook for 5 minutes.

Arrange the chicken in the centre of a warm platter and surround it with the artichokes. Add the wine to the pan juices while scraping the bottom with a spatula, and cook over high heat for 1 minute. Pour this over the chicken and serve immediately.

Poulet en Gelée
Chicken in aspic

This is a delicious dish, perfect for a summer meal or a buffet. The vegetables, white wine, lemon juice and herbs impart a subtle flavour to the chicken, and the jellied mound looks inviting garnished with crisp greens. Though never perfect aesthetically (the jelly will be cloudy), this dish is delectable when properly seasoned.

For 6 people

3 tbsp oil (half peanut, half olive)	2 tsp thyme
3 carrots, sliced	2 bay leaves
2 celery stalks, sliced	salt
2 onions, chopped	freshly ground pepper
5 garlic cloves, finely chopped	1 2.25-kg/5-lb roasting chicken, cut
115 ml/4 fl oz white wine vinegar	into serving pieces
225 ml/8 fl oz dry white wine or	2 egg whites, beaten stiff
dry vermouth	2 tbsp sherry
juice of 3 lemons	1 bunch watercress or several
225 ml/8 fl oz water or stock (made	lettuce leaves
with wings, neck, gizzard, bay	3 lemons, cut in wedges
leaves, salt and water)	2 tbsp chopped parsley or chives

Heat the oil in a heavy-bottomed saucepan and add the carrots, celery, onions and garlic. Reduce the heat and cook for 15 minutes. Add the vinegar, wine or vermouth, lemon juice, water or stock, 1 teaspoon of the thyme, bay leaves, salt and pepper and simmer for 15 minutes. Correct the seasoning (the stock should not be bland).

Place half of the pieces of chicken in a large saucepan and sprinkle with salt and pepper. Lay the vegetables on them, put the rest of the chicken on top and sprinkle with the remaining thyme, salt and pepper. Pour the stock over the chicken and vegetables so that they are barely covered. Bring to a boil, cover and simmer slowly for 2–3 hours. Cool.

Remove the chicken from the pan. Bone and skin carefully with a sharp knife and cut into 25-mm/1-in cubes. (If the wings, neck and gizzard were used, discard them or use for soup.)

Boil the stock, uncovered, over high heat for 15 minutes or until it has thickened. Add the egg whites. Reduce the heat and simmer for a few minutes so the egg whites will rise to the surface along with the scum. Remove the froth. Strain the stock through a sieve lined with cheesecloth and let it cool. Remove as much fat as possible and discard all vegetables except the carrots and bay leaves. Check the seasoning and add the sherry.

Oil a shallow bowl and arrange the carrots and the bay leaves in the centre. Place the chicken on and around the carrots and pour the cool stock on them. Refrigerate for several hours until the stock has jelled.

When ready to serve, run a knife around the rim of the bowl, then turn it upside down on a platter. Place watercress or lettuce leaves all round the mound of chicken in aspic and garnish with lemon wedges. Sprinkle with parsley or chives.

To serve, scoop out portions with a large serving spoon and put a lemon wedge, to be squeezed on the chicken, on each plate.

Poulet à la Niçoise

Chicken cooked with onion, tomato, olives and white wine

This is an uncomplicated dish that is light and refreshing. It can be made ahead of time and reheated, so that all the flavours are absorbed by the chicken. Serve it with *Fenouil Braisé* (p. 169), *Courgettes Râpées* (p. 165), *Févettes à la Verdure* (p. 171) or *Épinards aux Pignons* (p. 167).

For 6 people

1 1.8-kg/4-lb chicken, cut into
   serving pieces
juice of 1 lemon
2 tsp thyme
salt
freshly ground black pepper
5 tbsp olive oil
85 g/3 oz chopped lean streaky
   bacon
4 onions, finely chopped

2 garlic cloves, peeled
5 tomatoes, quartered, or 370 g/
   13 oz canned
2 bay leaves
115 ml/4 fl oz dry white wine
85 g/3 oz black olives (Nice's
   unpitted olives or pitted oil-
   cured olives)
20 g/¾ oz chopped parsley or basil

Dry the pieces of chicken thoroughly and sprinkle with lemon juice, thyme, salt and pepper. Set aside.

Heat the olive oil in a large heavy-bottomed frying-pan. Add the bacon and chicken. Sauté for 15 minutes, turning the pieces on all sides with tongs. Remove the bacon and chicken from the pan with a slotted spoon and add onions, adding more oil if necessary. Cook over a low heat for 10 minutes. Add the garlic cloves, tomatoes, bay leaves and wine and cook for 10 minutes. Return the bacon and chicken to the pan and cook slowly, uncovered, for 35–40 minutes, basting frequently. Check the seasoning.

Five minutes before serving, remove the bay leaves and garlic cloves and add the olives. Sprinkle with the parsley or basil and serve at once.

Poulet en Saupiquet

Marinated chicken cooked in an anchovy and garlic wine sauce

I love the traditional *lapin en saupiquet*, but since not everyone enjoys rabbit, I decided to create a variation using chicken. This is a rich, wonderful dish. I use only the breasts and thighs of the chicken, and marinate them overnight to allow various flavours to penetrate the meat before it is cooked. The sauce is cooked separately, then added to the chicken so that it retains its own full flavour.

This is a superb dish, strong in flavour, yet not heavy. Serve it with *Pâtes à la Verdure* (p. 202) or *Gnocchi* (p. 196) and perhaps *Courgettes Râpées* (p. 165) or *Épinards aux Pignons* (p. 167), accompanied by a dry white wine.

For 6 people

3 1.25–1.8-kg/3–4-lb chickens (use only the breasts and thighs), cut into serving pieces
5 tbsp olive oil
1 tsp rosemary
5 garlic cloves, peeled
2 bay leaves
3 tsp thyme
3 onions, chopped
10 peppercorns
450 ml/16 fl oz dry white wine

4 chicken livers
flour for dredging
8 anchovy fillets, chopped
4 tbsp finely chopped parsley
2 tbsp capers
85 g/3 oz black olives (Nice's unpitted olives or pitted oil-cured olives)
4 slices bread for making triangular *croûtons* (p. 11)

Put the chicken in a bowl, sprinkle with 3 tablespoons of the olive oil and the rosemary. Peel and crush 2 garlic cloves and spread on the chicken. Add bay leaves, cover and leave overnight in the refrigerator to marinate.

The next day remove the chicken from the marinade and sprinkle with 1 teaspoon of the thyme. Heat the marinade in a heavy-bottomed frying pan, add the chicken and sauté on all sides for 10 minutes. Remove from the pan and set aside.

Add the onions to the frying pan and sauté for 5 minutes. Return the chicken to the pan, add the remaining thyme, peppercorns and wine. Simmer uncovered for 30 minutes, or until the chicken is tender and there is only about 225 ml/8 fl oz of juice left in the pan. Remove the skin from the chicken and discard it. Put the chicken and juices aside in a bowl.

Dredge the chicken livers lightly with flour. Heat the remaining olive oil in the frying pan, add the livers and sauté for 3 minutes. Purée the livers, anchovies and remaining garlic cloves in a blender or food processor for 2 minutes, adding some of the cooking juice to make the blending easier. Stir in half the parsley, capers and olives. (This should be a rather thick purée.) At this point the dish is fully cooked. It can rest for a few hours before serving.

When ready to serve, place the pieces of chicken in the pan.

Combine the liver purée and the chicken juices, stir carefully and check the seasoning. Pour over the chicken and heat, uncovered, for 20 minutes. Meanwhile prepare the *croûtons*.

To serve, spread the *croûtons* along the sides of a warm platter and put the chicken in the centre. Pour the sauce over the chicken and garnish with the remaining parsley.

Rôti de Porc Provençale

Roast pork with fennel

There are a few imaginative ways to enhance the taste of pork, but to my mind this combination of sage and fennel is the most successful. This must be prepared a day in advance and is especially good with *Fenouil Braisé* (p. 169), *Pois Gourmands à la Paysanne* (p. 182), *Papeton d'Aubergines* (p. 181), or *Carottes Paysanne* (p. 162).

For 6 people

2 fennel bulbs
1 1.25-kg/3-lb pork loin joint,
   boned
2 tsp dried fennel or anise seed
2 tsp sage
salt

freshly ground black pepper
225 ml/8 fl oz dry white wine
2 tbsp peanut oil
1 tsp anise extract or Pernod
2 tbsp chopped fresh fennel leaves

Slice the fennel bulbs into 25 × 35-mm/1½-in strips. Make slits over the whole surface of the joint and insert a strip of fennel and a little of the fennel or anise seed into each cut. Rub the roast with 1 teaspoon of the sage, salt and pepper. Place it in a bowl and add the wine. Let it stand overnight, turning it over once.

The next day, remove the meat from the marinade and rub it with more salt and pepper, the remaining sage and the remaining fennel or anise seed. Bind it securely with a string.

Preheat the oven to 200°C/400°F/Gas mark 6. Oil a roasting pan and add the peanut oil. Place the pork in the pan and roast for 15 minutes. Reduce the temperature to 190°C/375°F/Gas Mark 5 and cook for 1½ hours. Transfer the meat to a warm platter and let it stand for 5 minutes. Remove the string and slice it.

Pour the marinade into the pan and cook for 2 minutes over high heat, scraping the bottom with a fork. Add anise extract or Pernod and pour over the carved slices of pork. Sprinkle with fennel leaves and serve.

Roustissouns

Pork sautéd with herbs and red wine vinegar

This is a light and zesty dish. Serve it with *Pâtes à la Verdure* (p. 202) or *Gnocchi* (p. 196) and, if you want a lighter meal, with *Céleri Paysanne* (p. 163), *Fenouil Braisé* (p. 169) or *Courgettes Râpées* (p. 165).

For 6 people

1.25 kg/3 lb lean pork (loin or other cut carefully trimmed of fat)	salt
	freshly ground black pepper
2 tsp thyme	3–5 tbsp red wine vinegar
2 tsp sage	2 tbsp chopped parsley, basil or
1 tbsp peanut oil	fennel

Cut the pork into 50-mm/2-in cubes and sprinkle with the thyme and sage. Let it stand for 1 hour.

Heat the oil in a heavy-bottomed frying-pan and add the pork. Sprinkle with salt and pepper and cook for about 30 minutes, browning evenly on all sides. Add the vinegar and scrape the bottom of the pan. Cover tightly and cook for 30–40 minutes, or until tender, checking to be sure there is enough liquid in the pan. Add a few tablespoons of water if necessary.

Check the seasoning, sprinkle with parsley, fresh fennel or basil and serve.

Tian de Boeuf aux Légumes

Baked beef with onions, mushrooms and garlic

This is a lovely dish in its own right, and nobody will ever guess it is based on left-overs.

For 6 people

450 g/1 lb mushrooms, sliced
6 garlic cloves, finely chopped
6 shallots or 3 spring onions, finely chopped
25 g/1 oz breadcrumbs (preferably home-made)
20 g/¾ oz chopped parsley

salt
freshly ground black pepper
8–10 slices beef (use what you have – exact proportions are not essential)
115 ml/4 fl oz dry white wine
1 tbsp olive oil

In a large bowl, mix the mushrooms, garlic, shallots or spring onions, half of the breadcrumbs, parsley, salt and pepper.

Preheat the oven to 190°C/375°F/Gas Mark 5. Oil a large baking dish and spread half of the vegetable mixture in it, spread the meat on it and cover with the rest of the vegetables. Add the wine. Sprinkle with the rest of the breadcrumbs and the olive oil and bake for 30 minutes.

Les Légumes
Vegetables

Vegetables are the core of Niçois and Provençal cooking. Gastronomy in the South of France begins with vegetables instead of meat. They are very often the main dish, and a variety are served with dips (*bagna cauda* is an outstanding example) instead of potato crisps or biscuits. Soups and sauces are thickened with vegetables instead of cream or egg yolks.

Some Niçois claim they know more than seventy ways to cook vegetables. Often three or four of them are demonstrated in a single meal; there may be a vegetable dip, salad, soup, stew and gratin. Vegetables are always treated with the utmost respect and imagination. The following recipes are designed to enhance their natural flavour, never to overpower it.

The crispness of the raw material is essential to the success of all these dishes. So select vegetables carefully and, if possible, cook them the same day you buy them. I never use frozen vegetables except spinach, which is wonderful for stuffing (as in ravioli, *toutnus, poche de veau, tourte de blettes*), and baby broad beans, which are crisp and rather tasty.

Most of Nice's vegetables are cooked in the Chinese and Indian way – quickly sautéd in oil that seals in the flavour as well as vitamins. The vegetables retain their taste, texture and nutritional qualities. Otherwise, the best way to cook vegetables is to steam them until just tender.

Vegetable dishes are garnished with a mixture of fresh herbs – mint, basil, chives, Italian parsley – either shredded with a *hachoir* or with kitchen scissors or pounded in a mortar.

The following are the vegetables most commonly used in the South of France.

Artichokes: *les artichauts*

The large globe artichoke is delicious in *artichauts à la barigoule*. The small and tender purple or green ones are eaten raw or just blanched, and are used in *omelette aux artichauts, salade niçoise* and *poulet aux artichauts*. Artichokes must be firm, unspotted and evenly coloured, and squeak when you squeeze them. Never serve anything but cool water, or perhaps cold beer, with artichokes – wine tastes awful with them.

Asparagus: *les asperges*

The little thin asparagus found wild in olive groves and woods in the South of France are superb in omelettes. The large ones are served warm with vinaigrette or are eaten dipped in a soft-boiled egg. Always choose asparagus with closed tips and firm stalks and peel the stalk up to about 50 mm/2 in from the tip (a vegetable peeler is handy for this chore).

Aubergine: *l'aubergine*

The little dark-purple aubergines of Nice are cooked unpeeled, but the very large, lighter ones are generally peeled, salted and drained. For both kinds, the skin should be shiny and smooth. It is a wonderfully versatile vegetable that can be used for fried *beignets*, sautéd and stuffed *farcis*, puréed *caviar provençale*, simmered ratatouille and baked *tians*.

Beans: *les haricots*

The flattish green beans are good for *soupe au pistou*; the round plump ones are delicious warm with vinaigrette; all the green and yellow beans are good with *aïoli* or in a marinade. They must always be fresh enough to snap between your fingers when you break them and be served crisp, not overcooked. Steam them for the tastiest and healthiest results. If you do not have a multi-tier steamer, you can put them in a large amount of salted boiling water, bring to a second boil, then uncover and simmer until just tender; drain at once and rinse in cold water. This process seals in the colour and the flavour.

Cauliflower: *le chou-fleur*
This goes perfectly with *aïoli*. It can be eaten warm with vinaigrette or raw dipped in *bagna cauda*. Cauliflower must have a firm, heavy head and a creamy colour. Before cooking, break it into florets or cut off the stem and leave it whole.

Celery: *le céleri*
At Christmas time we eat celery raw in salad; in the summer we dip the stalks in *bagna cauda* or *aïoli*. We cook it in *soupe au pistou* and in marinades, or serve it braised.

Courgettes: *les courgettes*
Never buy limp courgettes; they must be shiny, smooth and firm. Cook in soups, *farcis* and omelettes, or grate them raw for *beignets*. Courgettes should always be thoroughly scrubbed and left unpeeled.

Fennel: *le fenouil*
There are two kinds: the sweet fennel with a fleshy bulb, and the wild fennel with seeds and stalks. The light liquorice-flavoured bulb with its feathery green leaves is wonderful braised with pork or cooked with fish. It is fresh and lovely raw, dipped in *bagna cauda* or finely chopped in salads. The dried stalks of wild fennel are harder to find. In Nice we add its special flavour to fish by using it for stuffing or as a bed for grilling or by simmering it in bouillabaisse. It can be replaced by finely chopped fresh fennel or fennel or anise seed.

Mushrooms: *les champignons*
In Nice there is a rich variety of edible mushrooms. The most common are *mousserolles, girolles, sanguins* and *cêpes,* and each variety is prepared in all ways imaginable. White caps are abundant around Nice and are always eaten unpeeled, either raw with *bagna cauda, citronnette* or *aïoli,* or sautéd with parsley and garlic, marinated,

stuffed or added to various salads. Cultivated mushrooms should have plump, smooth, creamy-coloured caps.

Olives: *les olives*

There are 300 varieties in Provence and almost as many ways to eat them. In Britain, there are unpitted little black olives from Nice and black olives packed in oil or brine with and without herbs from Italy, Greece and Spain. Olives canned in water are tasteless and should not be used for the recipes in this book.

In Niçois cooking, olives are used raw with hors-d'oeuvres and salads, cooked with meats (*poulet en saupiquet, boeuf niçoise*) or with fish (*estockaficada, daube d'Avignon*).

Onions: *les oignons*

The small white onions (about 35 mm/1½ in in diameter) are used in omelettes or with fresh peas in spring. The larger yellow ones are for *pissaladière*, stews, soups or *farcis*. The red Spanish onions are for *court bouillon* and marinades. When you make a sauce, grate or finely chop the onion so it cooks quickly into a smooth purée and thickens the juices of the sauce.

Peppers: *les poivrons*

The little narrow Italian green peppers are delicious raw in salads. Plump red, green and yellow bell peppers are for *estockaficada, salade rouge* and *farcis*. Choose peppers that are firm and shiny. Before you peel a pepper, set it 50 mm/2 in below the grill for 5–10 minutes, turning it once with tongs. Peel under running water with a sharp knife, and seed.

Spinach: *les épinards*

Frozen spinach is perfect mixed with ham or rice. Use 900 g/2 lb for 6 people. When fresh spinach is available, use 1.8 kg/9 lb for 6 people.

Spring onions: *les cébettes*

Delicious with *bagna cauda, salade niçoise,* in omelettes, with *pâtes verdure* and *gnocchi vert*, and with broad beans in *févettes à la laitue.*

Squash: *la courge*
Widely used in Niçois cooking in *soupe de courges*, *tians* and *tarte de courges*. Pumpkin and acorn or butternut squash need lots of salt, so double-check the seasoning.

Swiss chard: *la blette*
The white ribs are eaten blanched or braised, and the green leaves are prepared like spinach. A staple in Niçois cooking, it is rather difficult to find here, but it can be successfully replaced by spinach. It is used in *pietsch*, ravioli, *tian*, *caillettes* and omelettes, and is also part of a curious mixture of sweets and nuts for *épinards aux pignons* and *tourte de blettes*.

Tomatoes: *les tomates*
To peel them, submerge each tomato in boiling water for 5 seconds, then slip off the loose skin with a sharp knife. Select firm tomatoes for *salade niçoise* and *farcis* and very ripe ones for all other dishes.

Artichauts à la Barigoule I

Artichokes stuffed with herbs, carrots and ham and simmered in wine and vegetables

In this version of *artichauts à la barigoule* (or *farigoule*, which is the Provençal word for thyme) small amounts of cooked vegetables and ham are wedged between the artichoke leaves, then the artichokes are simmered in white wine, vegetables and herbs. It is a savoury and delicate dish, perfect for a luncheon's main dish.

For 6 people

6 large artichokes or 12 very small ones	salt
	freshly ground black pepper
juice of half a lemon	1 tsp thyme
5 tbsp olive oil	2 garlic cloves, crushed
3 onions, chopped	2 carrots, chopped
20 g/¾ oz chopped parsley	bouquet garni (p. 14)
170 g/6 oz chopped prosciutto, country ham or lean streaky bacon	115 ml/4 fl oz dry white wine
	115 ml/4 fl oz water

If using large artichokes, wash them, cut off the stems and remove the outer leaves. Cut off the hard tips of the leaves with kitchen scissors. Add the lemon juice to a large saucepan of salted boiling water and scald the artichokes for 5 minutes. Set aside to cool.

Force open the inner leaves and scoop out the fuzzy choke with a spoon, knife or melon scoop. Scrape the bottom to clean it out as much as possible. It is not necessary to blanch the small artichokes, which have no chokes, but do trim the leaves and stem.

To make the stuffing, heat 2 tablespoons of the olive oil in a large frying-pan and gently cook a third of the chopped onions until tender, adding a little salt so they won't stick to the pan. Turn off the heat and add the parsley, ham, salt, pepper, thyme and garlic. Stir well and check the seasoning.

When the artichokes have cooled, put them upside down and press to force the leaves to open. Push the stuffing between the layers of leaves, forcing it down as deeply as you can. (The distribution need not be precise, but be sure to use all of the filling if possible.) Sprinkle the artichokes with a little olive oil, pepper and salt (omit this if you used bacon), and place in a heavy-bottomed casserole or *doufeu*.

Sprinkle the carrots, the remaining onions, and 3 tablespoons of the olive oil around the stuffed artichokes in the casserole. Add the bouquet garni and cook over a moderate heat until the vegetables just begin to turn brown. Add the wine and let it come to a boil. Simmer, uncovered, for 3–5 minutes, then add the water. Cover and cook gently for 45 minutes (you may need to add more wine or water if the sauce becomes too thick).

Place the artichokes in a covered shallow dish to keep warm. Force the carrots and onions through a sieve with a large spoon or pestle. Put the purée back into the wine broth, simmer for 5 minutes and pour over the artichokes.

Artichauts à la Barigoule II
Artichokes stuffed with herbs and garlic

This cruder version of the *barigoule* is designed only for the small artichokes. It is a lovely first course.

For 6 people

12 small artichokes	salt
20 g/¾ oz finely chopped parsley	freshly ground black pepper
1 tsp thyme	2 tbsp olive oil
3 garlic cloves, 1 crushed and 2 left whole and unpeeled	2 onions, chopped
	1 bay leaf

Trim the artichokes of their tough outer leaves and tips and cut off the stems. Press each one upside down so that the leaves are forced apart. Combine the parsley, thyme, crushed garlic, salt and pepper and stuff the mixture between the leaves of each artichoke.

Place the artichokes in the olive oil in a cast-iron frying-pan or *doufeu*. Scatter the onions around the artichokes in the pan with the 2 *unpeeled* garlic cloves. Cook slowly over a low heat for 5 minutes. Add about 25 mm/1 in of warm water and a bay leaf and simmer, covered, for 1½ hours.

Beignets de Légumes
Vegetable fritters

Always choose the smallest vegetables possible and serve them like hot bread in a basket lined with a bright napkin. I have selected the vegetables traditionally used for this dish. You can, of course, add anything you wish: asparagus tips, green beans, carrots, celery, mange-touts, bell peppers.

For 6 people

2 egg yolks	1 fennel bulb, cut into strips
2 tbsp olive oil	12 firm mushrooms
170 ml/6 fl oz beer	½ head cauliflower, broken into florets
115 g/4 oz flour, unbleached	1 tbsp thyme
salt	2 tbsp olive oil
freshly ground pepper	8 courgette flowers (if available)
1 small narrow aubergine, peeled and sliced lengthways into 6-mm/¼-in strips	2 egg whites
	20 g/¾ oz chopped parsley
3 small unpeeled courgettes, sliced into 6-mm/¼-in strips	peanut oil for deep-frying
	Coulis (p. 74)

Prepare the batter. With a wire whisk, beat the egg yolks, then very slowly add the oil, beer and flour, beating constantly to prevent lumps. Season with salt (½ teaspoon) and pepper and set aside, covered, for 1 hour in a warm place.

Blanch the aubergine, courgettes, fennel bulb and mushrooms* for 3 minutes in salted boiling water and drain. Blanch the cauliflower florets for at least 5 minutes and drain. Dry them all and marinate in salt, pepper, thyme and olive oil for 1 hour or until ready to cook. Remove the stems of the courgette flowers, rinse and drain them carefully.

Preheat the oven to 150°C/300°F/Gas Mark 2. Beat the egg whites until stiff but not dry, and fold them gently into the batter. Add the parsley and marinated vegetables.

Heat the peanut oil in a large frying-pan. Test the oil with a drop of batter – if it sizzles, it is ready. Using tongs, pick the vegetables out of the batter, one at a time, shaking off excess batter. Dip the courgette flowers in the batter one by one. Drop into the oil and fry about five pieces of vegetable at a time, turning them once gently with the tongs after 1–2 minutes. (Do not cook too many fritters at one time because the temperature will drop and the fritters will stick together. Each fritter should have room to puff and roll over easily.) Fry for 4–5 minutes, or until the fritters are golden brown. Drain them on layers of kitchen towels placed on a baking sheet and cover them with another layer of towels.

When all the fritters are made, place them on a large serving dish or in a basket lined with a folded napkin. Sprinkle with salt and pepper. Serve as soon as possible, as they will lose their crispness if they wait. Serve with a warm *coulis* in a separate bowl.

---

* Mushrooms can be blanched for 4 minutes in 115 ml/4 fl oz of dry white wine and the juice of half a lemon instead of water. But if they are very fresh, do not blanch them at all.

Capoun

Cabbage stuffed with ham, rice, vegetables and herbs and simmered in white wine

This is a hearty cold-weather dish and a good way to use left-over ham, beef, rice or vegetables. The stuffed cabbage is baked slowly on a bed of vegetables in a wine and herb stock. When served, the cabbage is sliced like a melon and looks most appetizing, with the green leaves surrounding the colourful stuffing. This is a meal in itself.

For 6–8 people

1 large head green cabbage	85 g/3 oz diced lean streaky bacon
½ tsp cumin	255 g/9 oz chopped cooked ham,
salt	boiled beef or pork
freshly ground pepper	1–2 thick slices of country ham or
2 onions, finely minced	prosciutto, diced
6 tbsp olive oil	½ tsp Spanish saffron
3 garlic cloves, peeled and crushed	3 carrots, sliced
55 g/2 oz finely chopped parsley	2 onions, sliced
2 eggs, beaten	1 garlic clove, peeled
140 g/5 oz cooked rice	170 ml/6 fl oz dry white wine
115 g/4 oz peas (fresh or frozen),	170 ml/6 fl oz water or beef stock
cooked	bouquet garni (p. 14)

Remove the tough outer leaves of the cabbage. Wash and shred them. Wash and cook the head of cabbage for 10 minutes in a large saucepan of salted boiling water. Drain in a colander and, when cool enough, gently peel off the leaves and spread each one on a kitchen towel. Sprinkle with cumin, salt and pepper.

Sauté the onions in 4 tablespoons of the olive oil for 5 minutes and put them into a large bowl. Add to the bowl the crushed garlic, parsley, eggs, rice, peas, all the meats and the shredded cabbage leaves. Add the saffron, salt and pepper and mix thoroughly with your hands. Taste to see if it is well seasoned.

Take a large piece of cheesecloth and place 4 or 5 of the biggest cabbage leaves in a circle in the centre of the cloth. Place all the stuffing in the centre of the leaves, and cover with the rest of the leaves. Pull up the corners of the cheesecloth and tie tightly with a piece of string so that you have a firm, melon-shaped ball.

Preheat the oven to 180°C/350°F/Gas Mark 4. Sauté the carrots, onions and the whole peeled garlic clove in a deep roasting pan for 5 minutes. Add the wine, the water or stock and the bouquet garni, and place the stuffed cabbage on top of the vegetables. Cover with aluminium foil and cover the pan. Bake for 3–4 hours, checking now and then to see that there is enough liquid. When a knife slides through the cabbage ball easily, it is done. Remove the bouquet garni. Skim off the fat and remove the string and the cloth from the cabbage.

Place the cabbage ball on a warm shallow serving dish. Slice it in large wedges as you would a melon. Pour a little of the cooking juices over each slice and sprinkle with salt and pepper.

Note: Cutting the *capoun* will be easy if you use the kind of chopping board described in Techniques and Tools (p. 20).

Carottes Paysanne
Carrots sautéd with parsley and garlic

In every province in France except Provence carrots are sautéd in butter. In Provence olive oil, parsley and garlic are added to contrast with, instead of to enhance, the natural sweetness of the carrots.

For 6 people

1.25 kg/3 lb small carrots	225 ml/8 fl oz water
5 tbsp olive oil	2 tsp sugar
salt	freshly ground black pepper
2 garlic cloves, peeled and crushed	2 tbsp finely chopped parsley

Wash and peel the carrots and slice them on the bias into 12-mm/½-in slices. Heat the olive oil in a frying-pan and add the carrots. Sprinkle with salt. Cover, and cook over a low heat for 10 minutes, shaking the pan from time to time. Add the garlic, water, sugar, more salt and pepper and cook for 20 minutes. Add the parsley and toss gently. Check the seasoning before serving.

Céleri Paysanne

Celery braised in white wine

The fresh flavour and the lightness of this dish make it one of my favourites. Served in individual dishes and sprinkled with cheese, it is a lovely first course, and as an accompaniment to lamb, pork or chicken, it gives spirit to the meat. Make sure the celery you buy is as crisp as possible.

For 6 people

1.25 kg/3 lb celery (about 3 heads) – do not use the tough outer stalks	1 garlic clove, peeled
	2 onions, chopped
	4 carrots, chopped
2.7 l/4¾ pt salted water	3 bay leaves
salt	225 g/8 fl oz dry white wine
freshly ground black pepper	juice of 1 lemon (optional)
2 tbsp olive oil	
115 g/4 oz diced lean streaky bacon	

Wash the celery, remove as many strings as possible, and cut into 25-mm/1-in pieces. Steam or cook in boiling salted water for 15 minutes. Drain and sprinkle with salt and pepper.

Heat the olive oil in a large cast-iron frying-pan. Add the bacon, garlic, onions and carrots and cook gently for 10 minutes, or until tender but not browned. Add the celery,* bay leaves, wine, salt and pepper. Simmer, covered, for 40 minutes and then uncovered for about 5 minutes, or until the liquid has thickened. Remove the bay leaves and garlic and check the seasoning. You may wish to sprinkle the juice of a lemon on top of the celery before serving.

* If you want the dish to have a thicker consistency, you may put the coarser celery stalks through a Mouli food mill and stir the purée into the cooked vegetables.

Note: This dish can be reheated quite successfully. If this is to be a first course, use individual china or copper bowls, slightly oiled. Add 1 heaped tablespoon of celery purée to each bowl and stir. Sprinkle with a little grated cheese and bake at 190°C/375°F/Gas Mark 5 for 15 minutes. The dish can be prepared in advance, of course, and baked at the last minute.

Champignons Farcis
Stuffed mushrooms

In Nice mushrooms are cooked in innumerable ways. This recipe is a wonderful first course, served piping hot. Select firm, cream-coloured mushrooms for this dish.

For 6 people

450 g/1 lb mushrooms (about 50 mm/2 in in diameter)
salt
3 tbsp olive oil
2 thin slices bread, crusts removed
2 tbsp milk
2 tbsp finely chopped parsley

2 garlic cloves, peeled and crushed
1 egg, beaten
40 g/1½ oz finely chopped ham
freshly ground black pepper
1 tbsp breadcrumbs (preferably home-made)

Rinse the mushrooms, dry them well and remove the stems. Rub the caps of the 12 largest with salt and 1 tablespoon of the olive oil so that they are thoroughly coated. Finely chop the rest of the mushrooms along with the stems.

Dip the slices of bread in the milk, then squeeze out the excess moisture.

Heat 1 tablespoon of the olive oil in a large frying-pan, add the chopped mushrooms and cook gently for 5 minutes. Remove the pan from the heat and add the parsley, garlic, bread paste, egg, ham, salt and pepper, and blend well. Check the seasoning.

Preheat the oven to 180°C/350°F/Gas Mark 4. Fill the mushroom caps with the mixture. Sprinkle with breadcrumbs and the remaining olive oil and place them in an oiled baking dish. Bake for 20 minutes, then set the dish under the grill for 3 minutes to brown the top.

Champignons Provençale
Mushrooms sautéd with parsley and garlic

The dish can be served with almost any meat, fish or fowl and is a good substitute for potatoes and other starches. All ingredients must be super-fresh.

For 6 people

900 g/2 lb mushrooms
115 ml/4 fl oz oil (half olive, half peanut)
5 g/¼ oz butter
20 g/¾ oz finely chopped parsley (preferably Italian)

25 g/1 oz breadcrumbs (preferably home-made)
salt
freshly ground black pepper
2 garlic cloves, peeled and crushed
juice of 1 lemon

Rinse the mushrooms and dry them thoroughly. Finely chop the stems (with ends cut off), and slice the caps or quarter them if they are small. Heat the oil and butter in a frying-pan and add the mushrooms. Cook, stirring occasionally, for 5 minutes, or until browned. Reduce the heat and add the parsley, breadcrumbs, salt and pepper and cook for about 3 minutes.

Put the mushrooms on a warm platter and sprinkle with garlic and lemon juice.

Courgettes Râpées
Grated courgettes sautéd in olive oil

This is a quick, delicious dish. Make sure the courgettes are firm, smooth and glossy.

For 6 people

8 small courgettes
3 tbsp olive oil
20 g/¾ oz finely chopped parsley
   or basil
salt
freshly ground white pepper

Scrub and dry the courgettes. Slice off the stems and tips but do not peel them. Grate them coarsely and sprinkle with salt. Drain them on a tea-towel for 30 minutes, then fold the towel over and squeeze out as much water as possible, or take handfuls of the courgettes and squeeze.

Heat the oil and add the courgettes and parsley. Sauté over a medium heat for 15–20 minutes, tossing gently with a wooden spoon. Add salt and pepper to taste.

This dish can be prepared in advance and quickly reheated before serving.

Chou-fleur Rouge

Cauliflower, potatoes and onions simmered with tomatoes and saffron

With its subtle counterpoint of flavours, this is one of the most interesting of vegetable stews. The cauliflower should remain crisp and the potato slices firm. The vegetables are delicious as a hot first course or as an accompaniment for plain grilled fish or meat.

For 6 people

2 tbsp olive oil
6 small white onions, finely chopped, or spring onions cut into 12-mm/½-in pieces
2 garlic cloves, peeled and cut in half
5 tomatoes (canned or fresh), chopped

2 heads cauliflower, separated into florets
2 tsp salt
a pinch of freshly ground white pepper
½ tsp Spanish saffron
4 large or 6 medium-sized potatoes, peeled and sliced

Heat the olive oil in a heavy-bottomed pan and sauté the onions and garlic for 3 minutes. Add the tomatoes and cook over high heat until they begin to bubble. Add the cauliflower and reduce the heat. Add salt, pepper and saffron (crush between your fingers and sprinkle). Cook, uncovered, over low heat for about 10 minutes. Add about 115 ml/4 fl oz water if the dish becomes dry. Add the potatoes and cook, uncovered, for 25 minutes, adding more water if necessary, until the potatoes are just cooked. Check the seasoning and serve.

Épinards aux Pignons
Spinach cooked with pine nuts and orange-flower water

The combining of greens and sweet ingredients in this way is known to be indigenously Niçois, though it would be difficult to trace its origin through the complex layers of Nice's history. The famous *tourte de blettes*, a thin pastry filled with Swiss chard, raisins, eggs, sugar, pine nuts and orange-flower water, is another example of this treatment.

Here is an intriguing dish, a perfect complement to almost any meat or fish.

For 6 people

900 g/2 lb fresh spinach, or 570 g/   2 tbsp orange-flower water
   1¼ lb frozen   1 tsp salt
3 tbsp olive oil   freshly ground black pepper
55 g/2 oz pine nuts

Cook the spinach until tender. Squeeze out as much water as possible and chop it (it should be quite dry). Put it in a pan and toss with the other ingredients. Cook, uncovered, only until the spinach is heated through and serve at once.

Farcis à la Niçoise
Lightly stuffed vegetables

Like the *crudités et bagna cauda* and *salade niçoise*, *farcis* are a summer staple in Nice. On Sundays and festive days housewives and children carry large trays of freshly stuffed vegetables to the village baker's oven, returning at noon to pick up their crisp, golden *farcis*.

Served at most picnics or buffets, *farcis* are usually prepared in large quantities, since they are delicious warm or cold. Be sure to choose small vegetables and not to overstuff them.

For 6 people

4 tbsp olive oil

3 medium-sized or 6 small aubergines, with stems removed and cut in half lengthways

6 green bell peppers, with the bottom end cut off and seeded

6 onions, peeled

6 small cucumbers, peeled

6 small courgettes, with stems removed

6 medium-sized tomatoes

1 onion, chopped

340 g/12 oz chopped beef, lamb or ham

85 g/3 oz chopped lean streaky bacon

450 g/1 lb cooked rice

40 g/1½ oz finely chopped Italian parsley

2 tsp thyme

2 garlic cloves, peeled and crushed

salt

freshly ground black pepper

2 eggs, lightly beaten

55 g/2 oz freshly grated Parmesan or Gruyère cheese

25 g/1 oz breadcrumbs (preferably home-made)

Preheat the oven to 180°C/350°F/Gas Mark 4. Lightly oil the aubergines and peppers with 1 tablespoon of the olive oil and place on an oiled baking dish (you may need two). Bake for 10 minutes. Scoop out the pulp from the aubergines and set aside in a large bowl.

Heat a large saucepan of salted water. Blanch the whole onions, cucumbers and courgettes for 10–15 minutes. Remove them with a slotted spoon.

Prepare the vegetable shells, which should be about 12 mm/½ in thick so that they are firm enough to hold the filling. Cut the onions in half crossways and remove the centres, leaving about 3 layers of skin. Cut the courgettes and cucumbers in half and scoop out the pulp. Cut the tomatoes in half lengthways, sprinkle with salt and leave them upside down to drain for 10 minutes; gently squeeze out excess juice and scoop out the pulp. Add the onion centres and the pulp of the courgettes, cucumbers and tomatoes to the aubergine pulp in the bowl, and set aside.

Preheat the oven to 190°C/375°F/Gas Mark 5. Heat 2 tablespoons of the olive oil in a large frying-pan and add the chopped onion. Cook gently for 5 minutes or until tender. Stir in the pulp of all the vegetables and then the meat, bacon, rice, parsley, thyme, garlic, salt and pepper. (Taste before adding salt because it may not be needed with bacon and ham.) Cook over a low heat, stirring occasionally, for 15 minutes. Turn off the heat and add the eggs. (The stuffing should be fairly solid, but if you think it is too dry, add a chopped tomato.)

Place the vegetable shells on one or two oiled baking dishes. Fill them with the stuffing and sprinkle with cheese. Sprinkle bread-crumbs only on the tomatoes and onions. Dribble the remaining olive oil over all the vegetables and bake for 30 minutes. Serve hot (preferably) or cold.

Note: I have added the cucumbers to this otherwise traditional recipe so that you can make it even when courgettes are out of season.

Fenouil Braisé
Braised fennel

This anise-scented vegetable will brighten your winter meals.

This dish can be reheated easily and it complements both lamb and fish. Here are two versions.

For 6 people

·········· Fenouil Braisé I ··········

6 large fennel bulbs	1 tbsp freshly grated Parmesan
3 1/6⅔ pt salted water	cheese
bouquet garni (p. 14)	salt
1 tbsp olive oil	freshly ground black pepper
	fresh fennel leaves, finely chopped

Cut off the stems of the fennel bulbs, remove the outer stalks and wash the bulbs well.

Preheat the oven to 190°C/375°F/Gas Mark 5. Bring the water to a boil in a large saucepan. Add the bouquet garni and the bulbs and cook uncovered for 25–30 minutes, or until tender but still crisp. Drain, cool and squeeze the bulbs gently to remove the excess water. Cut the bulbs in half lengthways and arrange them on a baking dish. Sprinkle with the olive oil, cheese, salt and pepper. Bake for 10 minutes.

Before serving, garnish with the fennel leaves, cut finely over the dish with scissors.

·········· Fenouil Braisé II ··········

6 fennel bulbs
2 tbsp olive oil
salt
4 tbs water or, preferably,

stock (which improves the
flavour and glazes the fennel)
freshly ground black pepper
fresh fennel leaves, finely chopped

Remove the outer stalks of the fennel bulbs, and wash and dry the bulbs. Heat the olive oil in a frying-pan. Add the bulbs, sprinkle with salt and simmer for 30 minutes. Add water and bring to a boil. Cover and simmer for 1–1½ hours, or until the bulbs are tender to the touch.

Slice each bulb in half lengthways, add salt and pepper to taste, and serve hot sprinkled with the fennel leaves.

Févettes à l'Ail

Baby broad beans sautéd with garlic

A delicious dish made with newly picked baby broad beans. Since fresh beans are not available all year round and the frozen ones are, this is a modified but still interesting version of the Niçois recipe. Fresh French beans, cut into 25-mm/1-in pieces, may be substituted.

For 6 people

570 g/1¼ lb frozen broad beans
5 tbsp oil (half olive, half peanut)
6 garlic cloves, peeled and sliced in
    half

25 g/1 oz breadcrumbs (preferably
    home-made)
salt
freshly ground black pepper

Blanch the beans according to package instructions and drain them.

Heat the oil in a large frying-pan and sauté the garlic until it is golden. Add the beans, breadcrumbs, salt and pepper. Cook, stirring constantly, for 3 minutes, or until the beans are coated with oil and crumbs. The beans should remain slightly crisp. Serve at once in a warm bowl.

Févettes à la Verdure

Baby broad beans simmered with lettuce, spring onions and thyme

Ideally, the broad beans used in this recipe should be fresh ones, but when they are unavailable, I use the frozen kind. Cooked with lettuce, spring onions and herbs, even frozen broad beans make one of the most refreshing of all vegetable dishes.

For 6 people

570 g/1¼ lb frozen broad beans	1 tsp thyme
225 ml/8 fl oz water	salt
2 large heads lettuce, shredded	freshly ground black pepper
4 spring onions, finely chopped, or	1 tbsp olive oil
20 g/¾ oz chopped chives	2 tbsp chopped basil and/or mint

Take the beans out of the freezer 1 hour in advance. Boil the water in a saucepan and add the beans, lettuce, spring onions or chives, thyme, salt and pepper. Cover and bring to a boil. Cook, uncovered, for 20–30 minutes over moderate heat. Check the salt and pepper.

Place the beans in a serving bowl. (There should not be any liquid left, but if there is, just leave it in the pot.) Add the olive oil and the basil and/or mint and serve.

Note: The left-overs can be used in *Capoun* (p. 161) or *Pietsch* (p. 139).

Mélange Printanier
Small artichokes with fresh peas

This is a dish to be served in the spring – both the artichokes and peas must be very young, crisp and sweet. It is glorious sprinkled with fresh mint leaves and served as a first course.

For 6 people

680 g/1½ lb fresh peas	3 tbsp olive oil
6 small artichokes	2 small onions, chopped
2 heads round lettuce, shredded	85 g/3 oz chopped lean streaky
1 tsp sugar	bacon
1 tsp salt	2 tbsp chopped mint or parsley

Shell the peas and keep about half of the empty pods. Pull off the transparent lining of the pods. Remove the outer leaves of the artichokes and the stems. Split the artichokes lengthways and remove the chokes.

In a saucepan of boiling water, cook the peas, empty pods and lettuce with sugar and salt for 20 minutes, or until they are tender.

Meanwhile, in a deep frying-pan, heat the olive oil and add the artichokes, onions and bacon. Cook for 20 minutes over medium heat until the artichokes are tender, then add the drained peas, pods and lettuce and cook for 5 minutes.

Sprinkle with mint or parsley. Serve as a separate course accompanied by good, fresh bread.

Ratatouille
Vegetable medley simmered with herbs

Ratatouille is an eminently versatile dish – you can serve it warm or cold, as the centre of a meal, or as an hors-d'oeuvre or accompaniment. You may want to prepare this a day or two ahead, since it is even better reheated. Some cooks feel strongly that the vegetables in a ratatouille should be puréed; I prefer it when the vegetables retain their shape because the flavour seems better.

For 6 people

2 large aubergines or 6 small ones	4 garlic cloves, peeled and crushed
salt	2 bay leaves
3 yellow or red peppers	2 tsp thyme
6 courgettes	freshly ground black pepper
6 tomatoes	115 ml/4 fl oz dry white wine
8 tbsp oil (half peanut, half olive)	40 g/1½ oz chopped fresh basil (or parsley)
3 onions, finely chopped	juice of 1 lemon

Peel the large aubergines; leave the small ones unpeeled. Remove the stem ends and cut the large aubergines in to 25-mm/1-in cubes; slice the small ones into 25-mm/1-in slices and cut each slice in half. Put them in a colander with salt and leave them to drain for 30 minutes. Press them down and blot with kitchen towels. Reserve.

Slice the peppers in half vertically. Remove the seeds and stems and cut into 25-mm/1-in strips. Cut off the stem ends of the courgettes and cut them into 25-mm/1-in slices. Quarter the tomatoes and squeeze them gently to extract the excess water and seeds.

Heat 1 tablespoon of the oil in a heavy-bottomed frying-pan. Add the onions, tomatoes, garlic cloves, 1 bay leaf, 1 teaspoon of thyme, salt and pepper. Cook for 10 minutes, or until the sauce thickens a bit. Pour the sauce into a bowl.

Clean the frying-pan with a kitchen towel and heat 3 tablespoons of the oil in it. Add the aubergine and cook for 5 minutes. Add salt and pepper, remove from the pan, and put in the bowl with the tomato–onion sauce.

Clean the frying-pan and heat 2 tablespoons more oil in it. Add the peppers, salt and pepper and cook for 5 minutes. Put them in the bowl with the aubergine. Clean the frying-pan again and heat 2 tablespoons more oil. Add the courgettes and cook until tender – about 10 minutes. Pour the entire bowl of vegetables on top of the cooked courgettes and sprinkle with 1 teaspoon of thyme. Add the wine, 1 bay leaf, salt and pepper to taste and stir well with a wooden spoon. Simmer uncovered for 1 hour, or cover and cook in the oven at 180°C/350°F/Gas Mark 4 for about 45 minutes.

Before serving, remove the bay leaves, carefully pour off the excess oil, check the seasoning and add more pepper and salt if necessary. Serve sprinkled heavily with basil – it will keep the dish fresh.

If you serve the ratatouille cold, add about 1 tablespoon of olive oil and the juice of a lemon just before serving.

Note: If you keep this dish in the refrigerator, allow the excess oil to stay floating on the surface. The oil will protect it and keep it fresh.

Omelettes Jardinières
A variety of vegetable and herb omelettes

The following nine recipes are for vegetable omelettes that can be eaten cold or warm. They are Nice's omelettes – fresher, lighter, tastier than their northern French counterparts. Wonderful for picnics or buffets, they can also be served warm for lunch. They look like plump pancakes – green, red or yellow, depending on whether you choose spinach (*troucha*), tomatoes (*crespeou*) or potatoes (*crique*). The process of cooking all these *omelettes jardinières* is the same.

Basic Omelette-making Procedure
Heat the olive oil (sometimes with a little butter). Pour the egg–vegetable mixture into the frying-pan and reduce the heat. After a few minutes the omelette will start to coagulate. Shake the pan gently. Put a large plate over the frying-pan (of course, the plate must be wider than the pan), then, holding the plate firmly against the pan, turn the omelette upside down on to the plate. Add a little oil to the pan, then slide the omelette back into it with the raw side down, and let it cook over a medium heat for about 5 minutes. Do not fold the omelette over – it should remain round so that it can be cut in wedges for serving.

The process may sound complicated, but once you have tried it, you will see how simple it is. If the omelette sticks to the pan, lift it with a large spatula and add a little oil.

Never wash the oiled frying-pan that you use for making omelettes; rub it with kosher salt and wipe clean with kitchen towels.

Omelette aux Artichauts
Artichoke omelette

Use only the fresh small artichokes for this omelette. Avoid canned artichokes. Frozen artichoke hearts are acceptable if they are rinsed with cold water, sprinkled with salt, pepper and olive oil and set aside for 10 minutes before cooking.

For 6 people

5 small artichokes	salt
2 tbsp olive oil	pepper
8 eggs, beaten with a fork	1 tbsp Parmesan cheese (optional)

Rinse the artichokes in cold water and quarter them. Cut off the tips of the leaves and remove any choke in the centre. Cut off any wilted or very tough leaves. Heat 1 tablespoon of the olive oil in a frying-pan and gently sauté the artichokes for 10 minutes. Season the eggs with salt and pepper and pour over the artichokes. Cook for 4 minutes, then turn on to the other side adding more oil to the pan (see Basic Omelette-making Procedure, p. 174) and cook for 2 minutes more. If you like, sprinkle Parmesan cheese on top of the omelette before serving.

Variation
Wild asparagus make a delicious omelette. Following this recipe, you may use them, trimmed and chopped, instead of the artichokes.

Omelette aux Courgettes
Courgette omelette

This is the simplest, quickest dish to make. The main point to keep in mind is to pick very firm, fresh courgettes.

For 6 people

4 tbsp oil (3 tbsp olive, 1 tbsp
   peanut)
7 small courgettes, unpeeled and
   sliced 6 mm/¼ in thick
salt

freshly ground black pepper
1 garlic clove, finely chopped
8 eggs, beaten with a fork
15 g/½ oz butter
a pinch of chopped parsley

In a frying-pan heat 2 tablespoons of the mixed olive and peanut oil and sauté the courgette slices over medium heat for 10 minutes, or until they are soft. Remove with a slotted spoon and drain on kitchen towels.

Place the courgettes in a large bowl, add salt, pepper and garlic and add the eggs.

Heat the remaining mixed oil with the butter in the frying-pan and pour in the egg and vegetable mixture. When the bottom is firm, turn the omelette over (see Basic Omelette-making Procedure, p. 174) and cook for 2 minutes. Sprinkle with parsley and a little olive oil before serving.

Crespeou
Tomato omelette

For 6 people

4 tbsp olive oil
1 onion, finely chopped or grated
4 ripe tomatoes, peeled, quartered
   and squeezed dry
1 garlic clove, peeled and crushed

2 tsp flour
salt
freshly ground black pepper
4 tbsp chopped parsley or basil
6 eggs, beaten with a fork

Heat 2 tablespoons of the olive oil in a frying-pan, add the onion and cook gently for 5 minutes. Add the tomatoes and garlic, sprinkle with flour, salt and pepper. Stir in half of the parsley or basil and cook over a low heat for 10–15 minutes, or until the mixture has become a little dry. Add the mixture to the beaten eggs.

Heat the remaining olive oil in a frying-pan, pour in the tomato mixture and cook for about 5 minutes before turning (see Basic Omelette-making Procedure, p. 174). Cook on the other side for 2–3 minutes.

Variation
Slice the tomatoes 50 mm/½ in thick, mix them with beaten eggs, salt and pepper and cook. The tomatoes remain very firm, making this one of the most refreshing summer omelettes.

Crique
Potato and onion omelette

This is a substantial omelette, quick to prepare, with the commonest ingredients. Freshly grated potatoes give it a creamy substance.

For 6 people

3 medium-sized onions	salt
3 medium-sized potatoes	freshly ground pepper
4 tbsp olive oil	6 eggs, beaten with a fork
3 tbsp chopped parsley	

Peel the onions and potatoes and grate them into a bowl. Place them in a tea towel and squeeze dry.

Heat 2 tablespoons of the olive oil in a heavy-bottomed frying-pan, add the potatoes and onions and sauté them, covered, for 10 minutes, stirring from time to time.

Add the potatoes, onions, parsley, salt and pepper to the beaten eggs.

Heat the remaining olive oil in a frying-pan, pour in the egg–vegetable mixture and cook slowly for 5 minutes (see Basic Omelette-making Procedure, p. 174). Then turn on to the other side and cook for about 1 minute. Sprinkle with olive oil just before serving.

Omelette Moissonière
Onion and clove omelette

This omelette is called *moissonière* because it was eaten cold under the trees after the harvest (*la moisson*). It can also be served warm.

For 6 people

3–4 large onions	8 eggs, beaten with a fork
3–4 cloves	salt
1 tbsp red wine vinegar	pepper
3 tbsp olive oil	

Peel the onions. With a sharp knife make an incision in each and put in a clove. Place the onions in bowl of water, add the vinegar, and marinate them for half a day. Then dip them in boiling water for a few minutes and drain. Remove the cloves and slice the onions into thin slices.

Heat 1 tablespoon of the olive oil in a heavy frying-pan. Add the onions and sauté them for about 5 minutes or until they are tender. Meanwhile, beat the eggs in a bowl and add salt and pepper. Add 1 tablespoon olive oil to the onions. Season the beaten eggs with salt and pepper and pour over the onions. Cook for a few minutes until firm underneath (see Basic Omelette-making Procedure, p. 174), then cook the other side for 1–2 minutes. Sprinkle with the remaining olive oil.

Omelette aux Oignons
Onion omelette

This can be served either cold or warm.

For 6 people

3 tbsp olive oil	salt
450 g/1 lb (about 10–12) small white onions, finely chopped	pepper
	8 eggs, beaten with a fork

Heat 1 tablespoon of olive oil in a frying-pan, add the onions, cover and cook over low heat for 30–40 minutes. The onions must remain pale, yet be very soft. Add salt, pepper and the onions to the eggs in a bowl.

Heat 1 tablespoon of oil in the frying-pan and pour in the onion–egg mixture. Cook for 6–8 minutes over low heat (see Basic Omelette-making Procedure, p. 174). Then turn on to the other side and cook for about 1 minute. Sprinkle with the remaining olive oil and serve.

Omelette Panachée
Mixed vegetable omelette

This is a typically Niçois omelette, best in springtime and eaten warm.

For 6 people

4 artichokes (use only the hearts)	salt
2 tbsp olive oil	pepper
140 g/5 oz frozen spinach or 285 g/	25 g/1 oz cooked peas
10 oz fresh spinach, blanched	8 eggs, beaten with a fork
and drained, chopped	2 tbsp chopped parsley or basil

Prepare the artichoke hearts: remove and discard the leaves and the fuzzy choke, and cut the hearts into 6-mm/¼-in slices.

Heat the olive oil in the frying-pan and add the artichoke hearts and the spinach. Add the salt, pepper and peas to the eggs in a bowl. Pour the egg–peas mixture over the artichoke hearts and spinach. Cook for about 5 minutes (see Basic Omelette-making Procedure, p. 174), turn it over and cook for about 3 minutes. Sprinkle with a little olive oil and basil or parsley before serving.

Omelette aux Pommes de Terre

Potato omelette

For 6 people

2 tbsp olive oil
85 g/3 oz finely chopped lean
  streaky bacon
3 potatoes, diced
1 onion, grated or finely chopped

20 g/¾ oz chopped parsley or
  chives
freshly ground black pepper
5 eggs, beaten with a fork

Heat the olive oil in a frying-pan and add the bacon, potatoes and onion. Cook, stirring gently from time to time and scraping the bottom with a spatula, for about 20 minutes, or until the potatoes are crispy and lightly browned. Add half of the parsley or chives and the pepper (no salt is needed because of the bacon), and pour in the beaten eggs. Cook until the underside is firm (see Basic Omelette-making Procedure, p. 174), then cook the other side for about 2 minutes.

Troucha

Spinach omelette

This is the buffet and picnic dish *par excellence* because it is delicious cold.

For 6 people

2 tbsp olive oil
85 g/3 oz chopped lean streaky
  bacon
½ onion, grated
5 eggs, beaten with a fork
1.1 kg/2½ lb frozen spinach, or
  2.25 kg/5 lb fresh spinach,
  cooked and squeezed dry

55 g/2 oz freshly grated Gruyère or
  Parmesan cheese
55 g/2 oz chopped parsley or basil
½ tsp nutmeg
salt
freshly ground black pepper

Heat the olive oil in a large frying-pan and sauté the bacon for a few minutes. Add the onion and cook for 5 minutes. In a bowl, mix together the beaten eggs, spinach, cheese, parsley, nutmeg, salt and pepper. Pour the mixture on top of the onions and bacon. Cook over a medium heat for 4–5 minutes, or until the underside is firm (see Basic Omelette-making Procedure, p. 174), then cook the other side for 2 minutes.

Papeton d'Aubergines
Aubergine mousse

This recipe was created in the fourteenth century by the French papal chef in Avignon. It was his response to the Italian pope's criticism of French cuisine. It is a delicate, unique way to serve aubergine – light and delicious. Be sure to select aubergines that are firm, shiny and smooth.

For 6 people

3 large aubergines, unpeeled and coarsely chopped
about 3 tbsp salt
3 tbsp olive oil
2 tbsp peanut oil
3 onions, finely chopped
6 eggs, beaten
55 g/2 oz finely chopped parsley

2 garlic cloves, peeled and crushed
½ tsp freshly grated nutmeg
1 tsp thyme
freshly ground black pepper
3 tbsp freshly grated Parmesan or Gruyère cheese
2 tbsp chopped basil or parsley
Coulis (p. 74) – optional *

Put the chopped aubergine in a colander or large bowl and toss with 1 tablespoon of salt. Let stand for 30 minutes to draw out the bitter juice. Rinse well under cold water and squeeze out as much moisture as possible with your hands.

Heat the oils in a large frying-pan. When they begin to smoke, add the onions and aubergine and reduce the heat. Cook slowly, uncovered, stirring occasionally, for 30 minutes, or until the

---

* This sauce is sometimes served with the dish, but I think the delicate *papeton* is overwhelmed by it.

aubergine is translucent and tender. Pass it through a Mouli food mill* into a large bowl and discard the seeds. The purée will be smooth and thick.

Preheat the oven to 180°C/350°F/Gas Mark 4. Oil a soufflé dish.

Stir the eggs, parsley and garlic into the aubergine purée. Add the nutmeg, thyme, remaining salt and pepper to taste. Pour the mixture into the oiled soufflé dish and set it in a pan of hot water 35 mm/1½ in deep. Bake for 40 minutes, or until a knife inserted comes out clean. Sprinkle the cheese on top and bake for 5 minutes more. Garnish with basil or parsley and serve.

Pois Gourmands à la Paysanne
Mange-touts sautéd with lean streaky bacon and chives

One of the quickest and freshest vegetable dishes. Make sure the mange-touts are fresh and crisp, and don't overcook them.

For 6–8 people

900 g/2 lb fresh mange-touts	4 tbsp finely chopped chives
3 tbsp olive oil	salt
55 g/2 oz diced lean streaky bacon	freshly ground pepper
2 garlic cloves, peeled and each cut into 3 slices	

Break off the ends of the mange-touts and pull off the strings. Wash and drain them.

Heat the olive oil in a heavy-bottomed frying-pan and add the bacon, garlic and chives. Reduce the heat and cook, tossing well, for 3–5 minutes. Add the mange-touts, salt and pepper and toss again. Cover and cook for 4–6 minutes, stirring occasionally. (The mange-touts should retain their bright colour and crispness.) Check the seasoning and serve.

---

* Instead of using the Mouli food mill, you can use a blender or food processor, set at high speed, to purée the aubergine, along with the eggs, garlic, onions, parsley, nutmeg, thyme, salt and pepper.

Pommes de Terre à l'Ail
Sautéd potatoes with garlic

An easy way to infuse potatoes with the spirit of Nice.

For 6 people

6 garlic cloves, unpeeled and cut in
  half
3 tbsp olive oil
3 tbsp peanut oil
12–18 medium-sized potatoes,
  diced

salt
freshly ground black pepper
20 g/¾ oz chopped fresh basil or
  parsley

Crush the garlic cloves on a board with your closed fist or the blade of a heavy knife.

Heat the oils in a heavy-bottomed frying-pan, add the garlic and sauté for 2 minutes. Add the potatoes, salt and pepper. Reduce the heat, cover and cook, turning often with a spatula, for 20 minutes or until tender.

Remove the garlic cloves and drain off the excess oil. Put the potatoes in a serving dish and add the basil or parsley. Toss gently and serve.

Pommes de Terre aux Herbes
Sliced potatoes baked with herbs and olive oil

This is a lovely, golden dish; some of the potato slices will be crunchy, some tender – all will taste delicious. It is one of my favourite accompaniments for *gigot d'agneau à l'aillade*, grilled fish, or plain grilled lamb chops.

For 6 people

8 medium potatoes, very thinly
  sliced
115–240 ml/4–5 fl oz oil (half olive,
  half peanut)

½ tbsp thyme
½ tbsp savory
2 tsp salt
1 tsp freshly ground black pepper

Preheat the oven to 220°C/425°F/Gas Mark 7.

Dry the potato slices on kitchen towels and place them in a large bowl. Add the oil, thyme, savory, salt and pepper and mix thoroughly with your hands to be sure each slice of potato is coated.

Spread the slices in two or three layers on a flat baking dish or baking sheet and bake 35–40 minutes, or until crisp and golden. Remove from the dish with a spatula. Check the seasoning and serve.

Purées de Légumes
Vegetable purées

Cook any of the following vegetables: potatoes, turnips, courgettes, chick-peas, white haricot beans, cauliflower, celery, carrots. Drain them and use your Mouli food mill to purée them. They will turn light and fluffy and have an interesting texture (whereas a blender would turn them into a sticky paste). Add a little stock, salt, freshly ground pepper and olive oil to taste. If you wish, add a little crushed garlic or finely chopped onion. Serve surrounded with *croûtons* (p. 11) as an accompaniment to any fish or meat dish.

If you have some left-over vegetable purée, you can prepare these simple but delicious little *boulettes*.

For 6 people

·········· Vegetable Balls ··········

1 onion	2 eggs, beaten
20 g/¾ oz finely chopped chives, mint, basil or parsley	salt freshly ground pepper
900 ml/1⅗ pt vegetable purée (of any one vegetable or a mixture of two or more)*	25 g/1 oz breadcrumbs (preferably home-made)
	peanut and olive oil for frying

---

* Cooked courgettes, cauliflower and celery put through the Mouli and mixed with egg are too watery to be made into balls, and need firming up with some potato or bean purée.

Grate the onion into a bowl and add to it the chives, mint, basil or parsley.

Whip the vegetable purée with a fork so it is smooth but not runny. Add it, along with the eggs, to the bowl and beat for a few minutes. Add salt and pepper. Form little balls the size of small plums with your hands and roll them in breadcrumbs.

Heat a little oil in a frying-pan and fry the balls, leaving enough space so you can turn them easily. Keep them warm as you fry successive batches. Serve as accompaniments for a leg of lamb, grilled fish, or by themselves as an hors-d'oeuvre with a bowl of warm *coulis* (p. 74).

Tian d'Artichauts

Baked artichoke hearts

This dish is common throughout Provence and is especially good with roast lamb or baked fish.

For 6 people

2 onions, chopped	1 tablespoon olive oil
20 g/¾ oz chopped parsley	salt
2 garlic cloves, peeled and crushed	freshly ground black pepper
4 slices bread, soaked in a little milk and squeezed into a paste	55 g/2 oz freshly grated Parmesan cheese
6 large globe artichoke hearts	

Put the onions and parsley in a bowl. Add the garlic and the bread paste and toss gently.

Preheat the oven to 190°C/375°F/Gas Mark 5.

Cut off the stem of each artichoke at the base. Cut each artichoke in half lengthways with a large, heavy knife, using a mallet to bang it if necessary. Pull off all the hard outer leaves of each half and then slice off the remaining inner leaves. Discard the leaves. With a little knife or spoon, scrape out the choke. Cut each heart in half again and sprinkle with a little of the olive oil, salt and pepper.

Line an oiled baking dish with half of the bread paste. Arrange the pieces of artichoke heart on this layer and cover them with the rest of the bread paste. Sprinkle with cheese, olive oil and pepper and bake for 1½ hours.

Tian d'Aubergines
Aubergine and meat gratin

In rural Provence this dish is prepared from left-over meat and fish and is often eaten at the end of the day for a light meal. It can be reheated in the oven at 180°C/350°F/Gas Mark 4.

For 6 people

3 large aubergines, peeled and diced into 12-mm/½-in cubes
salt
115 ml/4 fl oz olive oil
1 onion, chopped
170–340 g/6–12 oz chopped cooked meat or fish
2 tomatoes, chopped, or 140 g/5 oz canned

20 g/¾ oz chopped parsley
1 garlic clove, peeled and crushed
55 g/2 oz freshly grated Parmesan or Gruyère cheese
2 tbsp fresh breadcrumbs
2 tbsp chopped basil or parsley
Coulis (p. 74)

Sprinkle the diced aubergines with salt and let them stand in a bowl for 10 minutes to draw out the bitterness. Rinse under cold water, drain and pat dry.

Preheat oven to 190°C/375°F/Gas Mark 5.

Heat 55 ml/2 fl oz of the olive oil in a large cast-iron frying-pan. Sauté the aubergine over low heat, adding more oil as you need it, for about 20 minutes, or until tender and golden. (If the pan is not large enough, you may have to do this in two batches.) Drain the aubergine on kitchen towels and put them in an oiled baking dish. Put 2 tablespoons of the olive oil in the frying-pan and cook the onion slowly until transparent. Add the meat, tomatoes and parsley and cook for 5 minutes. Turn off the heat. Add the garlic and stir well. Spoon the mixture over the aubergine and sprinkle with cheese, breadcrumbs and the remaining olive oil. Bake for 30 minutes. Serve sprinkled with basil or parsley and with a bowl of warm *coulis*.

Tian de Courges

Baked courgettes, pumpkin or squash with rice and cheese

According to the season, this dish can be made with any of the three vegetables: courgettes, squash or pumpkin. Serve as a separate course or with a roast leg of lamb. It is a light, delicate dish, which deserves your good home-made breadcrumbs on top.

For 6 people

6 courgettes unpeeled, or 900 g/ 2 lb pumpkin* or squash, peeled
3 tbsp olive oil
1 onion, finely chopped
85 g/3 oz cooked rice

55 g/2 oz freshly grated Gruyère or Parmesan cheese
20 g/¾ oz chopped parsley
1 egg, beaten
salt
freshly ground black pepper
2 tbsp fresh breadcrumbs

Chop the courgettes, pumpkin or squash. Preheat the oven to 190°C/375°F/Gas Mark 5.

Heat 2 tablespoons of olive oil in a large frying-pan and gently cook the onion until tender. Add the courgettes, pumpkin or squash and cook for 10 minutes over low heat, stirring from time to time. Remove from heat and cool a little.

Blend the rice, cheese, parsley, egg, salt and pepper, and combine with the courgettes and onion. Spread the mixture in an oiled shallow baking dish. Sprinkle with the breadcrumbs and the remaining olive oil and bake for 20 minutes.

Variations

Before baking, cover the dish with 4 tomatoes, cut in half and gently squeezed to remove excess water and seeds; omit the breadcrumbs and sprinkle 20 g/¾ oz chopped parsley, salt, pepper and a little olive oil all over the top.

If you want to make a finer, more delicate version of this dish, pass the vegetables through a Mouli food mill before covering with the breadcrumbs and olive oil. Bake for only 15 minutes.

* Pumpkin is very bland, so it requires a fair amount of salt. Taste to be sure it is seasoned enough.

Tian d'Épinards et de Morue
Spinach and dried-cod gratin

This is a very fresh preparation, high in flavour because the spinach is cooked in olive oil. You may use frozen chopped spinach for this. A delicious luncheon dish.

For 6 people

225 g/8 oz dried cod (double this amount if you like a strong flavour)

1.1 kg/2½ lb frozen spinach or 2.25 kg/5 lb fresh spinach

4 tbsp olive oil

1 large onion, grated

3 garlic cloves, finely chopped

salt

freshly ground pepper

20 g/¾ oz chopped parsley

3 tbsp fresh breadcrumbs

Soak the cod in water for several hours or overnight, according to the instructions on the package. When adequately soaked, shred the cod with your hands. Thaw frozen spinach at room temperature, then squeeze out all excess water. If you are using fresh spinach, steam it until tender.

Preheat the oven to 180°C/350°F/Gas Mark 4. Heat 2 tablespoons of the olive oil in a heavy-bottomed frying-pan and add the onion, spinach, garlic, salt and pepper. Cook, stirring with a wooden spoon, for 10 minutes. Remove from heat and add the parsley. Put half of the spinach into an oiled shallow baking dish. Add the cod and cover with the rest of the spinach. Sprinkle the breadcrumbs and remaining olive oil on top and heat in the oven for 1 hour.

Note: For a more substantial dish, add 70 g/2½ oz cooked rice to the spinach before baking it.

Tian de Navets Rosés
Pink turnip gratin

Little pink turnips have a lovely subtle flavour. This *tian* is light and tasty and can be served with pork, lamb or fish, or as the main course.

For 6 people

1.25 kg/3 lb small pink turnips (about 24; 50 mm/2 in in diameter)	freshly ground black pepper
	70 ml/2½ fl oz water (or more if needed)
2 onions	3 tbsp freshly grated Gruyère or
2 garlic cloves, peeled	Parmesan cheese
salt	

Peel and slice the turnips and onions as thinly as possible and put them in a large bowl.

Preheat the oven to 190°C/375°F/Gas Mark 5. Oil an ovenproof baking dish.

Crush the garlic into the bowl, add salt and pepper and mix together. Spread the vegetables in the baking dish and pour the water over them. Bake, covered, for 1 hour. Uncover and cook for 30 minutes more. Stir once with a spatula during the baking so that the vegetables on top are moved to the bottom of the dish. When the turnips are uniformly tender, sprinkle the cheese on top and bake for 5 minutes.

Note: This can be fully baked (except for the very last step) ahead of time and kept for a few hours at room temperature. When ready to serve, sprinkle the cheese on top and bake for a few minutes until it melts.

Tomates Provençale
Baked tomatoes with parsley and garlic

In this traditional recipe the tomatoes are cooked on top of the stove *before being baked*, so that all their excess water is cooked away and they look transparent – like candied fruit. In Provence they say the tomatoes must look like a *vitrail* (stained-glass window). This dish is sometimes eaten cold in Nice, but I prefer it warm.

For 6 people

6 large firm tomatoes, cut in half
3 tbsp olive oil
salt
freshly ground black pepper

25 g/1 oz breadcrumbs (preferably
   home-made)
3 garlic cloves, finely chopped
20 g/¾ oz parsley, finely chopped

Preheat the oven to 190°C/375°F/Gas Mark 5.

Put the tomato halves upside down on kitchen towels and drain the excess juice.

Heat 1½ tablespoons of the olive oil in a large frying-pan. Add the tomato halves and cook them, six halves at a time, cut side down for 5 minutes over a medium heat. Sprinkle with salt and pepper and carefully turn them over with a spatula. Cook for 3 minutes, then delicately remove the tomatoes with a spatula and put into an oiled baking dish. This can be done in advance to this point.

Just before serving, sprinkle the tomatoes with breadcrumbs, salt, pepper, and the remaining olive oil and bake for 10 minutes. Sprinkle with garlic and parsley and serve immediately.

Les Farineux

Pasta and Grain Dishes

Ever since Marco Polo brought back pasta from China we have tried to improve on it. In Nice pasta is always home-made and offered with a light sauce so that the fresh taste of the dough is never smothered by its accompaniment. And pasta is often served as a main course as a good alternative to meat or fish.

When I was a child we used to make pasta once a month. It was quite a production. The kitchen, the pantry and the entire guest room would be strung with sheets of drying noodles. They were draped from beds, tables, chairs and brooms propped up like clotheslines. The air would be misty with flour and rich with the smell of the fresh dough.

Making pasta has now become a weekly routine in my kitchen. With the aid of an Italian pasta machine, the arduous production has become a simple production. Like baking bread, pasta-making is time-consuming, but its rewards quickly compensate for the labour involved. And it is addictive: after you have made your own, all commercial pasta will seem a poor substitute.

Pasta is the basis for many delicious and economical meals, particularly for large groups of people. It takes about 2½ hours to prepare: 15 minutes to mix and knead the dough; 1 hour to let it rest; 15 minutes to roll it through the machine; 30 minutes to let it rest; 15 minutes to cut it; and 5 minutes to cook it.

Always remember to boil the pasta with a tablespoon of oil, to prevent it from sticking, and salt to add flavour. When the pasta has boiled for 3–4 minutes, start testing to be sure it will be served *al dente*.

Drain and pour the pasta into a warm bowl and add a little olive oil, toss quickly with two forks, and then add whatever sauce you choose: *pistou*, *coulis*, walnut, *saussoun*, *tapenade*, or plain grated Parmesan or Gruyère cheese.

Barba Jouan

Pastry filled with cheese, ham, rice, herbs and pumpkin

These delicious little turnovers can be served with drinks, as a first course, or as a main course warm or cold. Why they are called *Barba Jouan* (Uncle John, in the Niçois dialect) is truly a mystery.

It will be best to use a pasta machine for the pastry.

Makes 6 turnovers and a tourte, or pie (to serve 6 people)

················· Pastry ·················

225 g/8 oz unbleached flour
4 tbsp olive oil
4–5 tablespoons warm water
1 egg, beaten
salt

Place the flour in a large bowl. Make a well in the centre, add the olive oil, water, egg and salt, and mix well with a fork. Flour your hands and knead until the dough becomes smooth (this will take about 5 minutes). Form a ball and let it rest in the bowl for 1 hour under a clean towel. Meanwhile, prepare the filling.

················· Filling ·················

1.6 kg/3½ lb raw pumpkin
or 450 ml/16 fl oz canned
unseasoned pumpkin
purée
1 tbsp olive oil
2 large onions, chopped
5 garlic cloves, chopped
salt
2 tsp savory, oregano or thyme

225 g/8 oz grated Parmesan cheese
(Roquefort or any blue cheese,
or any strong Italian or Greek
cheese may be used instead)
1 egg, beaten
115 g/4 oz cooked rice
55 g/2 oz finely diced prosciutto,
country ham or very lean streaky
bacon
freshly ground black pepper

Using a heavy knife, cut the pumpkin into several pieces and scrape out the seeds. Peel each piece and cut into 50-mm/2-in cubes. Heat the olive oil in a heavy-bottomed frying-pan, put in the onions and garlic, and sauté for 1 minute. Add the pumpkin and sprinkle with salt and the savory, oregano or thyme. Cover and cook slowly for 1 hour, stirring from time to time. When the pumpkin is soft (this will take 45 minutes–1 hour), put it through a Mouli food mill and then into a sieve and let it drain for 10 minutes over a bowl. Press it to help it drain. Put the pumpkin purée into a bowl and add the cheese, egg, rice and ham. Add salt and pepper to taste.

Put your pasta machine on a table or a counter. Place one small ball of dough, the size of an orange, in the machine. Pass it through Nos. 1, 3, 5 and 6, adding flour each time so the dough will not stick to the metal. Let this thin sheet (about 100 mm/4 in wide) rest on a floured tray or counter and repeat the process until all the dough is used up. Set aside half of the sheets for making the pie. Cut the other half in large circles (about 100 mm/4 in in diameter) or into 100-mm/4-in squares with a pastry wheel or a knife and use for making the turnovers.

To make the turnovers
Preheat the oven to 190°C/375°F/Gas Mark 5. Put a square or circle of dough in your left hand and place a teaspoon of the filling in the centre. Fold the dough over and seal the edges with fingers dipped in water. Pinch the edges to make a thick, curly edge. Continue to do this until all the pastry is used. Place the turnovers on an oiled baking sheet. Dip your fingers in olive oil and brush their surface. Bake in the oven for 20 minutes, or until they are golden.

To make the pie
Preheat the oven to 190°C/375°F/Gas Mark 5. Oil a baking sheet and place on it half of the reserved thin sheets of dough side by side and spread the pumpkin filling evenly on them. Cover with the rest of the sheets of dough and seal by pressing the two layers together with wet fingers. With a fork, prick the top of the pie so the steam can escape. Brush with olive oil. Bake for 45 minutes, or until the pie looks golden and crisp. This is better warm but it is often eaten cold at picnics and buffets.

Fada Riquet

Rice, spinach and cheese

A truly delicious dish adored by children and appreciated by all. It is often made with left-overs and can be reheated many times. If any amount is left over, it can be used for *Tout-Nus* (p. 207), *Capoun* (p. 161) or *Suppions Farcis* (p. 120).

For 6 people

900 g/2 lb frozen spinach or	2 eggs, beaten
1.8k g/4 lb fresh spinach	½ tsp freshly grated nutmeg
100 g/3½ oz uncooked rice	salt
115 ml/4 fl oz milk	freshly ground pepper
4 tbsp freshly grated	2 tbsp olive oil
Parmesan or Gruyère cheese	

Thaw frozen spinach for at least 1 hour before cooking, or steam fresh spinach until tender. Bring a saucepan of salted water to a boil. Add the rice and cook for 15 minutes. Add the spinach and cook for 10 minutes more. Drain the rice and the spinach in a colander, pressing out as much liquid as possible. They should not be overcooked.

Place the spinach and rice in a heavy-bottomed frying-pan and add the milk. Cook over low heat and, stirring rapidly, add the cheese and eggs. Add the nutmeg, salt and pepper. After 4–5 minutes, add the olive oil and blend well. Serve with a bowl of grated cheese on the side.

Note: To make this dish out of left-overs, you will need about 200 g/ 7 oz of cooked rice and 625 g/1¾ lb of cooked spinach. Chop the spinach and combine with the rice and milk in a heavy-bottomed frying-pan, and follow the remaining steps of the recipe.

Gnocchi

Potato gnocchi

This is a favourite with children, and is also a succulent, delicate accompaniment to any meat or fish dish which most adults will love. It can be very elegant as a first course served in individual dishes and sprinkled with freshly grated cheese.

For 6 people

5 medium-sized potatoes (about
    900 g/2 lb), as mealy as possible
2 egg yolks
55 g/2 oz butter
½–1 tsp freshly grated nutmeg
2 tsp salt (or more)
freshly ground white pepper
170 g/6 oz flour
1 tbsp peanut oil

3 tbsp olive oil
one of these sauces: *Pistou* (p. 81);
    Sauce aux Noix (p. 79); *Coulis*
    (p. 74); juices from a roast
    deglazed with white wine
freshly grated Parmesan or Gruyère
    cheese
3 tbsp finely chopped chives, mint
    or basil

Scrub the potatoes and cook them in boiling salted water until they are tender. Protect your hands by using a tea-towel or an oven mitt and peel the potatoes while they are still hot. Immediately put them through a Mouli food mill (do not use a blender because it would turn them into a sticky paste).

Slowly beat in the egg yolks, butter, nutmeg, salt and pepper. Add the flour gradually, beat with a wooden spoon or an electric mixer. The finished dough should be soft and smooth but not too sticky. Add more flour if it is too moist. Dust your hands with flour and divide the dough into balls the size of small apples. Roll each one out to a cylindrical shape about 12 mm/½ in in diameter, then cut it into pieces about 12 mm/½ in long.

The dish can be prepared in advance up to this point; cover the *gnocchi* with a towel and keep in the refrigerator or at room temperature for a few hours.

Bring a large saucepan of salted water to a boil. Put in the *gnocchi* and the peanut oil. Cook them for 7–10 minutes, or until all have floated to the surface. They should be elastic to the touch.

Drain well and place in a warm shallow dish. Sprinkle with the olive oil and stir gently, then add your favourite sauce and cheese. Sprinkle with the chives, mint or basil just before serving.

Variation
The *gnocchi* can be made to resemble shells – they not only will look prettier but will absorb the sauce better. To make the shells, put each piece of dough on the topside tines of a fork and press down. Cook the shells for only about 3–4 minutes.

Panisses
Chick-pea 'chips'

This is one of Nice's oldest recipes. Each morning, pasta and ravioli shops sell *panisses* freshly made and displayed on dozens of unmatched saucers. Every family saves a precious collection of chipped saucers for the *panisse* preparation. These chick-pea sticks are the children's favourite lunch, favourite snack and, when sprinkled with sugar, favourite dessert. Fried *panisses* seasoned with freshly ground pepper are delicious with grilled chicken, leg of lamb or plain hamburgers.

For 6 people

170 g/6 oz chick-pea flour	1½ tbsp olive oil
680 ml/1⅕ pt cold water	peanut oil for frying
salt	grated Parmesan cheese (optional)
freshly ground white pepper	

Oil 6–8 saucers or 2 dinner plates. Put the chick-pea flour in a large bowl and stir in the cold water. Beat with an eggbeater or wire whisk for 1–2 minutes, or until you have a smooth paste. Stir in the salt, pepper and olive oil.

Pour into a heavy-bottomed saucepan and cook over medium heat, stirring constantly with a wooden spoon. After 5–10 minutes the mixture will thicken, then become lumpy and finally form a mass. Remove from the heat and beat until the dough is very smooth. Spoon into the oiled saucers or plates and allow to cool. (You need not spoon out equal amounts.)

When the *panisse* dough is cool, cut it into little sticks (12 mm/ 1½ in wide and about 50 mm/2 in long) as you would potatoes for chips.

In a heavy saucepan, heat 25 mm/1 in of peanut oil, and when it is very hot fry the little sticks in the same manner as you would chips, not cooking too many at one time. When they are crisp and golden, turn them very carefully with a spatula. (They will be done in about 4 minutes.) Remove and drain on kitchen towels. Put them on trays in a low oven (120°C/250°F/Gas Mark ½) while you fry the remaining *panisses*.

Sprinkle with salt and pepper and, if you like, a little grated Parmesan cheese and serve.

Pâtes aux Courgettes
Pasta with courgettes

This is a fresh and pleasant dish that can be prepared in a flash. Make sure the courgettes are very crisp and very small, and don't overcook the pasta.

For 6 people

3 small courgettes, unpeeled (try to find those that are 50–75 mm/ 2–3 in long)
115 ml/4 fl oz olive oil
2 tsp thyme
salt

freshly ground pepper
good commercial noodles or spaghetti
1 garlic clove, finely chopped
25 g/1 oz freshly grated Parmesan cheese

Wash and scrub the courgettes and slice them on the bias. Pat dry with kitchen towels. Heat the olive oil in a heavy-bottomed frying-pan and add the courgettes. Sauté them, stirring with a wooden spoon, over medium heat until they are golden brown. Sprinkle with thyme, salt and pepper.

Meanwhile, cook the pasta and drain it. Put the courgettes on top of the pasta and sprinkle with 1 tablespoon of the olive oil and the garlic and cheese. Toss with two forks and serve.

Pâtes aux Moules
Pasta with mussels, white wine and garlic

Mussels, olive oil and garlic make a pungent combination with noodles. This is a simple dish you can prepare all year round, since all the ingredients are readily available. It takes 15 minutes to prepare if you already have the pasta at hand.

For 6 people

1.25 kg/3 lb mussels
salt
3 tbsp olive oil
115 ml/4 fl oz dry white wine
4 garlic cloves, finely chopped

Pâtes aux Oeufs (p. 200) or good commercial egg noodles
3 tbsp chopped parsley, basil or mint

Scrub the mussels thoroughly, remove the beards and leave the mussels in a bowl of cold water for 10 minutes. Discard all the opened ones. Meanwhile, set a large saucepan of water to boil with salt and 1 tablespoon of the olive oil.

In another saucepan cook the mussels, covered, over high heat with the wine for 3–5 minutes, or until their shells open. When cool enough to handle, discard the shells and strain the mussel broth through a piece of cheesecloth that has been dipped in cold water and wrung out and then spread over a sieve. Heat the remaining olive oil in a heavy frying-pan and cook the garlic over low heat for 3 minutes. Stir in the drained mussel broth and cook for 5 minutes more.

Cook the noodles in the saucepan of boiling salted water until tender but still firm. Drain at once and put in a heated serving dish. Put the mussels into the frying-pan and heat briefly. Pour the mixture over the noodles and toss with two forks. Garnish with parsley, basil or mint.

Pâtes aux Oeufs

Fresh egg noodles

This is my favourite recipe for egg noodles. Children and adults alike love this dish. I serve it with *Pistou* (p. 81), *Sauce aux Noix* (p. 79), warm *Coulis* (p. 74), *Saussoun* (p. 50) or a meat sauce. I also serve it plain with unsalted butter and freshly grated Gruyère cheese. Delicious with *boeuf à la niçoise, agneau à la niçoise* or *porc à la sauge et aux câpres*.

For 8 people

450 g/1 lb unbleached flour	2 tbsp water
6 eggs, slightly beaten	2 tbsp olive oil
1 tbsp salt	1 tsp peanut oil

Put the flour in a large bowl and make a well in the centre. Put into the well the eggs, salt, water and olive oil, and with your fingers work it gradually into the flour. Place the dough on a counter or table and knead it for 15–20 minutes: flouring your hands and the counter or table often, push the dough away from you with the heel of your hand, then gather it back into a mass and repeat until the dough is smooth and elastic. Let it rest, covered with a towel, for 1–2 hours.

Divide the ball into eight parts (each the size of a fist). Roll each part through the pasta machine into thin layers, starting at No. 1, then 2, then skipping to 4, and finally 5 or, if you like thin noodles, 6. Sprinkle a little flour on the machine every time you put in a new sheet of dough so it will not stick to the metal. In using No. 6 be sure to reach underneath and pull out the thin strip as it is being rolled. If allowed to pile up under the machine, it will stick together. Sprinkle flour on all the trays you have (use counters and tables also) and let the sheets of thin pasta dry on them for 30 minutes. Then pass the sheets of dough through the machine to cut them into thin or wide strips, as you prefer. Dust lightly with more flour and let them fall loosely on to the floured surfaces.

Bring a large saucepan of salted water to a boil. Add the peanut oil and drop the noodles in the water. Cook, stirring twice, for 5–10 minutes over medium heat. Drain them in a colander and pour into a shallow dish. Add whatever you wish: olive oil or butter and freshly grated cheese, or any of the following sauces: *pistou*, tomato, walnut or your own meat sauce of the day.*

Note: Raw fresh pasta can be left overnight in a refrigerator, but will lose most of its quality. Better cook it *al dente* and reheat the left-overs with 115 ml/4 fl oz of milk the next day.

Pâtes Rouges et Vertes
Noodles with ham and herbs

The texture and flavour of fresh herbs, good ham and olive oil complement the subtle taste of the noodles. This is a beautiful, lively dish, made in minutes. Don't ever attempt it with dried herbs.

For 6 people

115 ml/4 fl oz olive oil
55 g/2 oz chopped cooked ham, country ham or prosciutto
2 large garlic cloves, finely chopped

25 g/1 oz finely chopped basil, mint, chives, thyme or parsley (or any amount you like)
Pâtes aux Oeufs (p. 200) or good commercial noodles
freshly ground pepper
salt

Heat the olive oil in a heavy-bottomed frying-pan and add the ham garlic and herbs. Cook, stirring, for 3 minutes over medium heat.

Meanwhile, cook the pasta and drain it. Pour into a warm shallow dish and spoon the ham-and-herb mixture over the noodles. Sprinkle with pepper and taste before adding any salt. Toss lightly with two forks and serve.

---

* Your meat sauce could be the juices from *Boeuf à la Niçoise* (p. 128), *Agneau à la Niçoise* (p. 126) or *Porc à la Sauge et aux Câpres* (p. 143). Or you can make it by pouring 115 ml/4 fl oz of white wine or vermouth into the pan in which chicken or a leg of lamb has been cooked, scraping up the bottom of the pan, and simmering the liquid for 3 minutes.

Pâtes à la Verdure
Fresh herb pasta

This is a delicious pasta. The addition of fragrant fresh herbs – mint, basil, chives, thin spring onions, Italian parsley – to the dough gives a lively flavour to the noodles. The dish can be served as a main course with a little olive oil and some grated cheese. Sauces should not be used, as they would smother the fragrance of the herbs.

For 6 people

25–50 g/1–2 oz finely chopped fresh herbs (choose one or two: mint, basil, chives, very small spring onions, Italian parsley)
450 g/1 lb unbleached flour
6 eggs, slightly beaten

3 tsp salt
4 tbsp olive oil
1 tsp peanut oil
freshly grated Parmesan or Gruyère cheese (optional)

Dry the chopped herbs thoroughly in a kitchen towel. If you prefer a paste, pound the herbs in a mortar.

Place the flour in a large bowl. Make a well in the centre, add the eggs, salt and 2 tablespoons of the olive oil, and gradually work the flour into the eggs and mix well. Add the herbs and place on a counter or table and knead for about 20 minutes. Flour your hands and the work surface as often as necessary to prevent the dough from sticking. Keep pushing the dough away from you with the heel of your hand, then gathering it back into a mass, until the dough is smooth and elastic. Make a ball of the dough, cover with a towel and let it rest for 1 hour.

Divide the ball into three parts. Roll each part through the pasta machine to make thin layers. Pass it through the No. 1 plate, then 2, then 4, then 6, adding flour each time so the dough will not stick to the metal. If No. 6 seems too thin for your taste, set it on 5 instead. Let the layers of dough rest on a floured surface (trays, tables, counters) for 30 minutes, then pass them through the machine to cut them in strips. Let them fall loosely on the floured tray. Sprinkle with flour.

Add salt and peanut oil to the water in a large saucepan and bring to a boil. Add the pasta and cook, uncovered, for 5–10 minutes, depending on how tender you want it to be.

Pour the pasta into a colander to drain well. Pour into a large bowl, add the remaining olive oil, and toss with two forks. Serve with a bowl of cheese.

Polente aux Champignons
Corn-meal mush with mushroom sauce

Polente comes from Italy (where it is called *polenta*). In Nice it is accompanied by good pork sausage, small wild birds or vegetables, but here I am recommending a mushroom sauce to accompany it.

For 6 people

·················· Polente ··················

1–2 tsp salt
1.4 l/2⅖ pt water
10 tbsp coarse corn meal

Add salt to the water in a heavy saucepan. When the water comes to a boil, slowly add the corn meal while stirring with a wooden spoon. Lower the heat to medium and stir frequently for 25–30 minutes. It should be quite thick and detach itself from the sides of the pan. Pour it into a shallow dish oiled with peanut oil. When cool, cut into 50-mm/2-in squares.

········· Mushroom Sauce ·········

2 tbsp olive oil	3 tbsp chopped parsley
450 g/1 lb mushrooms, sliced	2 bay leaves
3 onions, finely chopped	½ tsp thyme
3 fresh or 225 g/8 oz canned tomatoes, chopped	salt
2 garlic cloves, finely chopped	freshly ground black pepper
	2 tbsp grated Gruyère cheese

Preheat the oven to 180°C/350°F/Gas Mark 4.

Heat the olive oil in a heavy-bottomed frying-pan. Add the mushrooms and sauté briskly for 3 minutes, stirring often. Add the onions, tomatoes, garlic, parsley, bay leaves, thyme, salt and pepper, and cook for 5 minutes.

Pour the sauce over the squares of *polente*. Sprinkle with the grated cheese and bake for 15 minutes.

Ravioli à la Niçoise

Beef and spinach ravioli

Inspired by the dish Marco Polo brought back from China, *raïoles* have been a traditional treat in Provence for centuries. The little squares of dough can be filled with beef, veal, ham, lamb's brains, pumpkin or rice. The Niçois version is truly superb, as light as it is fragrant. The secret here is the savoury combination of *boeuf à la niçoise* (with its wine and orange flavour) and spinach.

This is not a quick dish to prepare, but it is well worth the time. Frozen spinach and a pasta machine are great helpers. The *boeuf à la niçoise* must be prepared a day ahead, then chopped for the ravioli.

So with recipe in hand and a little time, you can now produce a most wonderful dish.

For 6 people (about 80 ravioli)

·············· Filling ··············

340 g/¾ lb beef stew (*Boeuf à la Niçoise*, p. 128)
85 g/3 oz lean streaky bacon
570 g/1¼ lb frozen spinach or 1.1 kg/2½ lb fresh spinach
1 onion
1 tbsp olive oil

1 garlic clove, peeled and crushed
½ tsp freshly grated nutmeg
2 eggs, lightly beaten
55 g/2 oz freshly grated cheese
1 tsp thyme
salt
freshly ground black pepper

Prepare the beef stew, then dice the beef. Reserve the stew sauce. Chop the bacon. Blanch and drain the frozen spinach, or steam fresh spinach until tender; squeeze it dry and chop. Grate the onion.

Heat the olive oil in a heavy frying-pan and add the bacon and onion. Cook for 5 minutes. Place the beef, spinach, onion and bacon in a blender in three batches until it becomes a paste, or chop them on a board as finely as you can. Pour into a large bowl and add the garlic, nutmeg, eggs, cheese, thyme, salt and pepper. Check the seasoning and stir well. You should have a smooth and fairly dry mixture.

·················· Pasta ··················

340 g/12 oz unbleached flour
1 tbsp olive oil
2 eggs, beaten
5–6 tbsp water (or more as needed)
2 tsp salt

Sift the flour into a large bowl. Make a well in the centre and pour in the olive oil, eggs, water and salt. Mix with a fork until all the flour is absorbed, adding another tablespoon of water if necessary. Knead for about 10 minutes, either in the bowl or on a floured table or counter, until the dough becomes smooth and elastic. Form a ball of dough, place it in an oiled bowl, cover with a clean cloth and let it rest for 1 hour.

Put your pasta machine on the table or counter and flour it. Divide the dough into 4 balls the size of small apples. Roll each ball through No. 1, then 3, then 5, then 6 or 7, sprinkling a little flour on the machine every time you put in a new sheet so it will not stick to the metal. Reach underneath and pull out the thin strip as it is being rolled. If allowed to pile up under the machine it will stick together. Lay the paper-thin sheets of dough on a floured tray or table to dry for about 10 minutes.

If you do not have a pasta machine, roll each small ball of dough on a floured board as thinly as you can. Let the sheets rest for 10 minutes. (Left longer they will become difficult to work with.)

Filling the ravioli
Place a sheet of dough on a floured surface. Put a teaspoon of filling every 50 mm/2 in along the entire sheet, making two long rows. Place another sheet of dough on top of the mounds and carefully press around each little heap with your fingers, sealing the two layers together. With a pastry wheel, cut around each heap so that you have neat little squares that look like plump cushions. If

the pasta strips have become too dry to adhere to one another, dip the pastry wheel into warm water and work them together. When all the squares are cut, sprinkle them with a little flour and allow them to rest for 1 hour before cooking.

To serve

Bring a large saucepan of water to a boil. Add 2 tablespoons of salt and 1 tablespoon of olive oil. Reduce the heat and gently slide the ravioli in. Simmer them gently for 5–10 minutes. When they rise to the surface they are ready. Take them out with a slotted spoon and drain them in a colander.

Arrange the ravioli in a warm dish, alternating layers of ravioli with a layer of warm beef stew sauce or grated cheese and olive oil, or *sauce aux noix*.

Variation

If you have roasted a chicken or leg of lamb, deglaze the pan with a little white wine while scraping the bottom of the pan. Use this sauce with the ravioli, which can accompany the chicken or lamb.

Note: With the left-over filling prepare *Tout-Nus* (p. 207) for the next day.

Riz aux Herbes

Rice with herbs

Use long-grain rice for this dish.

For 6 people

6.25 l/11 pt salted water	2 tsp thyme or rosemary
300 g/10½ oz uncooked rice	3 tbsp olive oil
3 bay leaves	freshly ground pepper

Bring the water to a boil in a large saucepan and add the rice while slowly stirring with a fork. Add the bay leaves and 1 teaspoon of the thyme or rosemary. Boil, uncovered, for 20 minutes. Rinse under cold running water and drain in a colander. Transfer to another saucepan, add the olive oil, and fluff the rice with two forks. Sprinkle with the remaining thyme and pepper.

Reheat, stirring lightly with the two forks a few times, for 5 minutes just before serving. (Do not remove the bay leaves.)

Riz au Safran

Saffron rice

For 6 people

a large pinch of saffron	450 ml/16 fl oz hot water
2 tbsp olive oil	½ tsp freshly grated nutmeg
1 large onion, finely chopped or grated	2 bay leaves
	salt
200 g/7 oz uncooked rice	freshly ground black pepper

Crush the saffron into 2 tablespoons of hot water and let it stand.

Heat the olive oil in a heavy-bottomed frying-pan. Add the onion, cover and cook slowly for 3–5 minutes, or until the onion becomes transparent. Add the rice and stir over low heat until all the grains are coated with oil. Add the dissolved saffron and the hot water and stir. Add nutmeg, bay leaves, salt and pepper. Bring to a boil, then reduce the heat and simmer, covered, for 15 minutes. All the liquid should be absorbed and the rice tender. Fluff the rice with a fork and remove the bay leaves. Just before serving, add a dash of olive oil and check the seasoning again.

You can keep this warm over simmering water until ready to serve.

Tout-Nus

Spinach, rice and meat balls

These little balls are called *tout-nus* (all naked) because basically they are the filling for ravioli, but without their coats of dough. You can prepare them from left-over ravioli filling made of spinach and *boeuf à la niçoise*, or spinach and any left-over meat, or spinach and lean streaky bacon or ham. In all cases, children will love them and they are wonderful for a buffet.

For 6 people

70 g/2½ oz cooked rice
300 g/10½ oz minced stewed beef
    and cooked spinach (see p. 204)
2 tbsp chopped parsley
1 egg, beaten
6 tbsp grated Gruyère or Parmesan
    cheese

salt
freshly ground black pepper
3 tbsp flour
2 tbsp olive oil

Put the rice in a large bowl and add the spinach and beef, the parsley, egg and 3 tablespoons of the cheese. Stir and add salt and freshly ground black pepper to taste.

Taking a tablespoonful of the mixture at a time, make small round balls. Sprinkle the flour on a tray and roll the balls in it.

Bring a large saucepan of salted water to a boil. Drop the balls in and cook over medium heat for 8–10 minutes (they are cooked when they rise to the surface). Drain them on kitchen towels and arrange them in a shallow dish. Sprinkle with olive oil and the remaining cheese. Check the seasoning and serve.

These balls can be cooked in advance and reheated in the oven at 180°C/350°F/Gas Mark 4 for 10 minutes.

Les Plats de Festin
Festive Dishes

Aïoli, bouillabaisse and *couscous* are the perfect party dishes. They each represent the menu itself. An assortment of *crudités* can precede them, and the dessert could be a basket of fruit, but nothing else is needed.

These superdishes require exuberance in the planning, many guests to enjoy them, a certain solemnity at the table and a long siesta to recover from them.

Perhaps Brillat-Savarin was thinking of these culinary joys when he wrote that 'the discovery of a new dish does more for the happiness of mankind than the discovery of a new star'.

Aïoli Monstre
A rich variety of vegetables, fish and meats served with a garlic mayonnaise

'*Aïoli* intoxicates gently, fills the body with warmth, and the soul with enthusiasm. In its essence it concentrates the strength, the gaiety, of the Provençal sunshine,' said Mistral, the Provençal poet. One of the most beloved dishes in Provence, *aïoli* is a legend, a festival. It offers a whole banquet by itself.

Traditionally, *aïoli* is eaten on Christmas Eve with boiled snails and on Ash Wednesday with dried cod, and its elaborate *monstre* version is always the star of village festivals.

In the summer every village and town in Provence celebrates its saint's day festival. The parades, dances and games last three days and end with the appearance of a huge *aïoli monstre*, shared by all on the village green. Long tables are set up on the plaza, and shop-keepers, farmers, dignitaries, tourists and children sit side by side to enjoy the virtually endless variety of fish, squid, meat, snails, eggs and raw and cooked vegetables. The *aïoli* sauce is passed separately in a bowl or in the marble mortar in which it was made.

When you prepare your own *aïoli* sauce, remember to allow about two cloves of garlic per person. It has to be almost unbearably strong to enhance the very bland food it accompanies. (If your guests fear for their breath, offer a sprig of parsley, a few mint leaves or a piece of dark chocolate after the meal.) The crisp garlic, the mortar (either marble or china), the pestle (either wood or china) and a good olive oil are the essential elements in making *aïoli*. Serve ice-water or a full-bodied red wine with this most exhilarating of dishes and be prepared to take a long siesta after the meal.

Remember that germinating garlic cloves, draughts and disloyal wives are supposed to cause an *aïoli* to fail.

For 8 people

·················· Sauce ··················

14 garlic cloves	450 ml/16 fl oz oil (½ peanut, ½
salt	olive)
2 egg yolks	juice of 1 lemon
1 tsp Dijon mustard	freshly ground black pepper

Make sure all the ingredients are at room temperature. Peel the garlic cloves and push them through a garlic press into a mortar. (Do not use a blender because it makes the sauce too fluffy.) Add the salt. Pounding steadily with the pestle, reduce the garlic and salt to a paste. Add the egg yolks and mustard, then very slowly add the oil. As the sauce becomes firmer you may increase the stream of oil.* When the sauce becomes firm and shiny, beat in the lemon juice and pepper and taste to see if you need more salt. Cover with cling film and refrigerate on a low shelf until ready to use.

* If your *aïoli* curdles, start again by putting an egg yolk into another bowl and very slowly beating in the sauce, *or* add a teaspoon of boiling-hot wine vinegar and stir vigorously until the sauce becomes firm and smooth again.

·············· Aïoli Garni ··············

a combination of the following:

900 g/2 lb snails, blanched in water
   flavoured with herbs
2 chickens, boiled or roasted
450 g/1 lb bottom round of beef,
   boiled
1 leg of lamb, roasted
1 large bass, baked
1.25 kg/3 lb octopus or squid
2 bay leaves
salt
freshly ground black pepper
900 g/2 lb dried cod
8 carrots
8 potatoes
8 beetroot

1 head celery
4 fennel bulbs
1.25 kg/3 lb French beans, trimmed
8 courgettes
1 large cauliflower, trimmed
900 g/2 lb chick-peas, boiled
8 artichokes
4 eggs
4 tomatoes
4 tbsp chopped Italian parsley
450 g/1 lb canned tuna or salmon
4 lettuce leaves
2 bunches parsley
1 lemon, sliced

Prepare the snails, chickens, beef, lamb or bass. Wash and cut squid or octopus into 50-mm/½-in strips, heat 700 ml/1¼ pt of water in a saucepan, add octopus, bay leaves, salt and pepper and simmer for 25 minutes. Drain and set aside.

Soak the dried cod overnight (follow instructions on the package). Place it in a pan of cold water, bring to a boil, reduce the heat, and let it cook for 20 minutes in barely simmering water. Peel the carrots, potatoes and beetroot. Cut the celery and fennel bulbs into sticks and refrigerate until ready to serve. Heat a large saucepan of water (or better, a *couscoussière*) and cook the carrots for 15 minutes, then add the potatoes and French beans and cook for 15 minutes more. Add the unpeeled whole courgettes and cook for another 15 minutes. Keep covered until ready to serve.

Boil the cauliflower and the beetroot separately. Heat the chick-peas, and if the artichokes are not tender enough to be eaten raw, cook them for 20 minutes in boiling water. Hard-boil the eggs, then peel and halve lengthways. Slice the tomatoes.

Place all your cooked vegetables in large round dishes according to colour and texture. Serve the raw vegetables surrounded with the eggs. Put the squid in a shallow dish, the cod on a platter sprinkled with chopped parsley, and the chilled canned tuna on a bed of lettuce. If you serve a boiled chicken or beef or poached fish, place this on a large platter with bunches of parsley at both ends and slices of lemon.

Pour the *aïoli* sauce into one or two bowls to be passed along with the various platters. *Bonne sieste!*

Note: You may also make an eggless *aïoli*, which is lighter. Peel the garlic cloves and boil and peel 1 potato. Crush the garlic and the potato in a mortar. When they have become a paste, slowly add the oil while stirring constantly. Add salt, pepper and lemon juice.

Bouillabaisse

The supreme fish and vegetable stew

Bouillabaisse is the noble 'golden soup', which embodies not only a whole region's ambience but a whole philosophy. You must invite at least eight guests, since bouillabaisse requires a large variety of fish and must be abundant. The success of a good bouillabaisse depends on the contrast of flavours and textures. Every home, every town, every restaurant has its own 'authentic' version, but remember, it originated as a simple stew made with whatever the fishermen brought home and quickly boiled with saffron, herbs and garlic. Although its preparation requires two separate operations, the process is very simple and the result truly superb.

Although many of the Provençal fish, such as *rascasse*, *fiela* and *grondin* may not be available, there is enough variety here to make a delicious bouillabaisse. Two types are essential: a firm, lean, strong-flavoured fish and a soft, delicate fish; and a hearty fish stock (I use the *Soupe de Pêcheurs*, p. 32). The stew must cook quickly (no more than 20 minutes) – bouillabaisse means 'to boil at top speed' – so that the olive oil becomes slightly emulsified.

Serve the stew accompanied by *rouille*, a garlic and cayenne pepper mayonnaise. It should be eaten in a relaxed, informal atmosphere with only a light hors-d'oeuvre to start and fresh fruit to finish the meal. Serve with a strong dry white wine or a light red wine.

For 8 people

900 g/2 lb flavourful fish (sea bass, snapper, cod, haddock, halibut, hake), cut into thick slices
900 g/2 lb delicate fish, such as flounder, whiting (as big a fish as possible), or red snapper, with skin left on
salt
freshly ground pepper
5 tbsp olive oil
2 tbsp *pastis* or 1 tsp anise extract
Rouille (p. 84)
2 onions, chopped
1 fish head and backbone
3 tomatoes, fresh or canned, chopped
1 tsp thyme or rosemary
a pinch of fennel seed or a branch of wild fennel

5 sprigs parsley
2 50-mm/2-in pieces dried orange rind
1 bay leaf
1 carrot
2 celery stalks, chopped
2 leeks, chopped (optional)
1.8 l/3⅕ pt water
900 ml/1⅗ pt white wine
1 tsp Spanish saffron
2–3 hard-shell crabs, whole
8 large potatoes, sliced 12 mm/½ in thick
8 slices French bread or 6 slices firm white bread for making *croûtons* (p. 11)
1 tbsp Pernod or 2 tbsp anise extract

Fillet the fish (save 1 fish head and 1 backbone) and sprinkle with salt, pepper, 1 tablespoon of the olive oil, and the *pastis* or anise extract. Set aside. Prepare the *rouille* sauce.

In a heavy frying-pan, heat 4 tablespoons of the olive oil. Add the chopped onions and sauté gently for 3 minutes. Add the fish head and backbone and sauté for another 3 minutes. Add the tomatoes, thyme or rosemary, fennel seed or wild fennel, parsley, orange rind, bay leaf, carrot, celery, leeks, salt and pepper. Cook for 5 minutes. Add the water and 680 ml/1⅕ pt of the wine (some claim white wine gives a bitter aftertaste, so you may use water instead) and bring to a boil. Simmer for 20 minutes. Crush the saffron between your fingers over the soup. Cook for 2 minutes and remove from heat. Place a Mouli food mill over a pan and pour two ladlefuls at a time of the soup mixture into it. Grind, adding a little stock whenever the mixture becomes too dry. Place a sieve over a large bowl and force the ground mixture through with a pestle or a large wooden spoon. Discard the residue.

Put the soup in a large saucepan, add the firmer fish and cook for 5 minutes, then add the potato slices and the more delicate fish, crabs, the remaining olive oil, the rest of the wine (the fish should be covered with liquid). Simmer gently for 20 minutes. Meanwhile, prepare the *croûtons* (you may want to rub the bread with garlic).

Just before serving the soup, add the Pernod or anise extract and check the seasoning. (The dish should be highly seasoned.) The traditional way to serve bouillabaisse is to place two or three *croûtons* in each soup plate and to ladle the soup, fish and potatoes on top of them. Serve the *rouille* in a separate bowl. Leave the tureen of bouillabaisse on the table throughout the meal so that the guests can help themselves, and pour some *rouille* into the soup itself, or spoon it over the fish.

You may also serve bouillabaisse as two separate courses: first, the soup over the *croûtons*; then the fish on a warm platter surrounded by potato slices with a ladleful of warm soup poured over them and served with a bowl of *rouille*.

Note: If you have any left-over fish, soup or potatoes, pass it through a Mouli food mill, add 70 ml/2½ fl oz of white wine, a dash of olive oil, and freeze – a thick soup will be ready for another day.

Variations

Bouillabaisse de Martigues
A black bouillabaisse with a very tasty, thick bouillon. Little 450-g/ 1-lb squids (together with their ink bags) are added to the fish.

Bouillabaisse Borgne
Add a poached egg to each plate. (*Borgne* means one-eyed.)

Bouillabaisse de Morue
Sauté in 3 tablespoons of olive oil: 2 leeks, 1 quartered tomato, 3 peeled garlic cloves, 900 g/2 lb dried cod (after soaking in water for 3 hours), 2 diced potatoes, a bouquet garni, a pinch of salt and freshly ground black pepper. After about 5 minutes, add a glass of water per person and boil it for 10 minutes.

Revesset
This is a green bouillabaisse. To a large saucepan of boiling salted

water (1.7 l/3 pt) add 225 g/8 oz Swiss chard, 225 g/8 oz spinach, and a few sorrel leaves. Boil for 10 minutes, then add 2 tablespoons of olive oil, 1 pound of sardines and cook for 10 minutes. Prepare *croûtons* (p. 11) and place in each soup plate. Pour the stock with the greens over them. Serve the fish separately with a sprinkling of red wine vinegar or lemon juice.

Bouillabaisse aux Poissons d'Eau Douce
Use eels, crayfish, trout or other freshwater fish. Follow the main recipe for bouillabaisse.

Bouillabaisse de Toulon
Add 3 more potatoes and 1.25 kg/3 lb of mussels to the main recipe for bouillabaisse.

Couscous
Couscous with chicken, meat, vegetables and a hot sauce

Although couscous is originally a North African dish, it has been incorporated in the Provence repertory for so long that it is now a traditional part of the cuisine.

Like *aïoli* and bouillabaisse, couscous is a spectacular creation, a feast in itself. It consists of many foods served on different platters: meat and vegetables, chicken and carrots, the couscous grain itself and the chick-peas. The assortment of dishes is served with a bowl of stock and a bowl of very hot red-pepper sauce.

The dish derives its name from the grain (hard wheat semolina) that is its principal ingredient. In North Africa a special semolina is rolled to prepare couscous, but in France and Britain, packages of ready-made couscous grain are available in whole-food and health-food shops.

The dish will take about 2 hours to cook. You will need three saucepans: one for cooking meats and vegetables, one for cooking the chicken and carrots, and a *couscoussière* (see Techniques and Tools, p. 20). If you do not have a *couscoussière*, line a sieve with a linen towel, place it over a large saucepan and cover with a lid.

For 10 people

900 g/2 lb lamb, shoulder or breast
900 g/2 lb short ribs of beef
225 ml/8 fl oz *Sauce Tomate* (p. 86)
Tabasco sauce
6 tbsp olive oil
2 beef or lamb bones
5 onions (1 finely chopped, 4 peeled and left whole)
4 tomatoes, fresh or canned, chopped
4 chilli peppers, finely chopped, or 2 tsp cayenne pepper
salt
8 medium-sized turnips, peeled

10 courgettes, seeded, or 1 pumpkin, peeled, seeded and cut into large pieces
1 clove
1 2.75-kg/6-lb chicken
1 celery stalk, cut into 50-mm/2-in sticks
5 carrots, peeled
freshly ground pepper
900 g/2 lb couscous grain
3 large heads green cabbage, quartered
225 g/8 oz chick-peas, cooked or canned
115 g/4 oz unsalted butter

Cut the lamb and beef into 35-mm/1½-in pieces, trimming as much fat and gristle as possible.

Prepare the *sauce tomate* and add Tabasco sauce to taste.* Set aside.

The following instructions for cooking the meat, chicken, vegetables, and couscous grain should be followed in such a way that everything will be ready at about the same time; this means that at some point you will have three saucepans cooking simultaneously.

Heat 3 tablespoons of the olive oil in a large heavy-bottomed saucepan and sauté the meat for 5 minutes. Add the beef or lamb bones, finely chopped onion, tomatoes, chilli peppers and salt. Pour in enough hot water to cover and simmer for 1 hour. Add the turnips and cook for 15 minutes. Add the courgettes or pumpkin and cook for 20 minutes over a low heat. Remove from heat and set aside.

Stick a clove in one of the whole onions and put it in a large saucepan with the chicken, celery sticks and carrots. Add salt and

---

* Or else prepare a different sauce: Crush 2 peeled garlic cloves into a mortar. Add ½ teaspoon cayenne pepper, ½ teaspoon ground cumin, ½ teaspoon crushed coriander seed, ¼ teaspoon ground ginger, and salt to taste. Pound and stir. Slowly add 5 tablespoons olive oil and stir, then add 225 ml/ 8 fl oz *Sauce Tomate* (p. 86). This sauce can be kept refrigerated for a few days.

pepper and cover with cold water and bring to a boil. Cook for 1 hour. Remove the chicken, take off the skin with a sharp knife and cut the meat into pieces. Discard the skin and bones, and put the chicken back in the stock until ready to use.

Meanwhile, pour the couscous grain into a large bowl and sprinkle it with 115 ml/4 fl oz of cold water. Toss it with your hands and let it rest for 30 minutes.

Take your *couscoussière* (or a large saucepan and a sieve) and fill the bottom part with 5.5 l/9⅗ pt of water, the remaining whole onions, the cabbage, salt and pepper. Place the couscous grain in the top part (or the sieve if you are not using a *couscoussière*). Bring the water to a boil and steam the couscous, covered, for 30 minutes. Remove the grain from the saucepan, sprinkle it with 115 ml/4 fl oz of cold water, 1 tablespoon of salt, 2 tablespoons of olive oil, and mix gently with your hands or two forks (the grains should not stick to each other). Allow to rest for 15 minutes. Put the grains back in the top of the *couscoussière* or saucepan and cook above the boiling stock for 30 minutes. Just before serving, heat the chick-peas with the remaining olive oil.

To prepare for serving, place the couscous grain in a large shallow dish. Dot with butter or sprinkle with olive oil and keep covered with a lid until ready to serve. Discard all the bones and place the meats and vegetables on one or two platters. Pour hot broth over them. Place the chicken on a large platter and pour some of the broth over it also. Pour six ladlefuls of the hot broth into a large bowl. Put the hot sauce in another bowl to pass around for pouring on all the various foods. Each person will put a ladleful of couscous grain on to his or her soup plate (this must be large and shallow), then take some of the meat, chicken and vegetables, and then spoon some hot broth and tomato sauce over everything.

Variations

The ingredients and the proportions will vary according to what you have on hand and according to your taste. Follow the general process as described in the main recipe and remember this is a simple dish you can improvise on and in which nothing needs to be absolutely precise.

Couscous aux Sept Légumes
Made with cabbage, squash, carrots, tomatoes, aubergines, chilli peppers, fresh broad beans and onions, with 2 teaspoons of saffron crumbled and sprinkled over the cooked vegetables a few minutes before serving.

Couscous aux Courgettes, Fèves et Navets
Made with courgettes, fresh broad beans, turnips, onions and lamb stew, flavoured with saffron and coriander.

Couscous aux Oignons et au Miel
Made with chicken and lamb, onions, cinnamon and honey.

Couscous aux Raisins Secs et Pois Chiches
Made with raisins, chick-peas, lamb, onions and saffron.

Couscous Medfon
Made with lamb, chicken giblets, onions, saffron and cinnamon.

Couscous aux Boulettes
Served with little meatballs seasoned with cumin and simmered in the stock for the last 15 minutes of cooking.

Les Desserts

Desserts

Most meals in the South of France end with cheese and fresh fruit. In fact, the Niçois term for dessert is *la frucha* (the fruit), and most of the time it comes from the family orchard. Fresh, stewed, dried, *confit* or kept in brandy, it usually replaces the elaborate cream-rich desserts of *haute cuisine*.

There is a traditional pastry based on honey, almonds and, of course, fruits, but it is not to everybody's taste.

There are *pompes*, shaped like plump crowns; *chichi fregi*, little circles of fried dough; *pogne*, the sweet brioche of Easter; *pan coudoun*, in which a whole quince wrapped in plain dough is slowly baked in the oven. There is *pain de Sainte Agathe*, in the shape of a breast (*le martyre de Sainte Agathe*); *oreillettes*, little ears of dough fried until crisp; *navettes*, little boats flavoured with orange-flower water, *muscardins*, *pignolats*, *tourtillons* and, of course, there is confectionery: *les calissons d'Aix*, made with candied fruit and almonds; *berlingots de Carpentras*, delicious hard mint candy; the *chiques d'Allaud*, soft honey candies; *suce-miel d'Aubagne*, a caramelized honey candy; and the famous *nougat de Montélimar*.

So, though they are simplicity itself, Provençal pastry and sweets do exist, and dessert can be other than the more prevalent *grata queca*, or baskets of seasonal fruit. Here is a selection of pleasing recipes.

Beignets de Fruits
Apple–raisin fritters

This apple–raisin *beignet* recipe is an old Niçois dessert. The lovely crisp fritters can also be made with bananas, peaches, apricots or acacia blossoms. Rum brings out the flavour of tart apples and raisins and enlivens this dessert. Since the fruit must marinate for 3 hours and the batter rest 1 hour, this is not a last-minute dish.

For 6 people

········ Fruit and Marinade ········

6 tart apples
140 g/5 oz raisins
115 ml/4 fl oz dark rum
65 g/2¼ oz sugar

Peel, core and dice the apples. Combine them with the raisins, rum and sugar and let them stand for 3 hours.

·············· Batter ··············

2 eggs, separated
about 140 ml/5 fl oz warm beer
115 g/4 oz unbleached flour
salt

10 g/⅓ oz butter, softened, or peanut oil
170 ml/6 fl oz (or more) vegetable oil
115 g/4 oz icing sugar

Separate the egg whites from the yolks and reserve them. Blend the yolks and beer and stir in the flour, salt and butter or oil. Stir well until the batter is smooth. Leave in a warm place (such as a turned-off oven) for 1 hour.

Preheat the oven to 150°C/300°F/Gas Mark 2. In a saucepan heat the vegetable oil. Beat the egg whites until stiff but not dry. Pour off the rum marinade from the apples and stir it into the batter, then very gently fold in the egg whites. The batter must be smooth. (It will be very liquid with the addition of the marinade. If you want slightly heavier, more rounded *beignets*, stir in 1–2 teaspoons of flour before you add the apples and raisins.) Very delicately but thoroughly fold the fruits into the batter and drop by tablespoonfuls into the hot oil. Fry the fritters until they are golden on both sides, turning them over with tongs after 3 minutes. Remove with a slotted spoon and drain on kitchen towels. Bits of the batter will break off and burn at the bottom of the pan. You will have to fish them out with a slotted spoon. Keep the fritters warm in the oven, changing the kitchen towels twice.

When all the *beignets* are ready, arrange them in a long basket or a platter lined with a napkin. Sprinkle icing sugar (or crushed crystallized sugar and a little dark rum) on top and serve.

Cloche Amandine
Bell-shaped almond brittle

Croquante, or *cloche amandine*, is usually served at Christmas and Easter in Provence. It is placed in the centre of the table and everyone breaks off little pieces to nibble. Left-overs are crushed and used on top of baked apples or pears or on ice cream.

215 g/7½ oz shelled nuts, almonds or a mixture of hazelnuts and almonds	170 g/6 oz honey (the best you can find)
400 g/14 oz white sugar	115 ml/4 fl oz water
200 g/7 oz brown sugar	115 g/4 oz butter
	1 lemon, cut in half

Preheat the oven to 150°C/300°F/Gas Mark 2. Place the shelled but unpeeled almonds on a baking tray and bake for 10 minutes until brown. Remove from the oven and chop them finely. Put them back in a turned-off oven.

Bring the sugars, honey and water to a boil and stir with a wooden spoon. When the mixture has heated to 150°C/300°F, add the butter and the warm nuts and pour onto a greased surface (marble or formica counter, aluminium baking tray, or aluminium foil). Smooth out and push with the 2 halves of the lemon until the entire sheet is very thin – 3–6 mm/⅛–¼ in thick. Lift off the mixture before it is completely cooled and hardened and mould it against the inside of a buttered marble or china mortar or a wide bowl. Let it cool, then unmould on a platter.

You may decorate it with crystallized violets or mimosa flowers (on sale in gourmet shops) or candied fruits or dribbles of icing. I prefer it plain.

Keep the left-over pieces wrapped in aluminium foil or in a closed glass jar. Never refrigerate.

Compote d'Abricots, de Pêches et de Prunes

Apricot–peach–plum compote cooked in lemon and orange juice

Peaches and plums are full of flavour, but apricots are sometimes rather bland. Poached in lemon and orange juice, however, they make a subtle combination perfect for concluding a hearty dinner or a rich lunch.

For 6 people

6 peaches	200 g/7 oz sugar
6 large or 10 small apricots	225 ml/8 fl oz orange juice
6 plums	2 tbsp cognac (optional)
1 lemon	2–3 sprigs mint (optional)

Peel, quarter and pit the peaches, apricots and plums. Cut and squeeze the lemon and peel off 2 75-mm/3-in strips of the yellow rind. Place the sugar, orange juice, lemon juice and rind in a saucepan and bring to a boil. Add the fruits to the boiling syrup and reduce the heat. Simmer, uncovered, for 10 minutes. Remove the fruit with a slotted spoon and put in a shallow bowl to cool.

Boil the syrup for 10 minutes, or until very thick, then spoon it over the fruit. Chill. Just before serving, add cognac and sprigs of mint on top.

Note: In Provence the fruit is never peeled because part of the flavour is lost in removing the skin. Try it both ways.

Compote de Fruits
Stewed fresh fruit

You don't need exotic fruits for this. It is usually made with fruit that is too ripe, too small or too blemished to be acceptable for serving in a *panier de fruits de saison* (basket of fresh fruits). So look round your market for good buys of seasonal fruits. There's no special list to follow, but you do need a varied selection.

For 6 people

1 lemon	3 apples, peeled and sliced
85 g/3 oz white or black grapes	200 g/7 oz sugar
3–4 ripe pears, peeled and sliced	225 ml/8 fl oz water
3 peaches (or apricots or plums), peeled and sliced	10 g/⅓ oz chopped mint (optional)

Cut the lemon and squeeze it. Peel 2 75-mm/3-in strips of the yellow rind. Rinse the grapes and remove the stems. Peel the pears, peaches and apples; remove the pits or seeds and slice them (quarter the fruit that is very ripe). Bring the lemon rind and juice, sugar and water to a boil.

Add the fruits to the boiling syrup and reduce the heat. Simmer, uncovered, for 10–15 minutes. Remove the fruit with a slotted spoon and put in a shallow bowl to cool.

Boil the syrup for 10 minutes or until it thickens, then pour it over the fruit. Chill. Sprinkle with chopped mint leaves.

Confiture Noire
Preserve made with a variety of fruits

Delicious preserves are made in Provence with interesting combinations of fruits, such as cherries with redcurrants, and watermelon with orange and lemon, but the best is *confiture noire*, or black jam. This can be made in any proportion you want of the following fruits and nuts:

fresh figs (if unavailable, use dried
   figs or omit figs altogether)
pears
melons
quinces

lemon rinds
walnuts
225 g/8 oz of sugar for each 450 g/
   1 lb of fruit

Choose very ripe fruits. Place the whole figs in a heavy-bottomed saucepan, sprinkle with sugar and bring to a boil. Remove from heat and drain through a piece of cheesecloth. Bring the juice to a boil and add the peeled and quartered pears, melons and quinces, lemon rinds and the shelled walnuts. Add sugar. Cook for 1 hour or more, or until the mixture is dark and sticky. Return the figs to the pan and cook for 15 minutes. Allow to cool. Place in a sterilized jar and seal.

Confiture de Tomates Rouges

Red tomato preserves

Curiously, in Aix the tomatoes are mixed with aubergines. For this recipe choose firm, ripe tomatoes.

> 2.25 kg/5 lb tomatoes
> 1.8 kg/4 lb sugar
> rind and juice of 1 lemon
> 2 tbsp dark rum (optional)

Drop the tomatoes in hot water for 5 seconds to loosen the skin and remove it with a sharp knife.

Cut the tomatoes in half and squeeze out the seeds. Place the tomato halves in a heavy-bottomed saucepan with the sugar and the lemon rind and juice. Bring to a boil and stir with a wooden spoon. Reduce the heat and simmer, uncovered, for 1 hour, or until the tomatoes have become transparent and sticky. Remove the lemon peel. You may add rum before putting the preserves in sterilized jars and sealing.

Serve as a dessert with plain biscuits or spread on toasted slices of home-made bread for a *goûter* or at teatime.

Confiture de Tomates Vertes

Green tomato preserves

2.25 kg/5 lb green tomatoes
1.8 kg/4 lb sugar
rind and juice of 1 lemon

Cut the tomatoes in half and squeeze out the seeds, then cut the halves into thin slices. Put them into a large glass or china bowl and sprinkle with the sugar. Allow to marinate for 24 hours. The next day, cook the tomatoes over a low heat in a heavy saucepan with the lemon juice and lemon rind for 2 hours. Stir from time to time with a wooden spoon. Allow to cool completely before sealing in sterilized jars.

Serve with thin biscuits for dessert or spread on toast for a five-o'clock *goûter*

Délices au Miel

Honey delights

This is a most unusual dessert, crunchy, sweet and light – a children's favourite.

For 6 people

225 g/8 oz flour
a pinch of salt
115 ml/4 fl oz water
115 ml/4 fl oz peanut oil
honey to coat the pastries

Preheat the oven to 120°C/250°F/Gas Mark ½. Put the flour in a large bowl, make a well in the centre and add salt and water. With floured hands, knead well until the dough no longer sticks to your hands. Form a ball and let it rest, covered with a towel, for 2 hours.

Oil a board or counter and knead the dough again for 5 minutes. Pull off a piece the size of a walnut. Pour a little oil in a saucer, dip in the piece of dough and place it on the oiled board. With an oiled rolling pin, roll the dough very thin and fold it in four; again roll it and fold it in four; then roll it out for the third time to a 100-mm/4-in square.

Heat the peanut oil to 180°C/350°F and put in the square of pastry. Cook about 2 minutes, or until golden, turn over with tongs, and cook for a few more minutes. Place on a heated plate, spread some honey on top and keep warm in the oven. Repeat the process, piling the squares one on top of the other.

Galette des Rois
A crown-shaped brioche with candied fruits

Epiphany, on the twelfth night after Christmas, is celebrated throughout Provence. Three clay figurines, representing the *Rois mages* (the three kings, Melchior, Balthazar and Gaspard), are added to the *crèche* in each home. Families and friends celebrate *la fête des Rois*, which ends with a big cake in which a tiny china figure or dried white bean is hidden. Whoever finds the figure is the sacred king of the day. He chooses his queen, receives a toast and must invite the whole group the following week to share a second *galette des Rois* and drink champagne or *vin cuit*. *Tirer les Rois* is a wonderful reason for gathering with friends to chat, drink and eat throughout the whole month of January.

Children in Nice are told that if they get up at midnight on Epiphany Eve, wear a wet nightgown, hold a tree branch and stand on the roof or on a high branch of a tree, they will see the Three Kings marching towards the church. A good thing they enjoy the *galette des Rois* before such an ordeal!

This is not a very sweet cake. The sweetness of the candied fruits and sugar on top is enhanced by the fresh, light texture of the cake itself. Start the cake the day before you plan to serve it. You can make the golden crown from some metallic Christmas paper or gilded cardboard – wonderful for a children's party. The proportions given here are for two large cakes. Whatever is left over can be frozen.

For 12–16 people

3¼ tsp dried yeast
70 ml/2½ fl oz lukewarm water plus
    water to cover
570 g/1¼ lb unbleached flour
225 g/8 oz softened butter
225 g/8 oz lukewarm milk
2 eggs
6 egg yolks
1 tbsp fresh orange rind, finely
    grated
1 tbsp fresh lemon rind, finely
    grated

1 tbsp salt
200 g/7 oz mixed glacé cherries,
    angelica, pineapple, melon,
    raisins
55 ml/2 fl oz lukewarm dark rum
8 pieces crystallized sugar or 8 tbsp
    sugar
2 egg whites mixed with 1 tbsp
    milk
1 white china figurine (about
    25 mm/1 in high) or a dried
    white bean

Mix the yeast with the lukewarm water and let it sit for 5 minutes. Put 85 g/3 oz of the flour in a bowl, make a well in the centre and add the dissolved yeast. Knead for 3 minutes, then make a ball of the dough. Cover it with more lukewarm water and let it rest in the bowl. Let it stand in a warm place for about 15 minutes or until the ball floats to the top.

Put the remaining flour in a large bowl, make a well in the centre and add half of the butter, all of the milk, eggs, egg yolks, orange and lemon rind, and salt. Blend them and knead well. Add the ball of yeasty dough and knead for 15 minutes. Knead in the remaining butter until the dough is smooth and no longer clings to the bowl. Place this in a greased bowl and cover with a damp towel. Heat the oven to the lowest temperature for 2 minutes, turn it off and place the bowl there (or another warm place) to let the dough rise until double in bulk – about 1½ hours. Punch it down. Let it double in size again – 1 more hour. Punch down and refrigerate overnight.

The next day, soak the glacé fruits in the rum for 2 hours. Remove the dough from the refrigerator and let it warm to room temperature.

Drain the fruits. Reserve about 10 cherries and some angelica to decorate the top. Flour the rest so they will not sink to the bottom of the dough during baking. Reserve the rum for garnish.

Knead the floured fruit into the dough and form two balls. Place each ball on a floured table and make a hole in the centre of each with your fingers, then stretch the dough to form a 50-mm-/2-in-wide ring with a diameter of 150–200 mm/6–8 in. Place both rings on a buttered baking tray with a cup or something similar in the centre to keep the hole open. With kitchen scissors, cut little notches all around the edge of the rings. Leave in a warm place for about 1 hour or until doubled in size.

Preheat the oven to 200°C/400°F/Gas Mark 6. With a wooden mallet or a bottle, coarsely crush the crystallized sugar (or use plain sugar instead) and add to the rum used for soaking the fruit.

Paint the surface of the rings with the mixture of egg whites and milk and sprinkle the sugar and rum on top. Bake for 30 minutes.

Carefully hide the figurine or bean inside the cake. Garnish the top with the cherries and angelica. Make golden paper crowns to fit the centre of each cake and place them in the hole before serving.

Gâteau aux Fruits
A soft bread and candied fruit dessert

This cake, originally intended for children's snacks, will become dressier and seem more important if you serve with it a bowl of *sabayon niçois, purée de fruits frais* or a *sauce á l'abricot*.

It is quick and easy to prepare, since you probably have all the ingredients at hand, and simply cannot fail. You may use a good firm bread or a slightly stale madeira or marble cake or even madeleines.

For 6 people

370 g/13 oz diced candied fruits
    and raisins or diced dried fruits
    (peaches, apricots, pears,
    prunes)
225 ml/8 fl oz dark rum
6 slices good firm white bread
    (preferably home-made) or stale
    cake
grated rind of 1 lemon
4 egg yolks

450 ml/16 fl oz milk
150 g/5¼ oz sugar
4 egg whites, beaten until stiff
a bowl of *Sabayon Niçois* (p. 236),
    Purée de Fruit Frais (p. 236) or
    Sauce á l'Abricot (p. 238)
3 tbsp granulated sugar or a little
    icing sugar

Place the fruits in a bowl and cover with the rum to marinate for at least 2 hours. Cut the bread or cake into small cubes and sprinkle the grated lemon rind on them. Preheat the oven to 180°C/350°F/ Gas Mark 4.

Butter a baking dish and line it with one thin layer of bread cubes, then a thin layer of the marinated fruits (reserve the marinade). Repeat until all the ingredients are used up.

Put the egg yolks, milk and sugar in a bowl and beat vigorously. Add to them the beaten egg whites and blend well. Add the rum marinade and pour over the fruits and bread cubes in the baking dish. Place the baking dish in a pan of hot water (reaching a level of 50 mm/2 in from the top of the dish) and place in the oven for 1 hour. Serve slightly warm or cold, with a bowl of *sabayon niçois*, *purée de fruits frais* or *sauce à l'abricot*, or sprinkled with sugar.

Glace à la Fleur d'Orangers
Orange-flower water ice cream

This is the most delicate and exquisite of desserts. You may sprinkle it with a few curls of bitter chocolate to provide contrast in colour and flavour with the light ice cream and surround it with mint leaves. Keep the left-over egg whites for *Soupirs aux Amandes* (p. 244).

For 6 people

680 ml/1⅕ pt milk
7 egg yolks, beaten
65 g/2¼ oz sugar
2 tbsp orange-flower water (or
    more for a stronger flavour)

½ tbsp vanilla extract
25 g/1 oz dark bitter chocolate
mint leaves

Scald the milk. In a heavy saucepan, beat the egg yolks and sugar until very thick and lemon-coloured. Stirring constantly, slowly pour in the hot milk. Put over a moderately low heat and stir constantly with a wooden spoon until the mixture thickens and coats the back of a metal spoon. Let the custard cool at room temperature, then chill it in the refrigerator. Stir in the orange-flower water and vanilla. Taste to see if the mixture is sweet enough and flavoured enough (freezing diminishes the taste, so it should be fairly strong). Place the mixture in an ice-cream freezer and turn until smooth and thick. Pack in a mould, cover with foil and place in the freezer for several hours or overnight.

Put a piece of chocolate on a sheet of waxed paper on the top of the cooker near the pilot light or on top of the lid of a saucepan of boiling water. When it has softened somewhat, shave off little curls of chocolate with a potato peeler or a sharp knife. Decorate a large platter with mint leaves. Run the mould quickly under hot water and invert on the platter. Sprinkle the chocolate curls on top and serve with a sweet wine (*vin cuit* or *vin à l'orange*) and *Soupirs aux Amandes* (p. 244).

Glace au Miel
Honey ice cream

For this recipe you must use honey that is strongly flavoured but not too sweet. The mixture of honey ice and toasted almonds is wonderful. Keep the left-over egg whites for *Soupirs aux Amandes* (p. 244).

For 6–8 people

680 ml/1⅕ pt milk	3 tsp thyme (optional)
7 egg yolks	55 g/2 oz coarsely chopped
510 g/1⅛ lb honey (the best you	unpeeled toasted almonds
can find)	fresh mint leaves
½ tsp salt	

Scald the milk. Beat the egg yolks in a heavy saucepan until they are thick and lemon-coloured. Very gradually stir in the hot milk and then the honey and salt. (You may stir in the thyme for a more accented flavour.) Put over a moderately low heat and stir constantly with a wooden spoon until the custard thickens and coats the back of a metal spoon. Do not let the mixture come anywhere near a boil (a 'thermospoon' is perfect for checking the temperature). Cool at room temperature, then refrigerate for 1 hour or until thoroughly chilled. Pour into an ice-cream freezer and turn until the custard is very thick and smooth. Dip a mould in cold water, pour in the honey ice cream, cover tightly with foil and freeze several hours or overnight.

Just before serving, run the mould quickly under warm water and invert on a chilled plate. Sprinkle with almonds and decorate the platter with mint leaves. Serve with *Soupirs aux Amandes* (p. 244).

Grata Queca

Snow flavoured with fruit syrup or liqueur

This is a perfect light dessert to serve after an *aïoli*, couscous or a hearty stew. Children love it. In Nice it is sold on all street corners. Easy to make, it is a refreshing substitute for brandy after dinner.

Good French and German fruit syrups are sold in speciality shops and delicatessens; most off-licences have the fruit liqueurs.

ice

fruit syrup (*sirop de fraise, de cassis*
   or *de framboise*) or fruit liqueur
   (*liqueur de cassis* or *d'abricot*,

or *crème de menthe* or *de cassis*)
or home-made berry syrup or
   fruit purée
fresh mint leaves (optional)

Shave a block of ice or crush ice cubes wrapped in a towel. Fill individual glasses with the shavings only, not the mush. Pour in the syrup or liqueur of your choice and garnish with fresh mint.

For an elegant occasion, serve in tall sherbet glasses with long-handled spoons.

Nougat Blanc

Honey, almond and egg-white confection

Christmas in Nice is not conceivable without having on hand at least two kinds of nougat – the black and the white. Since commercially made nougat is so remote from what it should be, it is well worth learning how to make this delicious and healthy confection. Besides, the whole process of making it – the smell, the colour, the taste – is a delightful experience.

200 g/7 oz almonds, peeled and quartered
130 g/4½ oz hazelnuts or pistachios, peeled and chopped or quartered

115 ml/4 fl oz water
265 g/9¼ oz sugar
225 g/8 oz honey
3 egg whites, stiffly beaten

Place the almonds and hazelnuts or pistachios on a baking tray in the oven at 150°C/300°F/Gas Mark 2. Stirring with a wooden spoon, heat the water and sugar until the sugar thermometer reads 143°C/290°F.

Meanwhile, in another pan heat the honey, stirring with a wooden spoon until the thermometer also reads 143°C/290°F.

Mix the honey and the sugar syrup slowly, and carefully add the beaten egg whites. Pour the mixture into one of the saucepans and cook over a very low heat for a few minutes. Add the warm nuts and stir with the wooden spoon.

Oil a loaf tin. Place a sheet of waxed paper in it and butter it. Pour the nougat mixture into it and place a buttered sheet of waxed paper on top. Wrap a piece of cardboard or wood the size of the loaf tin with aluminium foil. Put it on top of the nougat, then weight it down with something heavy (canned food, bricks or heavy pebbles). Or push another loaf tin into it and then weight it down with heavy jars.

Let the nougat cool at room temperature. Unmould, cut into 50-mm/2-in strips, and wrap in aluminium foil. This will keep well at room temperature. Do not refrigerate.

Nougat Noir

Black honey and almond confection

For 8–10 people

200 g/7 oz shelled almonds and hazelnuts, cut in half (do not remove the skins)

15–25 g/½–1 oz unsalted butter

450 g/1 lb honey (the most fragrant you can find)

3 tsp rosemary or thyme (optional)

1 lemon, cut in half

Place the almonds on a baking tray and heat them in the oven at 180°C/350°F/Gas Mark 4 for about 5 minutes. Reserve in the warm oven.

Butter two long and narrow loaf tins or, if you own one, a wooden nougat mould, and line with buttered waxed paper.

Heat the honey in a heavy-bottomed saucepan made of copper, cast iron or enamel. Stir with a long wooden spoon until it reaches the boiling point. (You may stir in the rosemary or thyme at this point.) Add the warm almonds and stir for about 30 minutes or until the honey turns brown and the almonds begin to crackle. At this point the sugar thermometer should register 150°C/300°F.

Pour the hot mixture into the prepared moulds and push it down with the lemon halves. The layer should be about 12–18 mm/½–¾ in thick. Cover with a sheet of buttered waxed paper. Cut a piece of cardboard or wood to fit the inside of the mould, wrap it in aluminium foil and weight it down with two cans. Let the nougat cool at room temperature overnight.

The next day, release the sides of the nougat with a knife. Unmould by holding the bottom of the mould over a burner for a minute. Peel off the waxed paper. Cut the nougat into 3 long strips, or leave it whole, and wrap in aluminium foil, or cut it in pieces and store it in a closed jar. It will become chewy and easy to eat. Keep in a cool place but not in the refrigerator.

Petits Biscuits aux Noix

Crumbly walnut biscuits

Like most of the pastry in Nice, these sinfully rich biscuits are made with walnuts, but pecans may be used instead if necessary. Make them small – the size of a walnut.

Makes 24–50 biscuits

115 g/4 oz finely chopped walnuts
115 g/4 oz butter
50 g/1¾ oz sugar
2 tsp vanilla extract

115 g/4 oz unbleached all-purpose flour
2 tbsp granulated sugar
2 tbsp icing sugar

Preheat the oven to 150°C/300°F/Gas Mark 2. If you use a blender to chop the walnuts, chop only a little at a time to prevent turning the nuts into butter. Cream the butter and stir in the sugar. Add the vanilla, nuts and flour. (All this can be done in a food processor in a few seconds.)

Butter two baking trays and dot with teaspoonfuls of dough, (about two-thirds of a teaspoon) spacing them 50 mm/2 in apart. Bake for 20–30 minutes. When the biscuits begin to turn pale brown, they're done. Remove from the oven and, with a spatula, lift the biscuits carefully on to a plate, table or tray to cool. Sprinkle at once with granulated sugar. When cool, sprinkle with icing sugar.

Poires au Vin Rouge

Pears in red wine and lemon juice

One of the easiest desserts to prepare. You can make it ahead of time and all the ingredients are often at hand. Quickly made, impossible to do poorly, always delicious. Serve it warm or chilled with *petits biscuits aux noix*.

For 6 people

6 large, ripe, firm pears
1 lemon
rind of 1 orange
450 ml/ 16 fl oz strong red wine
200 g/7 oz sugar

2 tbsp fresh strawberry or raspberry
   purée (see *Purée de Fruits Frais*,
   p. 236) or preserves
sprigs of mint or a handful of mint
   leaves

Peel and core the pears. Wash and dry the lemon and orange, and with a potato peeler, remove the rind, taking care to peel off only the zesty surface. Cut the orange rind and half of the lemon rind into fine strips. Squeeze the lemon and reserve the juice.

Simmer the wine, sugar and rind in a heavy saucepan, uncovered, for 5 minutes. Add the pears and simmer, covered, for 35–45 minutes, basting from time to time and turning gently with a wooden spoon so that they cook and colour evenly. Prick with a thin skewer to test for doneness. The pears should be tender but not mushy. Remove them with a wooden spoon and put in a serving dish. Add the fruit purée or preserves to the wine and simmer for 15 minutes. Stir in the lemon juice and pour over the pears. Or you may discard the wine syrup and simply serve the pears in fresh fruit purée. The pears may also be sprinkled with sugar and caramelized under the grill before serving. Garnish with fresh mint.

Pommes Surprise

Baked apples with raisins, honey and rum

This is a simple country dessert made with simple ingredients. You can make it more sophisticated by replacing the honey and the preserves with fresh strawberry or raspberry purée.

For 6 people

125 g/4½ oz raisins
3 tbsp dark rum
6 tbs honey
6 large sweet apples
juice and grated rind of 1 lemon

12 almonds (with skins left on),
   chopped or slivered
6 tbsp apricot preserve or redcurrant jelly

In a bowl, soak the raisins in the rum for 1 hour. Then mix in the grated lemon rind, lemon juice and honey. Preheat the oven to 190°C/375°F/Gas Mark 5. Wash and core the apples, but don't peel them. Cut off a thin strip at the base so the apples will remain upright. Put them in a baking dish and fill the centre of each with the raisin mixture. Sprinkle with the almonds. You can prepare this much ahead of time and cover with cling film or aluminium foil and set aside until ready to cook.

Pour 115 ml/4 fl oz of warm water around the apples, cover with a sheet of aluminium foil and bake for 1 hour. Remove the foil, pierce the skin of each apple two or three times with a sharp knife and bake for 10–15 minutes. Transfer the apples to a serving dish. Stir the preserves or jelly into the cooking-pan juices and pour over the apples. Serve warm or cold.

Purée de Fruits Frais
Fresh fruit sauce

Serve this fresh sauce with *Semoule aux Fruits Confits* (p. 238) or *Gâteau aux Fruits* (p. 228).

> 100 g/3½ oz sugar
> 70 g/2½ oz strawberries
> 70 g/2½ oz raspberries
> 3 tbsp kirsch

Put all the ingredients into a blender, food processor or through a Mouli food mill.

Sabayon Niçois
Nice's own sabayon

This is delicious served with *Gâteau aux Fruits* (p. 228), *Semoules aux Fruits Confits* (p. 238) or *Soupirs aux Amandes* (p. 244). If you serve it by itself, pour it into tall glasses.

For 6 people

6 egg yolks, beaten
100 g/3½ oz sugar
juice and grated rind of 1 lemon

225 ml/8 fl oz white wine, sherry,
port, Marsala or a mixture of
dark rum and water

In a bowl, beat the egg yolks and the sugar with an eggbeater. When the mixture turns pale and frothy, add lemon juice, grated lemon rind and the wine, and beat for 1 minute. Place the bowl over a saucepan of hot water and cook for 8–10 minutes, stirring constantly with a wire whisk or a fork. The mixture will thicken and become creamy. Don't overcook or it will curdle.

Pour into a warm bowl or into individual cups. Serve at room temperature, not chilled.

Salades de Fruits
Fresh fruit salads

Select as many fruits as you can, varying the flavour, colour and texture as much as possible. Serve the salad in a glass bowl – this will look very cool on a hot summer day – with perhaps a few mint leaves to decorate it.

Slice the large fruits but leave the small ones whole. Arrange the fruits in layers in a bowl, sprinkle with sugar, red wine, rum, kirsch and orange or lemon juice. Chill well, then toss gently just before serving.

Each of these combinations is a sample of the variety a salad bowl can have:

- Peaches, oranges (sliced, with rind left on) and strawberries with red wine
- Apricots, strawberries, pears and maraschino cherries with lemon juice
- Apples (sliced), bananas (sliced and quickly covered with lemon juice to prevent discolouring) and oranges with dark rum and orange juice
- Strawberries, raspberries and redcurrants with lemon juice and kirsch

- Black and white grapes (each grape washed and dried, but not peeled), pears and blackberries with red wine

Note: Never combine melon or watermelon with other fruits – it loses its crisp freshness.

Sauce à l'Abricot
Apricot sauce

Delicious on baked apples, semolina cake, bread cake or plain ice cream.

> 170 g/6 oz apricot preserves
> 6 tbsp dark rum

Place the preserves and half of the rum in a heavy-bottomed saucepan and bring to a boil. Reduce the heat and simmer, stirring with a wooden spoon, for 5 minutes. Add the rest of the rum and cook for 3 minutes more. Use this sauce warm or hot. It can be re-heated.

Semoule aux Fruits Confits
A semolina dessert with candied fruits

Prepared with the simplest of ingredients, this light, velvety dessert is also one of the healthiest. It is always a children's favourite. Adults will also love it when it is accompanied by *Sabayon Niçois* (p. 236), fresh fruit purée or apricot or redcurrant preserves heated with lemon and sugar.

For 6 people

25 g/1 oz raisins
2 tbsp dark rum
900 ml/1⅗ pt milk
65 g/2¼ oz medium-grain semolina
   (a hard wheat semolina wheat
   product)

2 whole eggs, beaten
150 g/5¼ oz sugar
150 g/5¼ oz diced candied fruits
   (cherries, melon, apricots)

Soak the raisins in the rum for 1 hour.

Bring the milk to a boil, then reduce the heat and sprinkle the semolina into the milk while stirring constantly with a wooden spoon. Cook for about 10 minutes or until the mixture thickens. Remove from heat.

Preheat the oven to 180°C/350°F/Gas Mark 4. In a large bowl, beat the eggs with a fork. Add the sugar, diced fruits, raisins and rum marinade. Add the mixture to the semolina and stir. Pour into an oiled baking dish and place it in a large pan containing about 50 mm/2 in of water. Bake for 20 minutes.

This can be served warm, spooned out on individual plates and garnished with *sabayon niçois*, fresh strawberry or raspberry purée (see *Purée de Fruits Frais*, p. 236) or *Sauce à l'Abricot* (p. 238). It can also be chilled and unmoulded before serving. It will keep a few days in the refrigerator.

Suce-Miels
Honey candies

Virtually impossible to eat, not easy to make, but these little sticks of cooked honey are a favourite in Provence.

Heat 450 g/1 lb of honey in a heavy enamel saucepan, a copper saucepan, or a metal mould used for making caramelized custard. Stir with a wooden spoon over a medium heat. For a more fragrant *suce-miel*, you may want to stir in 2 tablespoons of dried thyme. When the honey turns dark brown and liquid after about 15 minutes, remove from the heat.

Spread in little sticks on a buttered sheet of waxed paper. Cover with another buttered sheet and let them cool. Keep in a dry, cool place. With scissors, cut into pieces, a few sticks at a time.

Tian au Rhum
Rum and milk custard

This is a delicate and exciting traditional dessert, which is very easy to prepare. You can use the whites of the eggs later for *Soupirs aux Amandes* (p. 244); you will like the lovely combination of rum custard and almond wafers.

For 6 people

200 g/7 oz sugar
2 tbsp water
900 ml/1⅗ pt milk
3 whole eggs and 3 yolks
5 tbsp dark rum

Boil 100 g/3½ oz of the sugar with the water in a 1-l/1⅘-pt mould over a medium to high heat. Shake the mould from time to time. When the syrup turns from golden to amber in colour, place the bottom of the mould in a pan of cold water for 1 minute, then rotate it so the caramel runs and coats the entire bottom and part of the sides. Let it cool upside down for a few minutes over a plate that has been buttered to prevent the caramel from sticking.

Preheat the oven to 180°C/350°F/Gas Mark 4. Heat the milk in a large saucepan. In a large bowl, beat the eggs and yolks, gradually adding the remaining sugar. Very slowly pour in the hot milk while stirring vigorously. Stir in 4 tablespoons of the rum and pour the custard into the caramel-coated mould.

Place the mould in a large roasting pan and pour 50 mm/2 in of hot water into the pan. Bake for 40–50 minutes or until a knife inserted in the centre comes out clean.

Allow to cool, then run a knife around the edge of the custard to unmould it more easily. Place a flat dish over the mould and then, holding both dish and mould, turn them upside down to unmould the custard.

If some caramel is still on the mould, add 1 tablespoon rum to the mould and heat the caramel to dissolve it again. Pour this over the top of the custard. No garnish is needed.

Les Treize Desserts de Noël

The thirteen desserts of Christmas

Christmas, or *Calena*, in Nice is celebrated with a rich variety of rituals. It all starts on the fourth of December, when children place wheat and lentils in saucers and cover them with a little cotton wool so that they will sprout. The budding green is used for the *crèche*.

Displayed in the *crèche* are *santons*: little hand-painted clay figurines representing the most characteristic of Provençal villagers. There is the fish vendor with a large, flat basket of sardines on each arm, the miller carrying a bag of flour, the wine merchant with a barrel of wine on his shoulder, the simpleton, *ravi*, with his dried cod, the housewife with a full mortar of *aïoli*, the baker and his *pompe à l'huile*, the hunter carrying rabbits and a hare, the shepherd with a white lamb on his shoulder, and the old peasant women dressed in black and wearing shawls, the chair-cane weaver, the knife grinder. Curiously, there is also a drummer, a postman and a mayor.

A week before *Calena*, all the *santons* are unpacked and placed on a mantelpiece, a chest of drawers or a table. Rocky hills (brown wrapping paper), green meadows (the wheat and lentil sprouts) and snowy lanes (flour) create the setting. The little stable with Jesus, Mary and Joseph in it is put in, and then from all sides come the villagers, dressed in nineteenth-century Provençal costumes.

The theatres during that week play little pastorals (*presepi*) in which all the characters of the *crèche* take part: the gossipy linen washer, Tanta Giana, the Bastian Countrari (a sort of Mary contrary), Don Boutifa, the greedy monk and many others.

Decorations in the streets are minimal and food is the most colourful part of Christmas in Nice. On Christmas Eve the *gros souper* or *souper maigre* takes place. It is *gros* (big) because it is a celebration of all the good things we are thankful for and because it is an important family affair; it is *maigre* 'lean' for religious reasons – no meat is allowed.

Before the meal begins, the master of the house places in the fireplace a log (usually taken from a fruit tree) kept from the previous Christmas. He adds some pine cones and vine branches. Surrounded by all the guests, he lights the fire, dips a branch of celery in a glass of *vin cuit* and sprinkles the fire with it. The guests sip the wine as the glass is passed around.

The table is set with three white tablecloths. A large candle is brought to the table and throughout the meal everyone, from the youngest to the oldest member of the family, takes turns blowing it out and lighting it again.

The *gros souper* may begin with *aïgo bouido*, the light garlic and herb broth, or with raw celery dipped in an *anchoïade* sauce. Then there might be little grey snails or dried cod cooked in *raïto* or served with *aïoli*. A warm vegetable salad will follow – cauliflower or chick-peas or lentils. Ravioli made with vegetables or *tians* of vegetables will come next. A crisp green salad of chicory or celery follows, along with garlicky *chapons* seasoned with newly pressed olive oil.

The meal is long but is composed only of healthy natural foods and it ends with the traditional *treize desserts*, presented on a large tray or in little earthenware bowls.

############ Fresh Fruits ############

pale oranges from Nice

tangerines

winter melon (carefully turned to
    ripen evenly in the cellar since
    the autumn)

pears

apples

pomegranates

############ Dried Fruits ############

grapes that have been hung since
    the autumn and are wrinkled
    and sweet, almost like honey

figs, dried first in the sun, then
    kept indoors on screens and
    then between peach-tree leaves
    and bay leaves

hazelnuts

almonds, both the soft sweet kind
    and the hard-shelled bitter ones

walnuts

dates *en branche*, from Africa,
    candied on their branches

·················· Sweets ··················

calissons d'Aix, made with candied
    fruits and almonds
fruit *tourtes*
black and white nougats
quince paste (*pâte de coing*)

candied fruits
pompes à l'huile, a sweet cake
    enriched with orange-flower
    water and olive oil

The guests nibble the thirteen desserts, sip the sweet *vin cuit* (prepared in the autumn), gather around the *crèche* and sing while waiting for midnight mass.

Before leaving for church, the lady of the house places some of the thirteen desserts on a clean tablecloth ready for neighbours, beggars or even the souls of ancestors to taste while she is at church. She then pours the left-over wine on the fire, removes the log, wraps it and places it in a closet for the following Christmas.

Back from the mass the children are put to bed. Their shoes – here it is shoes and not stockings that Father Christmas fills – are stuffed with oranges, dates and sweets of all kinds.

Then the adults sit down for the *réveillon*. It can be either a small snack taken before going back to one's home or a large elaborate affair – *boudin blanc*, *foie gras* and other delicacies – lasting until dawn.

Traditionally on Christmas Day the godfather brings his godson a cake in the shape of a rooster, and his goddaughter a cake in the shape of a doll. The meal is also a family gathering; it often starts with chopped turkey heart and kidneys sautéd with olive oil, celery and black olives. Then comes the turkey or the goose, filled with chestnuts and ham, followed by a tart chicory salad seasoned with newly pressed olive oil. There may be a large tray of goat's cheese – creamy ones and little dry ones set on leaves. And finally, some of the thirteen desserts left over from the previous night. It ends with home-made liqueurs – *ratafia*, *liqueur de coing* – and songs.

Soupirs aux Amandes
Almonds wafers

These crisp little biscuits (they indeed deserve their name – *soupirs* means sighs) are made in Nice with a mixture of sweet and bitter almonds. Since bitter almonds may be difficult to find here, I add almond extract to the dough and leave the skin on the nuts. The biscuits go wonderfully well with *Glace à la Fleur d'Orangers* (p. 229), *Tian au Rhum* (p. 240) and all the fruit desserts.

Makes about 35 wafers

70 g/2½ oz almonds, with the skins left on
40 g/1½ oz unsalted butter at room temperature
100 g/3½ oz sugar

2–3 egg whites
5 tbsp unbleached flour
¾ tsp almond extract
¼ tsp salt

Preheat the oven to 230°C/450°F/Gas Mark 8. Grind the nuts in a blender or food processor at high speed for 2 minutes, or pass them through a Mouli food mill or chop them very fine by hand.

Cream the butter and sugar until the mixture is light and fluffy. Stir in the egg whites and blend well. Add the flour, almonds, almond extract and salt.

Butter a baking tray and drop the batter on to it by small teaspoonfuls, 50–75mm/2–3 in apart. Lower the oven heat to 200°C/400°F/Gas Mark 6 and bake for 5–6 minutes, or until the edges turn light brown.

Remove the biscuits immediately with a spatula and let them cool on wire racks or on a cold surface. When cold, store them in an airtight container to keep them crisp.

Tourte de Blettes
Apple, spinach and pine-nut pie

This is a curious blend of apples, raisins and spinach or Swiss chard (this is what is used in Nice) baked in a light pie. It is one of Nice's traditional and most beloved desserts, and although it may seem odd to you at first, it will probably become one of the staples for your picnics and buffets. It can be eaten warm or cold.

For 8 people

·················· Pastry ··················

340 g/12 oz unbleached flour
2 eggs, beaten
225 g/8 oz unsalted butter,
    softened

100 g/3½ oz sugar
about 1 tbsp salt

Working quickly with the tips of your fingers, mix all the ingredients together on a well-floured board. Pound and stretch the dough away from you with the heel of your hand to be sure all ingredients are well blended. Shape the dough into a ball, cover with a clean cloth and leave for 2 hours at room temperature.

·················· Filling ··················

4 large Golden Delicious or Granny
    Smith apples
3 tbsp raisins
2 tbsp dark rum
900 g/2 lb fresh or 570 g/1¼ lb
    frozen spinach, cooked,
    thoroughly drained and
    chopped
4 tbsp pine nuts

55 g/2 oz icing sugar
115–225 g/4–8 oz bland cheese,
    such as Gouda or a mild
    Cheddar, diced
2 beaten eggs
grated rind of 1 lemon
2 tbsp redcurrant jelly
3 tbsp icing sugar

Peel the apples and cut two of them into small cubes. Put the raisins and rum in a saucepan and bring to a boil. Cook for 2 minutes.

Preheat the oven to 190°C/375°F/Gas Mark 5.

In a large bowl, mix the spinach, raisins, apple cubes, pine nuts, sugar, cheese, eggs and lemon rind. Slice the remaining two apples. Divide the pastry into two unequal parts, the smaller being about a third of the larger amount. Roll the pastry as thin as you can.

Butter a deep mould and spread the larger circle of dough in the bottom, moulding it to fit the bottom and sides. Prick it all over with a fork. Spread the currant jelly on the bottom and add the filling. Cover with the apple slices and then with the smaller circle of dough. Fit together smoothly and cut off the excess dough. Prick the top crust with a fork and bake for 30 minutes or until golden. Remove from the oven and sprinkle with icing sugar.

Tourte aux Noix et au Miel
Walnut and honey pie

This recipe comes from the hills above Nice, where bees have fields of lavender and rosemary for making honey, cows have good pasture and walnut trees are luxuriant. It is a superb, richly flavoured dessert. Make sure when you prepare it that you have crisp walnuts (always keep them in the freezer so that they remain fresh) and flavourful honey. It must be made 3–4 hours before it is served to allow the taste to mature. Cut the pie in small slices, since it is quite rich. It will keep well.

For 8–10 people

·············· Pastry ··············

200 g/7 oz unbleached flour
140 g/5 oz unsalted butter, chilled
   and cut into pieces
2 tbsp peanut oil or lard

1 tsp salt
2 tsp sugar
4–6 tablespoons cold water, as
   needed

Put the flour on a counter and make a well in the centre. Add the butter, peanut oil or lard, salt and sugar. Blend with your fingers for 3 minutes, then add the cold water and knead briskly, pushing the dough down and then away from you with the heel of your hand, for a few minutes or until all the water is incorporated. When the dough is smooth, form a ball and wrap it in cling film or a towel. Chill it for 1 hour.

·············· Filling ··············

300 g/10½ oz sugar
115 ml/4 fl oz water
340 g/12 oz chopped walnuts

200 g/7 oz butter
225 ml/8 fl oz milk
115 g/4 oz honey

Put the sugar and water in a saucepan and cook it over a low heat for a few minutes. When the syrup turns light brown, immediately remove from heat (it can turn into caramel). Add the walnuts and the butter to the saucepan and stir. Add the milk and simmer over a low heat for 15–20 minutes. Stir in the honey and remove from heat. Set aside.

Preheat the oven to 200°C/400°F/Gas Mark 6. Roll the dough on a floured surface into two 275-mm/11-in circles. Place one of the circles in a well-buttered 250-mm/10-in pie tin and pour in the filling. Place the other circle of dough on top and seal the edges. Press and pinch the two layers together. With a thin knife, trim the crust and cut a few slits on top to allow the steam to escape.

Place on the centre rack of the oven and bake for 20 minutes. Let cool for several hours. Sprinkle with icing sugar and cut into thin slices.

Note: You may use strips of pastry on the top in a lattice pattern rather than a full crust.

Boissons de Ménage

Home-made Beverages

Most liqueurs and sweet wine were first prepared and their use justified as medicines. Quinces, cherries, oranges, herbs and blossoms were marinated in brandy or wine and prescribed (most of the time self-prescribed) for melancholy, toothache, gout and spring fever – anything from senility to growing pains.

I remember they were so good that every afternoon someone in my family would suddenly feel faint and whisper, 'I am hot and cold – I don't know what . . .' in full expectation that a delicious beverage would instantly appear to cure the mysterious discomfort.

As a child my passion was *ratafia d'oranges*. When my ailments became 'overwhelming', I was allowed to dip a lump of sugar in a glass of *ratafia*. The curative effect was very slow. Only after the third lump of sugar did I feel a barely perceptible improvement.

Now my two daughters seem to draw immense benefit from *vin de noix*. So every June I prepare a large jar of it. I also prepare grated quince marinated in brandy and sugar for my husband (he cannot quite explain how it helps or what it helps, but he knows it does help); lavender blossoms in white wine to fight severe winters; the *liqueur de lait* to fight severe summers, and a wide variety of *liqueurs de fenêtre* (called 'window liqueurs' because the fruits, brandy, wine and sugar are left on the window-sill to marinate and to let the sun mellow them). Thus no malaise ever catches us unprepared.

Ratafia d'Oranges

Orange liqueur with coriander

Ratafia can be made with sour cherries, strawberries, quinces or oranges. They are always served in ornate glass decanters and sipped in the afternoons or after dinner. They are good when one feels melancholy, anxious or even merry – truly wonderful for all occasions.

Makes 900 ml/1⅗ pt

> 6 oranges
> 450 g/1 lb sugar
> 450 g/1 lb whole coriander seed
> 900 ml/1⅗ pt brandy or cognac

Wash and dry the oranges. With a potato peeler, peel off only the zesty part of the rind and discard the white part. Chop it into small pieces. Squeeze the oranges and put the juice and rind in a bowl. Add the sugar, coriander seed and brandy or cognac, and stir. Pour into a large jar or a small barrel or a demijohn and close tightly. Let it rest in a dark, cool place for two months. Pass through a sieve, pour into bottles and store them, tightly capped, in a dark, cool place.

Vin Cuit

A sweet dessert wine

Vin cuit is served at Christmas with the *treize desserts*, at epiphany with the *gâteau des Rois*. In former times most families made their own *vin cuit*, but now it is made commercially and few bother to concoct it. Here is the recipe, however, for those who may be interested.

First of all, one must always choose the ripest black grapes (preferably *muscat de malvaisie*) picked during the heat of the day.

Crush the grapes. The unfermented grape juice, called must (*le moût*), is the base of the *vin cuit*. Pour 9 l/16 pt of must into a large copper cauldron. Simmer it until it has been reduced to 5.5 l/9⅗ pt. From time to time remove the scum that rises to the top. Pour the must into a large barrel or an earthenware jar. Stir vigorously with a long stick or spoon. When the liquid is cold, add 680 ml/1⅕ pt of brandy. Let it rest for 48 hours. Pass it through a sieve and pour into bottles. Seal and keep in a cool, dark place.

To this basic recipe, many additions can be made. While the must is boiling, 2 unpeeled quinces cut in half may be added. Anise seed, coriander, cinnamon and apricot pits may also be added to the must as it cools before the brandy is added. The proportions can be what one likes best. Each housewife in Provence prided herself on her own inimitable version of *vin cuit*.

Vin de Noix

A sweet red dessert wine flavoured with green walnuts

This is the most delectable of wines. It is prepared on the first day of summer and is ready at Christmas. Unbruised green walnuts can be picked during the month of June. Both the green kernels and the beige shells will be soft, so it should be possible to pass a long knitting needle through the whole fruit.

Makes 5.4 l/9⅗ pt

40 green walnuts with their shells
4.5 l/8 pt strong red wine
900 g/2 lb sugar
1 nutmeg, grated

1 clove
1 vanilla bean
900 ml/1⅗ pt brandy

Quarter the walnuts and place them in a large container. Add the wine, sugar, nutmeg, clove and vanilla bean. Cover the container tightly. Place in a dark room and let it rest for fifty days, shaking it a bit every fortnight. Add the brandy and pass the mixture through a sieve. Pour into bottles, seal tightly and leave them for about six months in a dark, cool place.

Vin d'Orange
An orange-flavoured dessert wine

This is a lovely wine to serve chilled with biscuits in the afternoon or as a dessert wine after dinner.

Makes 5.4 l/9⅗ pt

5 large oranges
1 large lemon
4.5 l/8 pt white wine, preferably
    dry, or red wine
900 g/2 lb sugar

900 ml/1⅗ pt brandy or cognac
1 vanilla bean (optional)
1 100-mm/4-in piece dried orange
    rind

Wash the oranges and the lemon and grate their skins on to a plate. Quarter the fruits into a demijohn or preserve jars or any other large glass containers. Add the grated rind, wine, sugar, brandy, vanilla bean and the piece of orange rind. Close the top and let it rest for forty days.

Pass through a sieve and pour into bottles. Seal tightly and keep in a cool place. Serve chilled.

Menus

Escoffier wrote that, like music, the grand structure of gastronomy is built upon the harmony and sequence of its elements. Preparing a menu is as important to me as preparing any given dishes. The seasonal fresh ingredients I find available always determine the core of the meal, and I organize the rest around them.

But the circumstances and the guests are also important. Do I want to prepare a substantial dinner for robust gourmands, an elegant lunch for dainty gourmets, a picnic *à la bonne franquette* for cosy friends? Do I have time to prepare only one dish? Several dishes? Shall I have someone to help in the kitchen, someone to wait at table, no help at all?

I don't attempt more than one challenge a meal; the rest are easy and often-tried reliable recipes. With the tone and core of the meal decided, I think about the sequence in which the courses will be served. I never have a Chinese-style series of delicious unrelated dishes. To me, not only the sequence but also the colour, texture, flavour and temperature are important. Each dish must contrast with the next. A crisp tossed lettuce salad in the middle of the meal will refresh the guests and allow a pause. I try to avoid repetitions. No *loup farci*, with its tomato sauce, after a *salade niçoise*. No meal starting with a *pissaladière* and finishing with *tourte de blettes*.

I usually plan not only special meals but also the whole week's menus to make sure of the variety of the meals, and because in the long run it is less time-consuming. Since so many good Niçois dishes are based on left-overs, I double the proportions of *gigot à l'aillade*, *boeuf à la niçoise*, *poisson au court bouillon*, and then prepare *salade de riz*, ravioli and *tian* the next day. The transformation of the basic ingredients is so total that nobody can guess they are making a second appearance.

Cooking and planning ahead also prevent impulse buying, the falling back on easily prepared but expensive cuts of meat and on convenient processed food, or subsisting on a boring repetitious diet.

While the pots and pans, the knives and Mouli food mill are being put to use anyway and the kitchen has become something of a battlefield, I feel I may as well win two or three battles simultaneously. The cleaning up will take only a little more time but the interesting menus we will have for days will take only a moment to produce – I will need to add only a tossed lettuce salad, a vegetable omelette, a tray of cheese or some of the cold salads I keep in the refrigerator.

So the soup cooks while the *boeuf à la niçoise* simmers and the *tian* bakes next to the *gâteau à la semoule*. Instead of a boring routine, a chore, those big cooking sessions are full of joy. My children love the excitement, the mess, the fun – they see me kneading and cutting, and they jump about helping me gather up peels, chop nuts, rinse vegetables. And they compose their own strange mixtures.

The kitchen is full of delicious smells – vinegar, thyme, lemon, garlic – and all the rituals of cuisine become vitalized by this magical chemistry practised *en famille*. Food and love always mingle easily. And children soon begin to realize the respect they should have for the variety and quality of food, and learn that like all other pleasure-giving activity, cooking and eating are serious matters.

When I serve my Niçois dishes, I always try to please the eye as well as the palate. Pretty earthenware, an assortment of baskets, bright napkins on which to place a *terrine* or *beignets* – everything is fresh, cheerful and more than merely functional.

However, keep the *faites simple* motto. Don't fuss, don't overdo. Gain confidence, plan carefully, consider your guests and the time you can spend, then enjoy yourself.

Here are a few suggested menus you may like to try. Soon you will learn the quality of each dish and you will enjoy creating the delicate balance each menu demands.

Le Déjeuner
Lunch

Soupe de Moules
Salade de Chou-fleur (Salade Blanche)
Compote de Fruits
Soupirs aux Amandes

Terrine de Campagne
Salade Amère
Tian au Rhum

Champignons Farcis
Tian d'Épinards et de Morue
Compote de Fruits
Petits Biscuits aux Noix

Artichauts à la Barigoule
Tian de Navets Rosés
Salade de Fruits
Soupirs aux Amandes

Pois Gourmands en Marinade
Pâtes aux Moules
Plateau de Fromages Variés

Caillettes de Nice
Tian de Navets Rosés
Salade Mélangée aux Noix
Pommes Surprise

Crique (Omelette Jardinière)
Salade de Haricots Verts
Gâteau aux Fruits

Le Dîner
Dinner

Moules aux Épinards
Canard comme à Nice
Champignons Provençale
Tian de Navets Rosés
Salade de Fruits

Salade de Moules
Poulet à la Niçoise
Gnocchi
Salade Verte
Tourte aux Noix et au Miel

Soupe de Moules
Brochettes de Nice
Riz au Safran
Glace à la Fleur d'Orangers
Soupirs aux Amandes

Ratatouille
Boeuf à la Niçoise
Salade Mesclun
Poires au Vin Rouge

Poisson Mariné
Farcis à la Niçoise
Glace au Miel
Petits Biscuits aux Noix

Poulet en Gelée
Salade de Riz Variée
Beignets aux Fruits

Barba Jouan
Estockaficada
Salade Mesclun
Pommes Surprise
Soupirs aux Amandes

Asperges Vinaigrette
Loup Farci à la Niçoise
Courgettes Râpées
Poires au Vin Rouge

Pois Gourmands à la Paysanne
Rôti de Porc Provençale
Tian de Navets Rosés
Compote de Fruits

Soupe de Lentilles
Agneau à la Niçoise
Épinards aux Pignons
Févettes à l'Ail
Tian au Rhum

Anchoïade
Estouffade
Pâtes aux Oeufs
Févettes à la Verdure
Panier de Fruits

Nu et Cru
Gigot d'Agneau à l'Aillade
Pommes de Terre aux Herbes
Tomates Provençale
Beignets de Fruits

Soupe de Pois Chiches
Caillettes de Nice
Riz aux Herbes
Céleri Paysanne
Pommes Surprise

Brandade
Artichauts à la Barigoule
Tourte de Blettes

Terrine de Campagne
Suppions à la Niçoise
Salade Amère
Glace à la Fleur d'Orangers
Soupirs aux Amandes

Plateau de Hors-d'Oeuvres Variés
Merlan Magali
Riz aux Herbes
Compote d'Abricots, de Pêches et de Prunes
Petits Biscuits aux Noix

Pissaladière
Gigot de Mer
Riz au Safran
Salade Verte
Poires au Vin Rouge

Soupe de Pêcheurs
Troucha
Beignets de Fruits

Pâtes à la Verdure
Capilotade
Courgettes Râpées
Grata Queca

Escargots à la Provence
Tian de Courges
Gâteau aux Fruits
Sabayon Niçois

Soupe de Courges
Capoun
Salade Verte
Tian au Rhum
Petits Biscuits aux Noix

Nu et Cru
Ravioli à la Niçoise
Salade Amère
Plateau de Fromages
Glace au Miel
Soupirs aux Amandes

Pissaladière
Merlan aux Moules
Riz aux Herbes
Salade Mélangée aux Noix
Pommes Surprise

Sardines au Vinaigre
Daube d'Avignon
Courgettes Râpées
Tian au Rhum
Petits Biscuits aux Noix

Papeton d'Aubergines
Poisson au Court Bouillon, Sauce Verte, Rouille
Salade de Riz Variée (au Fenouil)
Semoule aux Fruits Confits

Crudités et Bagna Cauda
Couscous
Plateau de Fruits

Anchoïade
Bouillabaisse
Salade Mesclun
Plateau de Fromages

Socca
Aïoli
Poires au Vin Rouge

Le Pique-nique
Picnic

Food for a picnic can be prepared ahead of time or barbecued on the spot. It must always be appetizing and easy to handle.

·········· Savoury Dishes ··········

Pissaladière
Farcis à la Niçoise
Omelettes Jardinières
Brochettes de Nice
Pan Bagna
Terrine de Campagne
Sardines Grillées
Caillettes de Nice
Pietsch
Crudités (with salt instead of
sauces)

·········· Sweet Dishes ··········

Tourte de Blettes
Tourte au Miel et aux Noix
Soupirs aux Amandes
Petits Biscuits aux Noix
Paniers de Fruits Frais
Plateau de Fromages
Nougat Noir
Nougat Blanc

Le Goûter
Snack

The most cheerful of meals for children. We call it *la merenda* in Nice.

·········· Savoury Dishes ··········

Socca
Pan Bagna.
Anchoïade

Saussoun
Pissaladière
Terrine
Toasted slices of bread spread with
congealed olive oil and eaten
with raw vegetables

············ Sweet Dishes ············

Panisses au Sucre
Beignets aux Fruits
Tourte de Blettes
Tourte aux Noix et au Miel
Semoule aux Fruits
Grata Queca
Nougat Noir
Nougat Blanc
Délices au Miel
Confiture de Tomates Rouges
Confiture Noire

Le Buffet
Buffet

There must be a rich offering of colours, textures and flavours, and
there must be both hot and cold dishes. Variety is important and
easy to have because all the dishes can be prepared ahead of time.

············ Savoury Dishes ············

Anchoïade
Crudités et Saussoun
Crudités et Sauce Verte
Caviar Provençale
Bagna Cauda et Crudités
Plateau de Hors-d'Oeuvres Variés
Poisson au Court Bouillon (with
three sauces)

Pissaladière
Terrine de Campagne
Pan Bagna
Salades Blanches
Salade Niçoise
Pois Gourmands en Marinade
Salade de Riz Variée

·············· Sweet Dishes ··············

Salades de Fruits
Pommes Surprises
Poires au Vin Rouge
Tourte de Blettes
Tourte aux Noix et au Miel
Tian au Rhum
Les Treize Desserts de Noël
Soupirs aux Amandes
Petits Biscuits aux Noix
Confiture de Tomates Rouges
Confiture de Tomates Vertes
Confiture Noire
Semoule aux Fruits (in individual
dishes)
Panier de Fruits Frais
Plateau de Fromages

Spécialités
Special Treats

Some Niçois dishes depend on local products and are impossible to recreate outside their home ground. The mushrooms of a certain wood, the fish from a particular cove, the ham from a village in the area – these are unique. And the traditional ways of curing meats, pressing olive oil and candying fruits are unique, too.

Can *poutine* (tiny undeveloped fish) be found anywhere but between Antibes and Menton? The privilege of fishing for these tiny sardines, herring and other minute fish dates back a hundred years. It is only valid for a month and each boat is entitled to bring back only 90 kg/200 lb of *poutine*. The *poutine* is rather thick and pasty; the *nonat*, another group of tiny fish, is transparent and slightly bigger. They are both prepared in various ways. Dusted with flour, they are fried in olive oil and served with lemon wedges. Fried as an omelette or a pancake, they form a golden crisp flat mass, which is sprinkled with red wine vinegar and chopped parsley and cut in sections like a tart. They can be cooked in individual dishes with little chilli peppers and garlic or be part of a *tian* made of vegetables, eggs and cheese. They can also be prepared in *beignets* and in soups. The closest British counterpart to these Mediterranean fish would be whitebait.

The *poutargue*, made with mullet roe, is another delicacy imposs- ible to find outside Provence. It is called 'the caviar of Martigues' (a small fishing town), and is gathered every spring when the sea is calm. Every year between the fifteenth of July and the end of August, the mullet leave their eggs along the Berre Pond, near Marseilles. Gathering the eggs is a delicate operation because great care must be taken not to tear the membrane surrounding the roe. The eggs are placed in a bowl and covered with rough salt. A heavy board is left on top of them for forty-eight hours to press out as much moisture as possible. After being rinsed with clear water, they are spread in the sun for four days, until they are perfectly dry. Then they are hung inside a large fireplace and smoked slowly (the wood is covered with sawdust to increase the smoke). After one hour of smoking each day for four consecutive days the *poutargue* is ready. It is eaten with oil and red wine vinegar as an hors-d'oeuvre, or is added in small pieces to chick-peas, then covered with a light nutmeg-flavoured mayonnaise mixed with finely chopped onions and parsley.

Snails in Nice are small and either pale grey or striped. Fed on fragrant herbs, such as fennel and thyme, they are often cooked in a hot tomato sauce with herbs or barbecued outdoors over an open fire. *Limaçons à la sucarelle* are first cooked in a herb-flavoured *court bouillon*, then mixed with a spicy sauce and put back in their shells, the bottom of which have been opened so that it is easier to suck the snail out of its shell. It is interesting that the Chinese use the same technique with periwinkles.

Some of the specialities are based on simple ingredients, easily available everywhere, but are prepared in ways that might startle most Britons. Among these is *galito denti* (which means a chicken with teeth), a curious dish loved by all. The head of a lamb is opened and washed, surrounded with quartered potatoes, sprinkled with herbs, and grilled; the brain and cheeks are great delicacies, and the potatoes cooked around the bones have a superb flavour. A goat's head spread with a paste of parsley and garlic is grilled the same way. A calf's head, simmered in tomato sauce with a little wine, is also delicious. A boar's head is more robust and also more elaborately prepared. The skull is emptied and washed carefully, and is filled with onions, thyme, chopped carrots, chopped tongue, ham and lamb cheeks and seasoned with cognac and white wine. It is first marinated, then cooked for eight hours in white wine.

There is *fressure d'agneau* (lamb kidneys, liver, heart and lungs simmered with olives and mushrooms); cockscomb stew; *bala de mouton* (by no means symbolic of 'women's lib's revenge' – this has long been considered a delicacy), sliced and fried and served with lemon wedges and parsley.

Anchovies in vinegar are a staple in a Niçois kitchen. Here is the way the Niçoise housewife prepares it:

Place 450 g/1 lb of fresh anchovies on a board and remove the heads and insides. Dry with kitchen towels. Bring to a boil 900 ml/ 1⅗ pt of red wine vinegar, add 2 cloves, 1 tablespoon of thyme, 1 teaspoon of savory and 3 peeled garlic cloves. Add the anchovies, bring back to the boiling point, then reduce the heat and simmer for 15 minutes. Remove from the cooker and let cool in its liquid. Place the anchovies in a glass jar. Close tightly and wait for two weeks before testing. These are served as an hors-d'oeuvre, in sandwiches and as an accompaniment.

Pissalat is sold everywhere in Nice packed in small jars with elaborate old-fashioned labels, but most Niçois still prepare their own. Here is the recipe in case you want to try it. Rinse and dry 450 g/1 lb of fresh sardines and 900 g/2 lb of fresh anchovies. Remove the heads and the insides. Place a layer of fish in a large bowl and sprinkle with rough (kosher) salt, a few peppercorns, a few cloves, branches of dried wild fennel and bay leaves. Repeat the procedure with the rest of the fish. Stir the mixture every day with a long wooden spoon. After a few days, the fish will turn pasty. After a month, push the fish paste through a sieve with a pestle. Fill glass jars with this purée and cover with a little olive oil before closing the top. Keep in a cool place. Serve with hot toast, cold meat, hot boiled potatoes or sliced tomatoes.

Baby thrushes and baby larks are called *chachas*. The insides (except for the gizzard) are kept and the birds are stuffed with a little butter, a few juniper berries and a grape or two. Wrapped in thin slices of salt pork or caul, they are cooked in white wine seasoned with crushed juniper berries. The stuffed birds are served on warm *croûtons*. With their little beak tucked under the wing, they can also be skewered and grilled over a fire of pine cones, vine prunings or rosemary sprigs. Toward the end of the cooking, large slices of bread are placed under them to gather the delectable juices, and the whole dish is served with a bunch of crisp watercress.

Panier de Fruits Niçois

A Look at Nice's Fruits

There is a staggering variety of fruits offered all year round in Nice's market-places. In summer there are melons and watermelons, *cantaloups*, *charentais*, *Verdons*. Madame de Sévigné on her visits to the South of France was fond of saying that 'it is indeed a strange thing, but if by an odd whim we were to demand a tasteless melon, we would have to have it sent from Paris. There are *none* here!' And southern melons are so fragrant that Alexandre Dumas offered his four hundred volumes of books in exchange for twelve southern melons a year.

There is also an abundance of peaches: the yellow peach of Nice with its pointed tip, strong delicious flavour and firm flesh; little vine peaches; the red peaches. There are yellow freckled apricots, *les muscats*, and big orange ones. There are pears with disconcerting names: *le trompe chasseur* (how can a pear cheat a hunter?); *cuissette de dame* (lady's little thigh), with a thin yellow-striped skin; and the *cuisse de dame* (lady's thigh), with a coarser skin but a melting flesh; and the *bon chrétien*, a very sweet but not very tasty summer pear. There are plums, the yellow *pistole* (after the Spanish money), the purple *perdigon*, with its mother-of-pearl flesh, the *reine claude* (the greengage), translucent and delicious. There are more than twenty varieties of fig: the purple-brown *belone*; the *barnissotte*, which looks like a black spinning top; the small green *marseillaise*; the big black *col de dame* (lady's neck). All are picked the very morning they are sold; dried in the sun, they are preserved with bay leaves in wooden cradles for the winter months and Christmas. There are grapes: the large white Saint Jeannet, which grows on lattices until

February; the large white *Servan*; the delicious white *muscat d'Alexandrie*; the black *muscat d'Hambourg*; the sweet *rolle*, which becomes the Bellet, the famous wine of Provence.

In winter there are the oranges of Nice, with their thick yellow skin and delicate flavour; the tangerines, the lemons of Menton; the kumquats (called *chinois*), kept in brandy or candied; the little bitter oranges (*oranges amères*), used for preserves and liqueurs or perfume. There are hazelnuts, walnuts, almonds – the sweet *pausane* and the delicate *princesse*, the hard-shelled bitter almonds (used for making pastry), the *coque dure*, the *Courrière*, the *Capronene*, the *Aberane*, the *Nathèrane*, the *Molière*. Around the hills surrounding Nice there are chestnuts – five varieties to be roasted in winter and eaten with sweet white wine. There are pomegranates, medlars, arbutus berries, persimmons, quinces for making pastry and liqueurs.

Les Fruits Confits
Candied Fruits

Nice's confectionery shops are full of baskets piled with *fruits confits*: superb glossy, mouth-watering melons, tangerines, strawberries and apricots. The fruits are preserved by replacing their own water with a sugary liquid, and remain beautiful and moist for months.

The process of treating the fruits is lengthy. It requires patience and precision and the help of a special instrument, a hydrometer, to determine the density of the liquid.

The first day The most beautiful, firm, ripe fruits are chosen and the pips removed. The fruits are blanched until a long needle inserted in them draws no water. They are then removed from the heat, rinsed in cold water and carefully drained.

The second day Sugar is melted in water (900 ml/1⅗ pt of water to every 1.25 kg/3 lb of sugar) and brought to a boil in a copper or heavy aluminium saucepan and simmered until a hydrometer dipped in it reads 20° density. The fruits are gently put in the syrup and boiled for a second, then removed from the heat and allowed to cool. Both the fruits and the syrup are then poured into a large bowl and left to rest for a day.

The fourth day The fruits are removed from the syrup, and sugar is added to the syrup to raise the density to 22°. The fruits are again cooked briefly in the syrup and then removed.

The sixth day The same procedure is followed as two days before, but the syrup must now be at 24°, so sugar is added accordingly. The fruits rest for a day.

The eighth day The syrup must be at 28°. The fruits rest for two days.

The eleventh day From this point on, glucose is added instead of sugar. The syrup must be at 32°. The fruits rest for four days.

The fifteenth day The syrup must reach 36°. The fruits rest for six days.

The twenty-first day The syrup must reach 37°. The fruits rest for eight days.

The twenty-ninth day The fruits are removed from the syrup and drained. The syrup (at 37°) is brought to a boil for a few seconds. The fruits are placed on a flat surface and the syrup poured over them is allowed to drain off. The fruits are now *confits* and will keep.

Whole melons, pears, apricots, lemons, oranges, figs and strawberries are candied by the above process until they become totally impregnated with sugar and glucose. The last pouring of syrup over them is to make them shiny. Flowers, such as violets, roses and mimosa, are also candied.

Fruits confits must be kept in a dry place and are usually sold in baskets or in wooden boxes.

Le Miel
Honey

Every spring the beehives are taken to the mountains around Nice and the bees feed on heather and on herbs – lavender, thyme, rosemary, sweet marjoram, sage – and on eucalyptus and flowering almond, apple, pear and orange trees. In September the honey is gathered and allowed to ripen for a whole month so that it will lose its excess of water. In November the hives are taken back to their original places, usually after the vine harvest is over. The liquid honey, which is blond at crop time, is poured into cardboard containers, where it solidifies and crystallizes. In winter the bees cease all activity. All through winter and spring they are fed with syrup and some of their own honey.

Lavender honey is amber-coloured and strongly flavoured. Rosemary honey is white and highly flavoured also. Acacia honey is pale yellow with a delicate taste, and heather honey is dark yellow. The best is thyme and wild thyme (*serpolet*) honey.

Honey is the base for most of Nice's desserts. It is used to cook fruits with, to make *Nougat Noir* (p. 233), *Nougat Blanc* (p. 231) and *Suce-Miels* (p. 239), and to sweeten tisanes (herb teas).

Huile d'Olive
Olive Oil

Olive oil, the most trendy of ingredients today, is at the core of Provençal life. It is not only its most essential culinary element, but it is also treasured as the enemy of cholesterol, and is thought to restore vitality to hair and skin. It is the only oil that is the natural juice of a ripe fruit rather than of a seed or nut.

A healthy olive tree is a thing of beauty, its silver-grey leaves like delicate lace. In Nice, where the trees are not regularly pruned, they grow in romantic shapes, like weeping willows, but in Provence they are tight and trim because of careful shaping. Olive trees produce only from their twenty-fifth year on. Around Nice the big trees produce small black olives with a bitter flesh, while the small trees bear larger, plump olives.

There are a great many kinds of olive: *olivière, lucques, pigale, verdale, rougette, picholine, saillerne, amelan, argentale, croniale, blancale, arabane, dent de Verrat, rose, redonale, moirale, caillet, rubeyro d'Antibes* and *coucourelle*, to name only a few. *Caillet* is the most widely found around Nice and Grasse. It has a purplish flesh, produces a fine pale-yellow sweet oil, and comes from big pyramidal trees.

Around Marseilles, fleshy green olives grow on small, stocky trees and produce a very tasty oil. Big, plump olives growing in the lower Alps make a heavy, very tasty green oil which is considered superb by some but unpalatable by others. There is a wide range of flavours, from the sweet yellow to the strong green, but the best oil is always made from perfectly ripe fruit. The more an olive matures and the more its water content diminishes, the better its oil will be. In August there is 40 per cent oil in the olives but the acidity is high, and oil made from these is of low quality. Olives picked too early taste too strong. The crop continues from August to September, and the oil is processed from November to April.

For picking eating olives, a double ladder (*caracons* or *escaracons*) is raised for the picker and the olives are received in an apron with a big pocket in the centre. Then they are spread on a large sheet in the shade of the tree. Olives to be used for making olive oil are knocked down with a long, flexible pole. Since the trees are in bloom in late spring, most of the blossoms are hurt by this method of picking and so a crop is available only every other year.

There are still some 150 olive mills in France and 60 of them are around Nice. Olives are brought to the mill (about 45 kg/100 lb from each tree) and put under a granite millstone, which reduces the pulp and the pits of 227 kg/500 lb of olives to a thick paste in about an hour and a half. The paste goes into a large 'mixing bowl' before being spread in large *scourdins* (round flattish sacks made of coco fibre). As many as sixty mats are piled 1.5 m/5 ft high under the heavy hydraulic press, which is usually run by water – only occasionally by electricity. All this must be done in a well-ventilated space. The first juice squeezed out is darkish. It is pumped into an *écrémeuse*, running 6,000 turns a minute, which separates the oil from the water. When the water is gone, what remains is a totally pure oil – the finest – officially labelled *Huile Vierge Première Pression à Froid*. Then comes the second pressing. The dried paste from the first pressing is covered with hot water and the process is repeated. This oil is labelled *Huile Vierge Deuxième Pression* and is sold either in pure form or mixed with other vegetable oils. The paste left over is covered with cold water. The pulp is used for soap, while the hard part, *les grignons noirs*, is burned in factories as fuel.

For purposes of cooking, oil from the first pressing must be bought because its acidity is never more than 1 per cent. The pale-yellow oil from Nice or Grasse is low in acidity and can be either very fine and sweet or more fruity if green olives are added to the local black ones. One should beware of all the other oils. In France *Olive Pure* means (legally, that is) that it is mixed with Tunisian oil. *Huile de Table* is made from left-overs, chemically treated oils, and by-products of various things, such as colza, soy and sunflower.

Because olive oil is such a fine product, it is best not to leave rosemary or basil leaves in it, or if used, to keep them in for only a short time. Grape-seed oil and peanut oil, which have very little flavour of their own, are better for flavouring in this way.

In Provence and in Nice we not only season almost every dish with olive oil, but we also nibble the olives as an appetizer, we stuff them with anchovies and capers, we use them in stews, *farcis* and dips. The pits left over from the process of crushing olives to extract the oil are used as fuel for cooking in the winter.

There are many ways to prepare olives, most of which you would find possible if you can buy uncured olives.

Olives cassées

Green olives have a very bitter taste when picked, so they must be cured. They are broken with a heavy piece of wood or a stone or gently squashed with a bottle, then thrown into water for nine days. The water is changed every day to hasten the curing. On the tenth day they are put in brine – salt water in which a bay leaf, a sprig of fennel, an orange rind and a few coriander corns have been boiled.

Olives à la picholine

Very plump, firm green olives are plunged into water. They are taken out when the flesh can be detached from the pit easily with a fingernail. The same weight of wood ashes as the olives is put in enough water to make a paste. The olives are left in the paste to neutralize their acidity. Then they are put in pure water for nine days, the water being changed every day. On the ninth day they are washed and put in brine made with 9 1/16 pt of water for 4.5 kg/10 lb of olives and 900 g/2 lb of salt, a bay leaf, an orange rind, a fennel branch, coriander and a clove and boiled for 5 minutes and then cooled before the olives are added. Completely covered with the marinade, the olives are kept away from light.

Olives farcies

First, *olives à la picholine* are prepared with very plump olives. The pit of each olive is removed and replaced with a caper wrapped in an anchovy fillet. Then the stuffed olives are put in a glass jar and covered with a good olive oil. They are kept in a cool place in the closed jar.

Olives piquées

Olives that have reached perfect maturity and are quite fleshy, oily and sweet are used for this treatment. They are put in a basket and pricked with a fork, then sprinkled with salt. Tossed from time to time and left in the basket for eight days, they lose some of their water. After fifteen days, when they have lost their bitterness, olive oil, pepper and bay leaves are added.

Olives en saumure

For this, not-too-ripe black olives are used. They are pricked with a needle and left in water for ten days, with the water changed every day. Finally, they are put in a cool brine spiced to taste and left there for five days.

Index